BEVERLY HARPSTER
SEPT, 2008

365 Days of Hope

365 Days of Hope

JONI EARECKSON TADA
DAVE AND JAN DRAVECKY

Authentic

Published in Partnership with World Vision Press

Authentic Media
We welcome your comments and questions.
129 Mobilization Drive, Waynesboro, GA 30830 USA authentic@stl.org
and 9 Holdom Avenue, Bletchley, Milton Keynes, Bucks, MK1 1QR, UK
www.authenticbooks.com

If you would like a copy of our current catalog, contact us at:
1-8MORE-BOOKS
ordersusa@stl.org

365 Days of Hope
ISBN: 1-932805-55-9

10 09 08 07 06 05 / 6 5 4 3 2 1

Published in 2005 by Authentic

Published in partnership with World Vision
34834 Weyerhaeuser Way South, P.O. Box 9716, Federal Way, WA 98063 USA
www.worldvision.org

The cover image, "Lower Lights," is an original oil painting rendered in 2002 by
Joni Eareckson Tada.

Cover design: Paul Lewis
Interior design: Angela Duerksen
Editorial team: Besty Weinrich

Printed in the United States of America

Dear Reader,

World Vision invites you to share your response to the message of this book by writing to World Vision Press at worldvisionpress@worldvision.org or by calling 800-777-7752.

For information about other World Vision Press publications, visit us at www.worldvision.org/worldvisionpress.

INTRODUCTION

*T*here is no doubt about it. Life can be painful. One only needs to open a newspaper or turn on radio to witness suffering of all kinds. For many of us, though, pain and trouble have become even more personal. If you've picked up this book, chances are you are already reaching out for hope and encouragement. You may be longing to feel God's presence. You may be looking for guidance from other people who understand what you're going through. You're looking for wisdom to steer you through the dark days.

That is why Joni Eareckson Tada and Dave and Jan Dravecky and World Vision have teamed up to bless you with this little book—365 days of encouragement and guidance that is based on the certain hope found in God's Word. They escort you through some of their best-loved passages of the Bible, beginning in Genesis and leading you all the way to Revelation. They will also share with you some of the insights they have gained through their own hardships. They have been there themselves. And collectively, they have years of experience in helping the hurting through their ministries, *Joni and Friends* and *Dave Dravecky's Outreach of Hope.*

HOW TO USE THIS BOOK

*E*ach of the 365 pages points you to a Bible passage for that day that you can read in your own Bible. There is also a short text from the *New International Version* of the Bible that narrows your focus to a specific truth from God's Word. After an inspirational reading by Joni, Dave, or Jan you'll find an interactive piece to take you one step further. **Points to Ponder** pose questions to deepen your thinking. **Take Action!** offers you positive steps toward personal growth. **A Path to Prayer** might give you the words you're looking for as you pray or prompt you to pray in your own way. **For Further Reflection** highlights other Biblical passages on that day's topic. Finally, **What Others Have Said** is a relevant quotation from famous and not-so-famous people who have wisely spoken on that topic.

And as you work your way through the 365 days of readings, open your heart and mind to the comfort of the God of all hope, the redemptive love of his Son, and the creative, renewing presence of the Spirit.

January

IN THE IMAGE OF GOD

Read: Genesis 1

So God created man in his own image, in the image of God he created him; male and female he created them. —Genesis 1:27

*E*specially when we feel depressed, it's vital to remember who God made us to be. If you look carefully through the first chapter of the Bible, you will see that every other creature was created "according to its kind"—but not human beings. They were made after the "image of God."

I will be the first to admit that I don't know everything that this little phrase is supposed to mean—or even most of what it means. But I do know this: If you are made "in the image of God," you are top-of-the-line merchandise. There is no higher "image" that you can be patterned after. You may be inspired by the mountains, thrilled by the stars, intrigued by the oceans, or mesmerized by this planet's wild variety of plants and animals, but none of them can come close to the wonder that is *us*. We are made in the very image of God! I am.

"But," someone will say, "isn't it true that Adam and Eve fell in the Garden of Eden through disobedience?" Yes, they sinned and dragged all of their descendants (including you and me) with them. But they were not "unmade" in God's image because of their sin. The image was marred but not destroyed or removed. To this day, all men and women are born into the world with God's image intact, and are therefore worthy of great respect.

Dave Dravecky

POINTS TO PONDER

* Read Colossians 3:9b–14. In verse 9b, Paul says that we are "being renewed in knowledge of the image of the Creator."

* What does that mean to you? What are the characteristics of the nature renewed in the image of God? (vv.12–14)

GOD GRIEVES

Read: Genesis 6:1–6

The Lord was grieved that he had made man on the earth, and his heart was filled with pain. —Genesis 6:27

B linded by our fallen nature, we have only the most vague notion of what consequences our disobedience and sinful choices are causing in the lives of others. But God has complete understanding. He is totally aware. He can see not only what is and will be, but also what might have been. He knows the full impact of our permanent impairment by sin.

And does he grieve? Does the God of the universe sorrow over human sin and the terrible effects they bring on themselves? Scripture indicates that he does feel anguish—deeper than you and I could ever understand.

In Judges 10:16 we are told that he "could bear Israel's misery no longer." In Hosea 11:8 he anguishes, "My heart is changed within me; all my compassion is aroused."

As Jesus approached Jerusalem, he mourned and wept over the devastation that was coming (Luke 13:34; 19:41–44). In Ephesians 4:30 Paul tells us that the Holy Spirit is grieved by our sinful ways.

Scripture refutes those who have imagined God as some kind of cosmic computer. He experiences emotions . . . and, therefore perfectly understands what we feel.

Joni Eareckson Tada

WHAT OTHERS HAVE SAID

We have a God who loves. That means that we have a God who suffers. —John Bertram (J.B.) Phillips

God's Smiles

Read: Genesis 9:8–16

I have set my rainbow in the clouds, and it will be the sign of the covenant between me and the earth. —Genesis 9:13

We live at the base of the front range of the Rocky Mountains. The sky is big and beautiful, and the cloud formations are breathtaking. Many storms form over the Rockies and then come over us. The lightning can be spectacular, and our family watches it as if it were a fireworks show. My favorite scene is after the storm rolls through—the sun finds openings in the clouds to peek its way through. The shining rays of sunlight color the drab landscape of the valley below with various shades of light.

While this heavenly play of light through dark clouds is a fairly common occurrence, it never escapes our notice. Many times Dave and I have been driving along the highway down the hill from where we live, and Tiffany will say, "Oh! Look! God is smiling down on us again." When the sun finally comes out, we often see a rainbow. The beauty of the rainbow after the storm reminds us of God's promises. The storm may be violent, dark—even frightening. Yet the Lord Jesus has promised never to leave us or forsake us. He will be with us always.

Jan Dravecky

Take Action!

With crayons, colored pencils, or markers, draw a rainbow. Beneath it, write a promise of God from Scripture that speaks to you. Post your drawing in a prominent place to remember how God smiles on you.

DO-IT-YOURSELF (NOT)

Read: Genesis 17

Then God said, "Yes, but your wife Sarah will bear you a son, and you will call him Isaac. I will establish my covenant with him as an everlasting covenant for his descendants after him."—Genesis 17:19–20

I admit it. I often line up with Abraham at the Do-It-Yourself Depot of life. Something's broke? Here, I'll fix that. Someone's hurting? I can solve that problem. Someone's mad? No worry, I'll talk to them. It seems I have an unflagging spirit to make right that which seems wrong.

Abraham desperately wanted a "fix" for his childlessness, so he asked God to bless Ishmael. But God would not abide by Abraham's solution. It was to be done God's way, as he had promised—Abraham and Sarah would have a son. He ultimately fulfilled that promise, but not without Abraham's regret seeding the ground of strife between Isaac and Ishmael. Abraham's do-it-yourself solution has repercussions even in our day.

What has God promised you? Are you attempting to fulfill that promise in your own energy and strength? Through your own schemes and strategies? No matter how tempting a solution appears, always, always stop to ask God. Compare it with his Word, his character, his Spirit. Anything short of complete trust in God's instructions will ultimately lead to regrets. "If only" living is not living at all.

Joni Eareckson Tada

PATH TO PRAYER

Take the predominant problem in your life to God this minute. Ask him to show you his will in this situation and how you should respond. Relinquish to God your anxiety and desperation, and ask for the wisdom to recognize how he is at work in your circumstances.

OF PERSPECTIVE AND PROMISES

Read: Genesis 21:1–7

Now the LORD was gracious to Sarah as he had said, and the LORD did for Sarah what he had promised. —Genesis 21:1–2

*T*he problem with pain is that it forces us to live in the moment, to deal with its unrelenting presence. That narrow, unpleasant perspective, like blinders on a horse, prevents us from clearly seeing the past (where God displayed his faithfulness to us) and the future (where the fulfillment of his promise awaits us). Bound by this thin sliver of time, we forget that God is not bound by time. He exists outside of its minutes and millennia. Promises that seem impossible from our limited perspective are totally possible from his. He will keep every promise he has made to his children, no matter how unattainable they seem at the time.

Dave and Jan Dravecky

WHAT OTHERS HAVE SAID

God does nothing in time which he did not design to do from eternity.
—William Jay

NOW I KNOW

Read: Genesis 22:1–19

"Do not lay a hand on the boy," [the angel of the LORD] said. "Do not do anything to him. Now I know that you fear God, because you have not withheld from me your son, your only son."—Genesis 22:12

W hy would God say, "Now I know that you fear [me]?" He already knew what was in Abraham's heart, long before the patriarch reached for the knife. Why put the old man through the test?

Simple: God didn't lack information about Abraham, *but Abraham may have lacked information about himself.* This is why God tests our faith: not that he might know what's in us, but that *we* might know. We say that we love God, that he is first in our lives, and that we trust and obey him. But we easily deceive ourselves. God wants us to know the actual, lived-out reality of our preference and inclination for him—not merely through words, but through gritty obedience.

You and I may imagine we are people of prayer and disciples that obey; but are we, in fact? What we believe must be lived out in reality. Trials are the best way of putting our love for God to the test. Our faith then becomes real.

Joni Eareckson Tada

POINTS TO PONDER

* Is there something that God is asking you to lay on his altar?

* In what way might God be testing you?

* What might he want you to do? What might he want you to learn? What might God want you to find out about yourself?

STONE OF REMEMBRANCE

Read: Genesis 28:10–22

Early the next morning Jacob took the stone he had placed under his head and set it up as a pillar and poured oil on top of it. He called that place Bethel.
—Genesis 28:18

*J*acob had a stone of remembrance. He never wanted to forget what had transpired the previous night at a place he named Bethel—"the house of God." He wanted to remember his encounter with the living God.

Back on our family farm in Maryland, I have a tree that serves the same purpose for me. It's an old, spreading maple growing by the springhouse. In October its leaves are resplendent in red, tinged with purple edges. By every October 15, my birthday, this maple reaches its peak of color. I call it my birthday tree.

Each year my tree marks how far I've come or what I have done or haven't done. Like Jacob's pillar, it is my stone of remembrance. Jacob's pile of stones was a visible, concrete reminder that God had touched his life.

What reminds you of growth in your life? Do you have some tangible reminder of how far you've come and how far you need to go? Be it a birthday tree, a photograph, or whatever, God wants you to be reminded of how he has met with you and touched your life.

Joni Eareckson Tada

WHAT OTHERS HAVE SAID

When remembrance of God lives in the heart and there maintains the fear of him, then all goes well; but when this remembrance grows weak or is kept only in the head, then all goes astray. —Theophan the Recluse

GROWING THROUGH ADVERSITY

Read: Genesis 29:31–35

Leah conceived again, and when she gave birth to a son she said, "This time I will praise the LORD."—Genesis 29:35

*L*eah suffered bitterly from Jacob's preference for Rachel, but she allowed God to bring joy out of her pain. Notice her growth: her responses progressed from misery to praise with each child she bore.

Hardships do not come into our lives to make us feeble, weak, lame and disabled. Such a thing is possible only if we allow it to happen. If we will choose instead to consider hardships as God's discipline and allow the difficulties of life to build into us the heavenly trio of holiness, righteousness and peace, we will watch ourselves grow from adolescence into spiritual maturity.

In my own growth it was important for me to understand that hardship was to be a part of my life because so many had told me that God did not intend for me to suffer. It was important for me to look at God as my Father, training me and disciplining me because he loved me, just as my earthly parents had. God will continue to train me, and he has chosen to use hardship as one of his primary tools.

Dave Dravecky

PATH TO PRAYER

Father, it is difficult to praise you in these hard times in my life, but I know that in spite of the sadness and discouragement that I feel, you are at work in me, disciplining me and helping me to grow. And so I praise you, Lord, for the way in which you can and will bring joy out of my pain.

Freedom in Admission

Read: Genesis 32

"Save me, I pray, from the hand of my brother Esau, for I am afraid he will come and attack me."—Genesis 32:11

*T*here is real freedom in admitting your fears. Jacob did just that, asking for God's protection from the wrath of his brother Esau and reminding God of his promises.

In my own life, being able to admit my fear and hear my wife say that she loved me for myself, not for what I could do on the mound, freed me. Do you know how much pressure was released when I realized that my wife didn't give a rip whether I was wearing a big league uniform or not? A lot. Do you know how freeing it was to have a wife to whom I could say, "Honey, I am scared! I am afraid, and the fear of failure is killing me," and have her accept me and affirm her love for me? That was one of the most freeing experiences I've ever had.

Dave Dravecky

Take Action!

Do you dare? On a sheet of paper or in your journal, describe some of the things you fear most. Now, after each one, write, "Save me, O Lord, I pray from _____. Offer that list to God and tear it up. Or, if you are able, share that list with someone close to you, a spouse, a friend, a pastor, or a counselor.

RECONCILED

Read: Genesis 33

But Esau ran to meet Jacob and embraced him; he threw his arms around his neck and kissed him. And they wept. —Genesis 33:4

Jacob had been a miserable brother to Esau. Esau had every reason and right, in human terms, to totally disown his brother. Jacob had tricked, taken advantage of, and stolen from his older brother. Then in cowardly fear, Jacob fled the country. The two hadn't talked for nearly two decades. God told Jacob to return to "your relatives" (31:3), but for all Jacob knew, Esau would kill him on sight. Nevertheless, Jacob obeyed the Lord and set out for home.

Human relationships are on God's "top ten" list (six of the Ten Commandments apply). But what about relationships that seem beyond repair? Jacob and Esau's reconciliation provides two key insights into how God knits back together what has become unraveled. The first element is obedience. Only God knows when "the time is right" for reconciliation because only God knows the condition of the human heart. Jacob returned *because God told him to.*

The second element is prayer. Jacob knew he needed God's help so he prayed with a fervent and humble heart. God honored Jacob's obedience and prayer, and paved the way for a tearful, but joyful reconciliation.

Dave and Jan Dravecky

POINTS TO PONDER

* Is there someone with whom you need to reconcile? Is God telling you it's time to "return" to that person?

* How can you pray with a "fervent and humble heart" about your relationship with this person?

DO NOT WORRY

Read: Genesis 32:22–32

Then the man said, "Your name will no longer be Jacob, but Israel, because you have struggled with God and with men and have overcome."—Genesis 32:28

God knows the devastating effects of worry on our lives. He knows how anxious thoughts can corrode our faith like acid. Worry robs us of joy; it steals our hope.

In Jesus' Sermon on the Mount, the phrase he repeated most often was, "Do not worry." The Lord was wise in repeating his warnings so many times. He knows the devastating effects of anxiety and how it can corrode faith like acid; robbing you of joy and stealing your hope.

I'm sure this is why Jesus said in the same sermon, "Therefore do not worry about tomorrow, for tomorrow will worry about itself. *Each day has enough trouble of its own*" (Matthew 6:34). The secret of being content is to take one day at a time. Not five years or ten at a time, but *one day*.

Jacob worried greatly about his reunion with Esau, but he did the right thing with those troubling thoughts. He poured them out before the Lord. He met his Lord face to face in an all-night prayer meeting and got up from his knees that morning with a new dependence on God.

Joni Eareckson Tada

PATH TO PRAYER

Lord, I admit that I'm so prone to worrying about things that happen in my life. Help me today to trust you. Receive glory as I turn from my anxiety and turn to you. Be near to me as you were near to Jacob that night on the banks of the river Jabbok. Lift the heaviness of my heart as I lean heavily upon you.

Return to God and Worship

Read: Genesis 34:1—35:3

"Come, let us go up to Bethel, where I will build an altar to God, who answered me in the day of my distress and who has been with me wherever I have gone."
— Genesis 35:3

*I*t was a time of trouble and heartache in Jacob's family. And in that dark season, God called Jacob to return to the place of their encounter so many years before. At that time, God had given Jacob a vision of a stairway reaching into heaven, with God standing at the top. The patriarch had awakened with divine words of protection, promise and provision ringing in his ears.

Now the Lord was telling him to go back to that place and to worship again. What good counsel that is! When the way before us seems clouded and confused, we need to return in our memories to those times and places when the Lord met with us and answered our prayers. He's still the same faithful God! He has not changed. And he is able to meet our needs today as he did in days gone by.

Joni Eareckson Tada

Points to Ponder

In a page of your journal or on a sheet of paper, list some of the occasions on which the Lord "met with you" and/or answered your prayers. List as many as you can remember. Keep your list available for you to review from time to time as a sort of "Bethel."

JEALOUSY

Read: Genesis 37

His brothers were jealous of him. —*Genesis 37:11*

J oseph's brothers didn't recognize (or didn't want to recognize) the death grip jealousy had on them. They sold the object of their jealousy, their own flesh and blood, for "twenty shekels of silver."

What we sell or what we lose when we allow jealousy to inject its venom into our lives is God's peace and joy. And there is only one effective antitoxin: confession. When we admit the hold jealousy has on our life, calling out for his mercy and grace, God will set us free. Until we do, we will live in a twilight world of fear, anger and paralyzing anxiety—somewhere God never intends his redeemed children to be.

Dave and Jan Dravecky

PATH TO PRAYER

If there is someone of whom you are jealous, confess it to God now. Ask God to free you of the torment of jealousy and its fear, anger, and anxiety. Ask God to give you instead a spirit of contentment and peace.

GOD'S SUSTAINING PRESENCE

Read: Genesis 39:1–22

While Joseph was there in the prison, the LORD was with him. —*Genesis 39:20–21*

*F*alsely accused and subsequently jailed, Joseph was (again) the victim of a terrible injustice. His plight was like that of the cancer victim abandoned by her spouse or the man permanently disabled by a drunk driver. He was innocent! But what is remarkable about Joseph's life isn't the series of injustices he endured, but rather how he responded in the face of those terrible trials. He never blamed God. He never turned away from God. He never lashed out at those around him. Regardless of the situation, Joseph's relationship with his Lord never changed.

"While Joseph was there in the prison, the LORD was with him." God doesn't give his children a "hall pass" to skip out on the negative effects of living in a sinful world. He gives us something much better: his own sustaining, encouraging presence.

Dave and Jan Dravecky

WHAT OTHERS HAVE SAID

God is above, presiding; beneath, sustaining, within, filling.
—Hildebert of Lavardin

GRACE IN TURN

Read: Genesis 48:1–12

Israel said to Joseph, "I never expected to see your face again, and now God has allowed me to see your children too."—Genesis 48:11

God had been gracious to Jacob, the old patriarch. On his death-bed, he said to Joseph, "I never expected to see your face again, and now God has allowed me to see your children too." Isn't that just like the Lord? What a kind and gracious God! Jacob, who had suffered much over the disappearance of his son, now had that son standing beside him—and grandchildren too!—at the hour of his death. And Jacob, in turn, is gracious in his blessing of Joseph and Joseph's children.

That's the way God intends it to be. He shows grace to us, and we, in turn, show grace to others. We who have been given much, give. We who have been forgiven much, forgive. We who have received thoughtful treatment, dispense it liberally in return. We who have been loved with such incomprehensible love, pour out our lives on behalf of others.

"Give," says our Lord, "and it will be given to you" (Luke 6:38). Yet how could we give anything at all if he had not given so much—his very life—to us?

Joni Eareckson Tada

FOR FURTHER REFLECTION

Consider these verses: 2 Corinthians 9:8; 1 Peter 4:10–11; Luke 6:31–38. What gifts of God's grace can you identify in these verses? What are some concrete ways in which you can pass some of these gifts on to others?

GOD INTENDS GOOD

Read: Genesis 50:15–21

"You intended to harm me, but God intended it for good."—Genesis 50:20

G od always exploits Satan's evil intentions and uses them in his own service. Satan plans to hinder the work of an effective missionary by arranging for him to trip in the jungle and break a leg; God allows the accident so that the missionary's godly response to pain and discomfort will bring glory to himself. Hoping to ruin her life Satan schemed that a seventeen-year-old girl named Joni would break her neck; God allowed the broken neck in answer to her prayer for a closer walk with him.

When we say that God allows Satan to do the things he does, we are not to imagine that once God grants permission, he then nervously runs behind Satan with a repair kit, patching up what the devil has ruined. The Lord is never forced into a corner. The Lord is never backed against a wall. Not only is God not frustrated or hindered by Satan's schemes, but God actually uses the devil's deeds to advance his kingdom and bring glory to himself. We can trust our sovereign God who works all things for our good and his glory.

When Satan causes calamity, we can answer him with the words that Joseph answered his brothers with when they sold him into slavery: "You intended to harm me, but God intended it for good."

Joni Eareckson Tada

PATH TO PRAYER

Lord God, I know that you are sovereign in all things and in my own life. Help me to trust you, to hold firmly onto the conviction that you will work all things for my good, even as I am tested by forces of evil that mean to do me harm. I pray that you will be glorified by my response. Amen.

ARGUING WITH GOD

Read: Exodus 3:1–4:17

"Now go; I will help you speak and will teach you what to say." But Moses said,
"O Lord, please send someone else to do it."—Exodus 4:12–13

Any time I'm tempted to argue with God, question his calling, or suggest he assign someone else to the task, I remember how far it got Moses. God had more than proved to Moses that he would back him up in Egypt. But Moses, like so many of us, didn't question God as much as he questioned *himself.* ("I am slow of speech and tongue," said Moses in verse 10).

I have no problem believing that God can do anything. I have serious reservations, however, about my abilities—or his desire to really use me as his instrument. But I don't ever want the Lord's anger to burn against me like it did toward Moses. All God really asked Moses to do was to carry a big stick and be obedient. God did all the heavy work. I think that's where we get our wires crossed. We think *we* have to do the heavy work. We underestimate God's goodness and provision for us. But I have learned (the hard way, of course) that one of my very favorite quotes really is true: "God will never lead you where his grace cannot keep you."

Jan Dravecky

POINTS TO PONDER

Look carefully at each question Moses asks God. What concern seems to be at the heart of his questions? How does God answer each time? What solution is at the heart of his answers? At what point does God become angry with Moses? Why?

A CHOICE

Read: Exodus 8:9–15

But when Pharaoh saw that there was relief, he hardened his heart and would not listen to Moses and Aaron, just as the LORD had said. —Exodus 8:15

Every plague God sent gave Pharaoh an opportunity to choose. But rather than acknowledge the sovereignty of the God of Moses, Pharaoh focused on trying to save face, maintain power, and control his economic well-being. Rather than learning from the awful plagues crashing down on him, he became hard and rebellious.

Through trials and hardships I may lose much. And yet I will never lose my opportunity to choose my *focus.* Do I focus on what I have lost, what "might have been," and what I am no longer able to do? Or do I focus on who I am right now and what I have to offer in Christ? That is a choice every man and woman must make, regardless of the loss. No one can take that choice away.

Dave Dravecky

POINTS TO PONDER

Thinking about the trial you are going through right now, take a sheet of paper and draw a line down the middle. On one side, write down some of things you have lost. On the other side, write out the words of 2 Corinthians 5:17. Think about who you are right now. Ask God to bring you to the place where you can focus on the "new creation" God is making of you in the midst of your trial.

BETWEEN A ROCK AND A HARD PLACE

Read: Exodus 14

"Do not be afraid. Stand firm and you will see the deliverance the LORD will bring you today . . . The LORD will fight for you; you need only to be still."
—Exodus 14:13–14

The Israelites could smell the dust and feel the ground shudder as the chariots approached. They were no match for the Egyptian army, and they knew it. With the sea on one side and pursuing army on the other, they were trapped. They wondered if God had delivered his chosen people only to destroy them days later. God's response to the Israelites' predicament was "you need only to be still."

We're no different than the Israelites. We get confused when circumstances don't pan out the way we want them to. We feel terror when our comfort zones are obliterated. And we feel forsaken when God doesn't act the way we think he ought to.

But I've learned that deliverance comes when we wait, when we step out of the way and let God be God. When we find ourselves between a rock and hard place, God's instructions are still the same to us as they were to the Israelites: "The LORD will fight for you; you need only to be still."

He may not part the sea of adversity for us, but he will comfort, instruct and prepare us for whatever lies ahead.

Dave Dravecky

TAKE ACTION!

Practice being still. See if you can sit for five minutes meditating on this verse. Can you make it all the way through that time without wandering back into your own thoughts?

FADING PRAISE

Read: Exodus 15

The LORD is my strength and my song; he has become my salvation. He is my God, and I will praise him. —Exodus 15:2

*E*xodus 15 is a glorious praise song to the Lord after he opened a path through the Red Sea. You can imagine the Israelites' amazement when they saw the water parted like giant, glass skyscrapers. Little wonder they sang on for 21 verses!

But a few verses later, their joy turned sour. Their song gave out. After three days of traveling in the desert without finding water, they grumbled, saying, "What are we to drink?" (v. 24). The song faded all too quickly when they ran into trouble.

Our own songs of praise fade all too quickly when we forget how God protects and provides for us. We need to take the advice God gave the Israelites in Deuteronomy 4:9: "Only be careful, and watch yourselves closely so that you do not forget the things your eyes have seen."

Joni Eareckson Tada

TAKE ACTION!

The next time you're tempted to grumble or complain, think of your favorite praise song and then sing it. It will be God's way of helping you not to forget his protection and provision in your life.

PROVISION FOR *TODAY*

Read: Exodus 16

Then the LORD said to Moses, "I will rain down bread from heaven for you. The people are to go out each day and gather enough for that day."—Exodus 16:4

"What is the greatest truth you've discovered in your cancer battle?" I asked Ellen, a successful businesswoman, wife, mother, and cancer survivor. "God will give you just what you need to get through each day," she replied. "When my thoughts wander into the future, when I begin to worry about tomorrow or next week or next year, God's peace evaporates like water in the desert."

How true. God's provision is for *today*. Like manna, it is fresh every morning. When I spend time with God in prayer and in his Word, I'm like the Israelites who gathered manna for the day. I receive enough of his direction, peace, wisdom, and comfort to see me through the day. Tomorrow is tomorrow.

Jan Dravecky

FOR FURTHER REFLECTION

For more insight into God's provision for today, read Lamentations 3:22–23; Matthew 6:11,34; and Philippians 4:6–7.

GOD OF THE DETAILS

Read: Exodus 22:1–15

"And even the very hairs of your head are all numbered. So don't be afraid; you are worth more than many sparrows."—Matthew 10:30

I often hear suffering people say they don't pray about "the minor stuff," the minutia of burdens that don't make the front page of conversation. When I ask them why, the answer is always the same. It goes something like this: "God has bigger problems to take care of. He isn't interested in *my* little worries and issues . . ."

My reaction is quick, intense and to the point: *"SAYS WHO?"* The God of Exodus 21:27 is concerned about missing teeth! The God of Exodus 22:5 has an opinion about grazing rights! In Exodus 22:6, he warns potential pyromaniacs that they could be held liable for damages caused by their dangerous obsession. He goes on to address wounded livestock, borrowing from neighbors, and missing garments. You can't get much more minor than that!

Believing that God doesn't care about our every burden is like a parent saying to a child, "Only come to me when your injuries require hospitalization. I don't do slivers, nightmares, or missing dolls." If God isn't interested in every detail of my life, why else would he number every hair on my head (Matthew 10:30)?

Dave Dravecky

PATH TO PRAYER

Praise God that he is all-knowing and everywhere present, that he is great enough and perceptive enough to be concerned even about the details of your life. Offer up to him the concerns that are on your mind today, even if they seem minor to you.

"I WILL DWELL AMONG THEM"

Read: Exodus 25:8–22

"Have them make a sanctuary for me, and I will dwell among them."—Exodus 25:8

S ince the Garden of Eden, God has been working to redeem his wayward children—and all for one purpose: *so that he could be with them again.* The whole activity, the heartbeat of heaven, is targeted at restoring our relationship with God. We were created for him, for his pleasure and for his glory. Every page of the Bible, every day of creation, every circumstance we encounter is divinely directed and dedicated to restoring what was lost in the garden: a love relationship between the Creator and his favorite creation. And we will forever be homesick until our hearts find their Maker. God told Moses, "Have them make a sanctuary for me, *and I will dwell among them"* (25:8). And how it must please God even more to say to us now, because of Jesus: "Open up for me the sanctuary of your heart. I want to dwell there."

Jan Dravecky

WHAT OTHERS HAVE SAID

There is only one being who can satisfy the last aching abyss of the human heart, and that is the Lord Jesus Christ. —Oswald Chambers

FACE TO FACE

Read: Exodus 33:7–14

The LORD would speak to Moses face to face, as a man speaks with his friend.
—Exodus 33:11

So often during my time in the wilderness, I longed for God to speak to me "face to face" as he did with Moses. I wanted answers. Reassurance. His presence. I wanted a burning bush, a glory-lit meeting, an encounter with God. But he never showed up . . . or so I thought. When we expect God to move in mighty ways through burning bushes, shaking mountains and pillars of fire, we may miss the gentle, more subtle ways he speaks to us.

So often he entrusts his love for us in far more "approachable" vessels, like the gentle touch of a human hand or the familiar sound of a friend's voice. God frequently chooses human couriers for his love. Using the kindness, love and compassion of family, friends and even strangers, God did meet me in my wilderness. But not in the way I'd expected.

Jan Dravecky

TAKE ACTION!

Make a point of looking for the face of God in those you meet today, his touch in those who touch you, and his voice in those who speak to you. If you feel alone, ask God to send someone to show you his love.

Following the Cloud

Read: Exodus 40:34–38

In all the travels of the Israelites, whenever the cloud lifted from above the tabernacle, they would set out; but if the cloud did not lift, they did not set out—until the day it lifted. —Exodus 40:36–37

Where's my cloud? Wouldn't it be easier to follow God if we had something like that big cloud to lead us? The good news is that we do! The God who inhabited that cloud now inhabits me! Because Jesus is my Savior, God's Spirit lives within me.

Wherever God dwells and reigns, there is peace, joy, and wisdom—the overflow of his character. When God's peace evaporates and his joy disappears, I know it's time to "check my position" with him. Have I been going off on my own? Have I been calling my own shots? Have I been depending on my own strength, my own abilities? No wonder I feel so empty! That's about the time I need to push for an immediate change in leadership. I need to wait on him, just like the Israelites waited for that cloud. I need to lay down my plans and hand over the reins of control so he can lead once again . . . and I can follow.

Dave Dravecky

Take Action!

Memorize the following verses from Proverbs: "Trust in the Lord with all your heart and lean not on your own understanding; in all your ways acknowledge him, and he will make your paths straight." (3:5–6)

OUT OF THE BOX

Read: Leviticus 9:22—10:3

Aaron's sons Nadab and Abihu took their censers, put fire in them and added incense; and they offered unauthorized fire before the LORD, contrary to his command. So fire came out from the presence of the LORD and consumed them, and they died before the LORD. —Leviticus 10:1–2

One of the greatest blessings to come out of a season of testing or a time in the spiritual wilderness is an enlarged view of God. The predictable, manageable box in which I have safely placed God is obliterated, and I am forced to readjust my thinking, to move the boundary lines I laid that fit him neatly into my life.

"Why has he allowed my suffering? I thought he was the God of mercy." "Why doesn't he deal with my troublemakers? I thought he was the God of justice." Just when I begin to grow comfortable with my "God in the box," I experience a trial or read a Scripture like Leviticus 10:1–2 that sends shock waves through my soul. His Spirit, like a gale-force wind, blows my box away. God wants me to know him, to plumb the depths of his being, to feel the beat of his heart, and to know intimately the nuances of his personality. He isn't content with my shallow, shadowy image of him. He knows that my ultimate happiness, the fulfillment of my every desire, is found as I discover who he really is.

Dave Dravecky

TAKE ACTION!

Draw a box about one-inch square on a piece of paper. Write as many attributes of God as you can fit in the box. How many can you fit inside? Continue to write attributes on the outside of the box to remind you that he is greater than you can imagine.

WAITING ON GOD

Read: Numbers 9:1–14

Moses answered them, "Wait until I find out what the LORD commands concerning you." —Numbers 9:8

*A*s one who leads both a ministry and a family, I often find myself on a decision-making tightrope. On one side, I'm inclined to use my God-given wisdom and keep moving forward. On the other side, I remember the value of "waiting on God" for specific direction.

But how does that work? How many decisions do I make on my own, and how many do I make only after I've waited for the Lord's direction? Someone on our staff shared this analogy: God's Word and the wisdom he gives me are like guardrails on a highway. They keep me heading in the right direction, prevent me from going in the ditch, and put me in company with others who are on the same journey. But guardrails don't tell you when to stop and help a stranded motorist! The Holy Spirit will be our guide within those guardrails, and I need to be listening for his counsel and his warnings all along the way. That's why Scripture tells us to "keep in step with the Spirit" (Galatians 5:25).

My relationship with God is a partnership. In his love, he will keep me moving in the best direction.

Dave Dravecky

FOR FURTHER REFLECTION

Read John 14:26; 16:13; Romans 8:26–28; and Galatians 5:22, and reflect on the work and character of the Holy Spirit. Reflect on the role of the Spirit in your decision-making.

STEPPING AHEAD OF GOD

Read: Numbers 14:20–45

Nevertheless, in their presumption they went up toward the high hill country, though neither Moses nor the ark of the LORD's covenant moved from the camp.
—Numbers 14:44

*D*ave and I have seen the casualties—bruised and bleeding, dazed and confused. They followed the formula and "claimed" God's promises for healing and prosperity. Like the Israelites, they stepped out to possess the promise . . . and met with crushing defeat.

The Israelites acted without first consulting God to see if the promise held true for that hour, for that situation and for those people. Was the promise a lie? No. God did bring his people to the promised land—but not *this* group of people.

Moses knew the heart of God on this matter. He knew the Israelites shouldn't attempt to possess the land at that time because God had told him so! And when I rashly "claim" the promises of God without first consulting the God behind the promises, I risk the same perilous results.

No matter how desperate I may feel, I still have to go to God with open hands and a trusting heart. He may say "yes," he may say "no," he may say "not this time," or he may say nothing at all. But whatever his will, that's right where I want to be!

Jan Dravecky

PATH TO PRAYER

Father, you know how often I want to charge ahead and take control of things. When I do, I pray that you will remind me to stop and come to you with my heart and mind open to your leading. Prompt me to consult with you so that I claim your promises only in your will and in your good time.

SUFFERING AS OCCUPATION

Read: Numbers 16:1–7

The LORD will show who belongs to him and who is holy, and he will have that person come near him. —Numbers 16:5

*K*orah was occupationally dissatisfied. Being one of the chosen that performed priestly duties just wasn't enough; he wanted *Aaron's job.* Korah refused to acknowledge that it is God who places us just where he wants us, and that knowledge brings great fulfillment.

My greatest desire was to play professional baseball, but God had something more in mind for me: he called me to a season of suffering. Maybe you've been called to the same occupation. You've tried to pray your way out of it, work your way around it, or search for some magic pill to make it all go away, but it refuses to leave. Like Korah, you can choose to rebel, cause a scene, and demand your "rights" to a better occupation.

Yet Christ himself chose this occupation. And aren't we glad he did? Now that my occupation has changed from suffering to one who encourages the suffering, I can look back at my previous job with a feeling of accomplishment. I got to know Jesus better during those dark days, and that remains the deepest desire of my heart.

Dave Dravecky

POINTS TO PONDER

What "occupation" or situation do you find yourself in? Has God called you to it? Are you satisfied in it or are you restless? Why or why not? Is God calling you to another occupation? Can and will you move on? Why or why not?

January 30

THE NOURISHING WORD OF GOD

Read: Deuteronomy 6:1–12

"These commandments that I give you today are to be upon your hearts."
—Deuteronomy 6:6

"How do you know so many Scriptures?" the troubled woman asked Penny. Out of Penny's purse came a palm-size, ornately stitched, handmade bag. She loosened the drawstring and a large collection of tattered, well-worn index cards fell onto the table. Each contained a Scripture verse, a Bible promise she was praying for either herself, a loved one, or a friend.

"When I find myself waiting somewhere or I'm feeling low," Penny explained, "I pull out my little bag and read, meditate, or pray over these verses." Penny's life and the ministry that flows out of it reflect her devotion to the Word. Like a compass, the Word of God aligns us with true north. It sets our mind and heart straight again, putting life and whatever may be troubling us back into perspective.

Just as we would never think of robbing our body of a continual supply of food and water, we should never consider robbing our spirit of its nourishment, the Word of God.

Jan Dravecky

TAKE ACTION!

Write a few "prayer words," such as "Jesus," "surrender," "peace," "eternity," "hope," and "patience," or other words of your choice on 3x5 inch cards and keep them in your purse or pocket. The next time you have to wait for an appointment or wait in line, take them out and give God the opportunity to speak to you through them.

WHEN WE WERE LOVELESS

Read: Deuteronomy 7:7–11

"The LORD did not set his affection on you and choose you because you were more numerous than other peoples . . . But it was because the LORD loved you."
—Deuteronomy 7:7–8

Just in case the Israelites were cherishing any false illusions, Moses set the record straight when he told them: "The LORD did not set his affection on you and choose you because you were more numerous than other peoples . . . But it was because the LORD loved you."

God loved us when we were loveless—and this means his love is completely uninfluenced by us. His love comes barreling at us at full speed, in a direct line from eternity past, in all its glorious, undiminished force. He has as much love for you and me as he has for the most godly of his saints. In fact, God loves us the way he loves his own Son, Jesus.

What's more amazing is that there is everything in us to repel God. We are sinful, depraved. No good thing dwells in us. Yet thankfully, that does not influence God. Rather he says in Jeremiah 31:3, "I have loved you with an everlasting love; I have drawn you with loving-kindness." Amazing love! How can it be?

Joni Eareckson Tada

WHAT OTHERS HAVE SAID

God's love is not drawn out by our lovableness, but wells up, like an artesian spring, from the depths of his nature. —Alexander MacLaren

February

EVERY DAY

Read: Deuteronomy 7:7–11

Know therefore that the LORD your God is God; he is the faithful God, keeping his covenant of love to a thousand generations of those who love him and keep his commands. —Deuteronomy 7:9

The sun is shining brightly with not a cloud in the sky. The birds are chirping. No personal struggles. No pressures. All bills are paid. Nothing but clear sailing. Little wonder you find yourself saying out loud, "Lord, this is great. You are wonderful!"

We get excited about God when circumstances are delightful. When things are good, God is good. But if circumstances turn sour, then . . . where is God? He must have forgotten about me!

We are so prone to let our circumstances—whether good or bad—dictate our view of God. But time and again the Bible tells us that God is *faithful*. He is not just a faithful God, but *the* faithful God. He is the same steadfast and good Father yesterday, today and forever. Scripture alone should be our frame of reference for who the Lord really is, rather than fickle, changing circumstances.

Whether the day is grand or gloomy, every day is a great day to give praise to our faithful God.

Joni Eareckson Tada

FOR FURTHER REFLECTION

Choose one of the following Scriptures to read and reflect on:

Read Psalm 103 and wonder at the faithfulness of God and how he has set creation in motion and keeps the world going everyday.

Read Isaiah 55 and meditate on the faithfulness of God in his plans and purpose.

Read Revelation 21:1–7 and rejoice in the new heavens and new earth that God will bring about in his faithfulness.

NOT BEYOND REACH

Read: Deuteronomy 30:11–20

"The word is very near you; it is in your mouth and in your heart so you may obey it."—Deuteronomy 30:14

The very word "obedience" causes my sinful nature to wince. Something in my flesh whispers, "Yeah, I'll obey . . . if I agree or if it suits my purposes. But if the act of obedience is costly or inconvenient, I can justify a way around it."

The Lord knows how many times I listen to *that* voice instead of the Holy Spirit's voice—especially if I don't feel well or I've let my spiritual life run down. How do you battle with such an intimate and familiar foe?

In some of his final words to Israel, Moses tells the people that the laws he has instructed them to obey are "not too difficult for you or beyond your reach." How can he say that? Because "the word is very near you; it is in your mouth and in your heart so you may obey it." When the Word of God is in my mouth, when I'm reading it, speaking it and meditating on it, transformation happens in my life. My ability to obey is a direct result of the time I spend applying the Word of God to my life.

Jan Dravecky

TAKE ACTION!

The only way the word can be in "your mouth and in your heart" is for you to make a commitment to read and memorize Scripture. Start by writing down a short passage on a 3x5 inch card and posting it in a prominent place for a week until you have it memorized.

APPLE OF GOD'S EYE

Read: Deuteronomy 32:1–14

For the LORD's portion is his people, Jacob his allotted inheritance. In a desert land he found him, in a barren and howling waste. He shielded him and cared for him; he guarded him as the apple of his eye. —Deuteronomy 32:9–10

Who's the apple of your eye? Your grandchild? Your son recently promoted? Your fiancée with those soft eyes and tender smile? Whoever is the apple of your eye, one thing's for certain: you *love* that individual with a fervent and intense love. That person gives you joy indescribable. In short, you *feel* something for this loved one.

You are the apple of God's eye. God actually *feels* powerful emotions when it comes to you. His joy and delight over you find their best expression at the cross: "God so loved the world that he gave his one and only Son" (John 3:16). Our Lord watched his Son's murder because he loves you. This means his joy and deep emotion for you is rugged, hard-won, and victorious. He is the admiral flying colors of victory over you. He's the hero who has carried you to safety from hell's burn. He is the joy-filled warrior who has brought you home. You are the apple of his eye.

Joni Eareckson Tada

PATH TO PRAYER

Spend some time meditating on this truth: You are the apple of God's eye. Imagine God's eyes of love resting on you. Stay in that thought until you feel a response welling up from your heart. Offer that response to God in prayer.

GET READY

Read: Joshua 1:1–9

"Be strong and courageous. Do not be terrified; do not be discouraged, for the
LORD your God will be with you wherever you go." —Joshua 1:7

Each day of life spreads before us like uncharted territory. Tonight at midnight you'll cross over into something new, like crossing the Jordan River. Tonight is a river of no return. Sounds a little like Canaan land, wouldn't you say? We could paraphrase Joshua 1:1–3 to read, "Get ready to cross into the new day that I am about to give you." And listen to the next line: "I will give you every place where you set your foot"!

Got that? God is about to give you the next 24 hours. He will give you every place where you set your foot (God doesn't present opportunities only to snatch them away). The thing is, you must step into those opportunities. God-blessed opportunities do not become yours until you take them. The land of Canaan was promised to the Israelites, but they had to step out and claim the ground. And that takes the strength and courage that comes from trusting God.

Joni Eareckson Tada

POINTS TO PONDER

* How do you define "opportunity"?
* How do you recognize opportunities?
* How can you be more aware of opportunities God gives you?
* What opportunity is staring you in the face right now?
* What do you need from God to help you step out in faith?

THE DAY THE SUN STOOD STILL

Read: Joshua 10:1–15

The sun stopped in the middle of the sky and delayed going down about a full day.
—Joshua 10:13

Breathtaking, the lengths to which God will go for his loved ones! Joshua made that wonderful discovery when five strong Amorite kings joined forces to attack Israel's allies, the Gibeonites. The terrified people of Gibeon sent a desperate S.O.S. to Joshua and his army (camped some distance away), and the general responded. Yet it's doubtful Joshua relished this new challenge, and it must have caused his heart to tremble, for God says to him, "Do not be afraid of them" (v.8).

But how could Israel have known the lengths to which God would go for them? Not only did the Lord hurl "large hailstones on them from the sky," killing more of the enemy than did Israelite swords, but to seal the victory Joshua asked God to keep the sun motionless until Israel had won a total victory—and he did, for a whole day! "Surely the LORD was fighting for Israel!" says a breathless Hebrew reporter (v.14).

When we recognize that God still fights for his people today, we too can conquer fear and move ahead. For who can guess the lengths to which our Lord will go to give us victory?

Dave and Jan Dravecky

TAKE ACTION!

Memorize the words of Psalm 27:1, 5:

The LORD is my light and my salvation—whom shall I fear? The LORD is the stronghold of my life—of whom shall I be afraid? For in the day of trouble he will keep me safe in his dwelling; he will hide me in the shelter of his tabernacle and set me high upon a rock.

WITH WHAT YOU HAVE

Read: Judges 6:7–24

The LORD turned to him and said, "Go in the strength you have and save Israel out of Midian's hand. Am I not sending you?"—Judges 6:14

I learned a lesson early in my career as a quadriplegic: work with what you've got. The occupational therapist taught me how to use muscles in a whole new way to make up for muscles that had been rendered useless. The good nerves in the upper part of my deltoids help me get a lot of work done that would otherwise be the responsibility of my biceps.

When you think about it, God's been in the occupational therapy business for ages. He has often come to weak, visionless people like Gideon and worked with what they had. Whether it was Moses' staff, Samson's jawbone, or David's sling, God simply took what was available and showed his people what was possible.

So what have you got? Make the list and show God. Short list? No matter; take it and apply to the needs and people around you. He'll take care of the rest.

Joni Eareckson Tada

WHAT OTHERS HAVE SAID

Do what you can, with what you have, where you are.
—Theodore Roosevelt

LET THE LORD DECIDE

Read: Judges 11:14–27

"Let the LORD, the Judge, decide the dispute this day."—Judges 11:27

Have you noticed? Relationships are complicated! And adversity only complicates them more. Often the pain of strained relationships is more difficult than the physical pain of our suffering. What do you do after you've done everything you can to patch things up—and hostility still radiates from the other party? You've forgiven, asked forgiveness for your actions, tried to talk it out, prayed for reconciliation, and acted with integrity and in love . . . but all you get in return is animosity, false accusation, and slander. What do you do? You heed the wise words of Judge Jepthah: "Let the LORD, the Judge, decide the dispute." You leave the dispute in with God, and continue to show the love of Christ. Scripture acknowledges that we are to do all we can do within our sphere of responsibility (Romans 12:18). Having done those things, we can leave all matters in his hands—including our anxieties.

Jan Dravecky

WHAT OTHERS HAVE SAID

Let us give up our work, our plans, our health, our lives, our loved ones, our influence, our all, into God's right hand. Then, when we have given over all to him, there will be nothing left for us to be troubled about, or to make trouble about. —J. Hudson Taylor

A CIRCLE OF BLESSING

Read: Ruth 3

"The LORD bless you, my daughter. This kindness is greater than that which you showed earlier." —Ruth 3:10

God's favorite shape must be a circle.

After all, he made so many round things: the sun; our earth; bubbles; flying dandelion seeds; eyeballs; peas; apples; sow bugs when they're all rolled up.

But maybe the best circular thing God ever made is the way he designed blessings to go 'round and 'round. The book of Ruth proves the truth of Proverbs 22:9: "A generous man will himself be blessed."

Ruth comes home to Naomi one day and tells her that a man named Boaz has been kind to her by allowing her to glean freely in his fields. Naomi responds with a hearty, "The LORD bless him!", declares that Boaz "has not stopped showing his kindness to the living and the dead" (2:20), and tells her daughter-in-law that he is her kinsman-redeemer. Some time later, when Ruth (following the instruction of Naomi) lets Boaz know of her personal interest in him, he responds with a gentle, "The LORD bless you, my daughter. This kindness is greater than that which you showed earlier" (3:10).

That is the way God intended blessings to flow: in a circle. That's how he means them to "get around"!

Dave and Jan Dravecky

TAKE ACTION!

Think of some of the ways in which you have been most blessed by others. A word of encouragement? A meal? A financial gift? Friendship? Close the circle of blessing today by reaching out to someone in some small (or large) way.

ULTIMATELY

Read: Ruth 4

"He will renew your life and sustain you in your old age."— Ruth 4:15

U ltimately, God brought great, surpassing blessing into the life of this poor widow who had seen so many days of sorrow. Yet her words coming into the land of Israel were haunting: "The Lord has afflicted me" (1:20). How can a good God allow his children to be afflicted? Notice that Naomi never asked this question. She accepted the reality that regardless of the source of her troubles, the sovereign God allowed them. She understood well that nothing slips by the throne of God and arrives at our door "by accident." How then, do we reconcile God's great love with the pain and suffering he allows into our lives? We can't. God's plans and purposes are too vast, too incomprehensible for our finite minds to put together. As Paul affirmed, his paths are "beyond tracing out" (Romans 11:35).

Ultimately, we have to trust that the God who created our souls and the limitless universe in which they reside knows what he is doing. And in time, like Naomi, we may even hear those near us praise God for his goodness to us.

Dave and Jan Dravecky

PATH TO PRAYER

Creator of my soul, I sometimes find it so hard to comprehend the how's and why's of suffering in this world. My finite mind cannot comprehend the vastness of your purposes. I long for acceptance like Naomi's, who had confidence that no trouble arrived at her door by chance. I pray now for your peace, and that others may see your hand in my life and praise you.

Expressing Grief

Read: 1 Samuel 1:1–20

"I have been praying here out of my great anguish and grief."—1 Samuel 1:16

Hannah didn't mince words or spare any tears, but rather poured her heart out to God in grief.

It's necessary to grieve over a major loss. God built us to express such grief. In my own case, I should have grieved over the loss of my arm. It would have been the natural thing to do. It would have been the healthy thing. But I didn't. Instead I had a cavalier attitude about it. I joked around before surgery and waved the arm in the air, playing like it was saying goodbye to everyone. After surgery I called out to my friend Bob: "Maybe now I can get a decent parking space; ya know, in one of those handicapped spaces."

My humor was a form of denial. I was afraid to face how I really felt about losing my arm. All the people I had been so critical of for denying reality—the faith healers, the positive thinkers, the sunshine-all-the-time Christians—how was I any different from them?

Take time to grieve your losses. And do it in your own way. It's the healthy thing to do.

Dave Dravecky

Points to Ponder

* What losses have you experienced (big *and* small)?
* Have you allowed yourself to grieve? If not, why not?
* What kind of space and time do you need to allow yourself to grieve?
* Do you need a pastor or counselor to help you grieve in a healthy way?

LOSS

Read: 1 Samuel 4:12–22

"The glory has departed from Israel, for the ark of God has been captured."
—*1 Samuel 4:21*

The Israelites had experienced loss upon loss. The ark was captured by the Philistines; Eli's two sons, along with thirty thousand foot soldiers had died. Eli died of grief, and then his daughter-in-law died in childbirth.

Loss is a part of our lives, too, woven into its very fabric. I'm grateful that my losses are redeemed by God. In my despair I have reached out to him and he has rescued me. As a result of yielding to Jesus at the time of my greatest loss, I've found great peace.

Sadly, some people turn away from God in their loss when Satan offers them a false peace through self-pity. It makes me so angry. If I were to dwell on it long enough, my frustration at the devil's dirty deeds would overwhelm me. But God has a hopeful word that sets my heart at peace: "The God of peace will soon crush Satan under your feet" (Romans 16:20). Now, we all know that Christ will reign victoriously. But the victory involves me personally. Somehow, on some future day, Satan will be crushed under my feet.

No matter how great your losses may seem, a day is coming when victory will be yours. As you believe this promise, you will experience peace in the face of your anxiety and anger. Surrender to God's future victory and find peace for your soul.

Joni Eareckson Tada

POINTS TO PONDER

* What do you think is the difference between grief and self-pity? How can you reach out to Jesus in your grief?
* What do you need to do to "yield to Jesus"?
* What do you think it means to surrender to a "future victory'?

EBENEEZER

Then Samuel took a stone and set it up between Mizpah and Shen. He named it Ebenezer, saying, "Thus far has the LORD helped us."—1 Samuel 7:12

When the Israelites defeated the Philistines, the prophet Samuel raised a memorial to commemorate the victory. He named it Ebeneezer, which means "stone of help." It was to remind everyone, including Samuel, that God was their help.

What are the memorials in your life, the tangible, physical reminders that God has given you of his ever present help?

My wheelchair is my "Ebeneezer." I've raised it up as a memorial to commemorate God's grace in my life. It reminds me (and everyone who sees me smile in it) that God is my help.

Look for the memorials, the stones or remembrances, in your life. Whatever they are—perhaps a ring, a family Bible, a pair of crutches, a pebble you picked up during a journey—they can be anchors to your soul. When pain becomes severe or sorrow crushing, you can remind yourself of that memorial set in place during a time of greater strength, and you can pray, "Oh, God, keep me faithful to that."

Joni Eareckson Tada

TAKE ACTION!

Do you have an "Ebeneezer"? If not, find one. If nothing occurs to you, find a small rock or a stone and with marker write on it *"Thus far has the LORD helped us,"* or some other appropriate saying. Display it in a prominent place to remind you of God's help.

ONCE AGAIN

Read: 1 Samuel 23:1–4

Once again David inquired of the LORD, and the LORD answered him.
—1 Samuel 23:4

*I*s that how my life story will read? Once again, Jan inquired of the Lord. Once again, Jan refused to make a decision until she prayed about it. Once again, Jan chose not to act impulsively but waited for God to give her direction. Once again, Jan did not take matters into her own hands, but fully released them to the Lord.

Like a boomerang, David always returned to the Lord. In season and out. While running for his life and running the nation. When he messed up and when he was victorious. And the Lord welcomed him every time.

Jan Dravecky

PATH TO PRAYER

Lord, please cause my own heart to continually be drawn back to you, regardless of where it has been or what it has done. Don't let pride or fear or indifference gain a foothold in me. May my dependence on you cause me to live a life that brings you great honor and glory. And if ever there is a narrative of my days written somewhere in heaven, I pray that it will include the words, "Once again . . ."

IN THE COURSE OF TIME

Read: 2 Samuel 2:1–7

In the course of time, David inquired of the LORD. —2 Samuel 2:1

*D*ave and I have a very mechanically inclined friend who recently installed a brand new engine in one of his cars. It really looked impressive under the hood—but it sounded terrible. That's when my friend explained the concept of "setting the timing." The more he adjusted and tweaked, the better it sounded.

I heard the awful results of a poorly timed engine. And I have lived with the disastrous results of poorly timed actions and decisions. God, who keeps the universe and all its moving parts humming, has perfect timing. I don't. I tend to react, rather than waiting for the right, Spirit-directed moment to speak or move. After Saul's death, David could have easily stepped in and filled the leadership vacuum he knew he was destined to fulfill. But he didn't. He didn't react to the circumstances. He moved in God's timing . . . and the result was powerful.

I want to be like David, one of the hearts in God's creation that moves in perfect harmony with his timing.

Jan Dravecky

WHAT OTHERS HAVE SAID

In the rush and noise of life, as you have intervals, step within yourselves and be still. Wait upon God and feel his good presence; this will carry you through your day's business. —William Penn

After God's Own Heart

Read: 2 Samuel 5:1–12

And he became more and more powerful, because the LORD God Almighty was with him. —2 Samuel 5:10

D avid was the most victorious warrior in the history of Israel. While the battles he fought were physical, some of the same principles apply to our spiritual and emotional battles. 1) David first sought the Lord's counsel. He didn't simply react to circumstances, assuming they were from God. Arrogance can cause us to step ahead of God because we think we know what he wants us to do. 2) David followed God's instructions implicitly, never stepping outside of God's boundaries and directives. God does have clear guidelines in his Word that we are to follow. When we don't, disaster follows. 3) He gave God the credit and glory for the victory that followed. Although God used him and worked through him, David knew he was just God's instrument, not the conductor.

At the heart of David's success in battle was his ongoing communication with God, dependence upon God, and love for God. Because his heart was right with God, his actions were in harmony with heaven's plans, and he was victorious.

Dave Dravecky

Points to Ponder

Think of a decision you have to make. In your journal or on a sheet of paper, rewrite the principles listed above in your own words. Follow each principle with the specifics of your own situation:

1) I will ask God to _____ .

2) I will follow God's direction by_____ .

3) I thank and praise God for _____ .

Remember, it may take some time for you to apply numbers 2 and 3. Wait on God until you know what to write down.

FOR THE SAKE OF A FRIEND

Read: 2 Samuel 9

"Don't be afraid," David said to him, "for I will surely show you kindness for the sake of your father Jonathan."—2 Samuel 9:7

By the standards of the day, David should have hunted down and killed Mephibosheth, because Jonathan's son represented a threat to the Davidic throne. But for the love of his dear friend Jonathan, David provided Mephibosheth a special place at the king's table.

Perhaps King David saw in this young disabled man's face the features of his departed friend. Maybe when Mephibosheth smiled, David could see a vestige of Jonathan's grin. The young man could have had his father's eyes. His inflections. Plus, the two had shared memories of the loved one they had in common.

In the same way, God the Father invites us to his table to commune with him, because he sees in our countenance the remembrance of his dearly beloved Son. There is something about us, those of us who are "hidden with Christ" (Colossians 3:3), that shows a trace of Jesus. Little wonder that God delights to welcome us to his table. It is for Jesus' sake that he raises us—like Mephibosheth—from poverty to nobility.

Joni Eareckson Tada

PATH TO PRAYER

Thank God, your Father and the Father of Jesus, that he has invited you to his banquet table. Thank him for raising you up from spiritual poverty to spiritual nobility. Pray that the Father will see Jesus' face reflected in yours. Praise him for loving you as his own child.

ON THE HEIGHTS

Read: 2 Samuel 22:1–37

*[God] makes my feet like the feet of a deer; he enables me to stand on the heights.
. . .You broaden the path beneath me, so that my ankles do not turn. —2 Samuel
22:34,37*

W hen I was a kid, my family once headed to the Rockies for vacation. After we crossed the border from Nebraska to Colorado, I searched the horizon for the first signs of the mountains. Soon I saw them, rising off the plain like a craggy, frightening fortress.

I worried that we would never make it to those high peaks in our old Dodge truck. And even if we did, all I could imagine was being stranded on some mountain spire. Was I in for a surprise when we reached the summit! The road sloped out onto a high, broad mountain plateau. Flat grassland with cattle grazing!

That's the Christian life. Our trials appear to be mountainous obstacles looming ahead of us. We see frightening heights from which we could fall, and pinnacles that make our heads spin. We wonder what awaits us at the crest of our trial. But once we arrive by God's grace, we find we have climbed to a higher plain.

Are you facing a mountainous trial today? The Lord knows where he's leading you. It's not some dizzying ledge; it's only higher ground.

Joni Eareckson Tada

POINTS TO PONDER

* What does the expression "standing on the heights" mean to you?
* What would it be like to be there?
* When have you been on "higher ground?" How did God lead you there?

February 18

A Wise and Discerning Heart

Read: 1 Kings 3:4–14

"So give your servant a discerning heart to govern your people and to distinguish between right and wrong."—1 Kings 3:9

Solomon asked the Lord for a "discerning heart." And the Lord was pleased with that request. The book of James tells us that God gives wisdom "generously" to those who request it (James 1:5). Wisdom is the ability to live skillfully, to see life situations through God's eyes, with his perspective and insight. It enables and equips us to make the best life decisions possible, whether life is calm and peaceful or deep in the throes of crisis.

After tasting and experiencing the benefits of God's great wisdom, Solomon wrote: "Wisdom is supreme; therefore get wisdom. Though it cost all you have, get understanding" (Proverbs 4:7).

Dave Dravecky

Take Action!

Using a concordance or Bible software, do a Scripture search on the word "wisdom." Find five verses that are the most meaningful to you. Write them on 3x5 inch cards or in your journal. Choose at least one to memorize.

ASK YOUR QUESTIONS

Read: 1 Kings 10:1–3

When the queen of Sheba heard about the fame of Solomon and his relation to the name of the LORD, she came to test him with hard questions. —1 Kings 10:1

The Queen of Sheba had serious questions about God and his ways and his will. Not content to sit on her questions, she set out on a spiritual quest that took her on a journey more than a thousand miles over land and sea. It was a lengthy and dangerous trip, especially for a woman.

But the queen's search was more than an intellectual exercise. She had to see for herself if Solomon could offer the answers for some of the most pressing questions on her heart.

If you have serious questions about God, his ways, and his will, don't sit on your curiosity. Let your thirst for God take you on a journey of questioning. It's okay to have doubts and to wrestle with spiritual issues. Remember, out of all the seekers in the Old Testament, our Lord picked this African woman as a model of spiritual thirst and hunger.

Joni Eareckson Tada

PATH TO PRAYER

Write down five questions you'd like to ask God. Bring one to God in prayer each day for the next five days and ask him to answer them in his own way and his own time.

GETTING ADVICE

Read: 1 Kings 12:1–9

But Rehoboam rejected the advice the elders gave him and consulted the young men who had grown up with him and were serving him. —1 Kings 12:8

*M*ost everyone loves to give advice. Just ask a new mother, a recent widow, or someone battling with a serious illness. They've heard it all. But how can you separate good advice from not-so-good advice? First and foremost, the counsel you receive must line up with Scripture. Second, you must carefully consider your sources. Are they trustworthy individuals? Do they live a life that reflects good judgment? Might they be cloaking a hidden agenda of some sort? Third, pray before acting on anyone's advice. Ask God to give you peace and confirmation about your decision. Solomon wrote in Proverbs 19:20, "Listen to advice and accept instruction and in the end you will be wise." But he also wrote Proverbs 12:5: "The advice of the wicked is deceitful."

Too late, Rehoboam learned about the peril of following bad counsel . . . and he lost a kingdom.

Jan Dravecky

PATH TO PRAYER

I praise you God, because you are the source of all knowledge, the Wonderful Counselor. I ask that your Spirit may dwell in me so that I can discern what is good advice or bad, so that in all things I will do your will and bring you joy.

GOD IS LISTENING

Read: 1 Kings 18:20–46

"Answer me, O LORD, answer me, so these people will know that you, O LORD, are God, and that you are turning their hearts back again."—1 Kings 18:37

I confess I've occasionally gone through dry times in prayer when I would swear God wasn't listening—or that he was preoccupied over some global crisis.

Meditations are sometimes barren and seem to yield no fruit. Dryness of soul provides a dangerous climate for sprouting seeds of doubt. We begin to wonder if it's all an illusion. But even Saint Teresa acknowledged that in every fifteen minutes of prayer there are fourteen minutes of distraction.

During such times, please remember that God is not busy or taking a snooze. His love is changeless and constant. His purpose for you is still on course. True, there may be times when he leads you through a stretch of dry wasteland, when his joys aren't as evident, but remember that even the Israelites who wandered in the desert for forty years were—the whole time—actually only a few days' journey from the Promised Land!

Joni Eareckson Tada

WHAT OTHERS HAVE SAID

For what is prayer in the last analysis? It is a conscious spreading out of my helplessness before God. —Al Martin

Needing God's Voice

Read: 1 Kings 19

After the earthquake came a fire, but the LORD was not in the fire. And after the fire came a gentle whisper. —1 Kings 19:12

E lijah was fresh off the victory at Carmel where God had spoken clearly and powerfully to the nation with fire falling from the heaven. But now the prophet was discouraged and depressed and needed to hear from God again, this time to receive encouragement and direction. God's response to Elijah perfectly fit the condition of the weary prophet's heart. Elijah needed a gentle, reassuring and fatherly interaction with God, not a message delivered via earthquake or windstorm. The depths of God's character and love are shown throughout Scripture as he responds to his children in just the way they need him most.

A broken heart needs a tender touch as surely as a rebellious one may require a heavy hand. The God who formed the hearts and souls of every person knows best how to speak to them. Our responsibility is to be in a position to listen.

Dave Dravecky

Points to Ponder

* What do you think it means to be in a position to listen to God?

* What attitude(s) might you assume if you were in that position?

* How might having a "broken heart" help you be in that position?

* What would it be like to have God speak to you in a gentle, fatherly way?

OPEN OUR EYES

Read: 2 Kings 6:16–17

And Elisha prayed, "O LORD, open his eyes so he may see." Then the LORD opened the servant's eyes, and he looked and saw the hills full of horses and chariots of fire all around Elisha. — 2 Kings 6:17

S ometimes I wish our eyes could be opened—if only for a moment or two—to see the heavenly realms all around us. The reality of heaven would spring to life for us if we could peel away this layer—thin as a veil—and take a peek.

Elisha calmly prayed that his frightened servant's eyes might be opened to see the heavenly realities all around him. What was true for the prophet is true for any believer. When we sing as a church, "Open my eyes that I may see/ Glimpses of truth Thou hast for me," we wouldn't believe our eyes if God actually answered our request. Our eyes would pop at all the hosts of angels, chariots of fire, archangels and cherubim, living creatures, and ministering spirits . . . a few of which are most likely within a hairsbreadth next to you right now.

Joni Eareckson Tada

PATH TO PRAYER

Everlasting God, you have ordained and constituted in a wonderful order the ministries of angels and mortals. Mercifully grant that, as your holy angels always serve and worship you in heaven, so by your appointment they may help and defend us here on earth through Jesus Christ our Lord, who lives and reigns with you and the Holy Spirit, one God for ever and ever. Amen. —The Book of Common Prayer

WHY SHOULD I WAIT?

Read: 2 Kings 6:33—2 Kings 7:2

"This disaster is from the LORD. Why should I wait for the LORD any longer?"
—2 Kings 6:33

"*I* am a quadriplegic," the caller said. "I had said I would kill myself in ten years if I could not find help. It is now the tenth year. This is my only hope."

Quickly we put together an "aid package" for the man and now we wait for God to heal his heart. His story is sad and shocking—but just as shocking is his patience. He gave himself (and God) ten years! Most people rarely take such a long-term view. They want relief, and they want it now, like the king in 2 Kings 6:33 who wailed, "This disaster is from the LORD. Why should I wait for the LORD any longer?"

The discouraged people who grab God's attention are those who intentionally set out to wait. They know it may take a while. They not only wait, they watch, because they know God will answer. Rather than standing on the corner of life waiting for God, they go about their days unencumbered. They are productive, joyful people, knowing that God will come in due time.

So wait. Wait patiently and eagerly. In the meantime, get busy with what you know to be your responsibilities.

Joni Eareckson Tada

WHAT OTHERS HAVE SAID

We must wait for God, long, meekly, in the wind and wet, in the thunder and lightning, in the cold and the dark. Wait, and he will come. He never comes to those who do not wait. —Frederick William Faber

INFINITE

Read: 1 Chronicles 2

How great is the love the Father has lavished on us, that we should be called children of God! —1 John 3:1

Genealogies! More than grains of sand or stars in the sky—surely that's how many people have lived on the earth. And that God has loved and continues to love every one is astounding. How could there be enough divine love to go around? Because we're touching on such astronomical numbers, perhaps God only loves the world in a general sense.

Not so. God's love is infinite. Spurgeon defines it this way: "In math, if you divide an infinite number by any other number, no matter how large, you still get an infinite result. Jesus' love is infinite, and even though it is divided up for every person on earth, His love is still infinitely poured out on each one of us."

That's enough love to take away your guilt, dissipate your anger, fill up your loneliness, and assure you of heaven. Love so infinite will more than meet your desires and longings. God's love may be divided up for an infinite number of people on earth, but because his love is eternal and without end, he can still infinitely pour out his love on you. Just for you.

Joni Eareckson Tada

WHAT OTHERS HAVE SAID

The person you are now, the person you have been, the person you will be—this person God has chosen as beloved. —William Countryman

February 26

"PAIN"

Read: 1 Chronicles 4:9–10

His mother had named him Jabez, saying, "I gave birth to him in pain."
—1 Chronicles 4:9

C an you imagine someone whose name is Pain? That's what "Jabez" means in Hebrew. Just think of the razzing little Jabez must have endured from his playmates!

Yet Jabez didn't let his name get him down. In fact, Scripture says he was more honorable than his brothers. It even says that when he cried out to God, the Lord blessed him and granted his request to be kept from harm.

Can you, like Jabez, turn around a negative, use it for good and not let it get you down? Can you let it push you into the arms of Christ? God has a special love for you, too, so look to him in your pain. Whether it be physical or emotional, you may find that you'll be as blessed as Jabez.

Joni Eareckson Tada

WHAT OTHERS HAVE SAID

I pray God may open your eyes and let you see what hidden treasures he bestows on us in the trials from which the world thinks only to flee.
—John of Avila

A PEACEFUL PLACE

Read: 1 Chronicles 4:40

They found rich, good pasture, and the land was spacious, peaceful and quiet.
—1 Chronicles 4:40

No matter what your name may be—Joshibiah, Elioenai, Jaakobah, or Henry, Susan or Pat—you have a powerful need to find "rich, good pasture" in a land that's "spacious, peaceful and quiet."

Everyone needs a place where he or she can kick back, relax, stretch out, and feel safe. Everyone needs to experience the grace of God in all its fullness, a place of green meadows and abundant, cool waters.

The good news is, God is in the business of providing just such a place!

Here in 1 Chronicles it's an actual locality (on "the outskirts of Gedor to the east of the valley"), but in Christ it may be found most anywhere—that is, as long as the Great Shepherd is present.

Do you need rich, good pasture today, a place that's spacious, peaceful and quiet? If so, then turn to the Savior, this moment, right where you are. And he promises, "I will give you rest" (Matthew 11:28).

Dave and Jan Dravecky

TAKE ACTION!

What would your perfect place of rest look like? Who would be there? Find some art supplies and draw a picture of your ideal place of rest. (Don't worry about your artistic ability—you don't have to show it to anyone!). Label it with 1 Chronicles 4:40, Matthew 11:28 or Psalm 23:1–4.

February 28

CALL ON HIS NAME

Read: 1 Chronicles 16:8–36

Give thanks to the LORD, call on his name; make known among the nations what he has done . . . Glory in his holy name; let the hearts of those who seek the LORD rejoice. —1 Chronicles 8,10

When God invites us to call on his name, we should never be at a loss as to which name to use. I call the Lord my Shepherd and Friend during those times when God's tenderness melts my heart and I cry to think how rich and full his love is.

Then there are times when I'm battling pride or wasting hours in daydreams. That's when God's Word slices through my sinfulness. It stings. His hand seems heavy. That's when I call the Lord my Refiner, my Purifier.

There are times when I feel helpless and frightened, when no one, not even my husband or best friend, seems to understand. Then I hide under the shelter of his wings. I snuggle safely in the cleft of the Rock. These are times when I call God my Tower, my High Fortress.

When it comes to God, one name just isn't enough. And because Scripture is full of different names for him, we can always know exactly how to relate to our Lord, whether we fall to our knees in awesome respect, or climb up in his lap to be held in his arms.

Joni Eareckson Tada

TAKE ACTION!

Do a Scripture search with a topical Bible, concordance or Bible handbook. Make a list of all the names for God you can find. How many are there? Put your list in your Bible or journal to help you remember God's names and to help you address God when you pray.

March

Two-way Communication

Read: 2 Chronicles 6:14–31

"Yet give attention to your servant's prayer and his plea for mercy, O LORD my God. Hear the cry and the prayer that your servant is praying in your presence."
— *2 Chronicles 6:19*

When you talk with someone, you share your thoughts and ideas and then listen. You listen to what your friend has to say. The same is true when we talk with God. The Lord is delighted when we arrive at his throne, having sought in advance his heart's desire in a matter. He loves it when we are ready to explain why we believe it is his will to do a certain thing or act in a certain way. When we pray that way, God can see we are attaching importance to our intercessions and petitions.

Before you offer your intercessions and petitions to God, take time to quietly sit before the Lord and listen. Ask him to reveal to you his heart's desire in a matter. Only then, when you offer your petition, will you be able to say that you are praying in his will. Pause during your praise and intercession for long moments just to . . . listen. Wait on the Lord to hear what Scriptures he places on your mind. Focus the ears of your heart on him, keeping distractions at bay and your wandering mind in check. This is listening. This is talking with the Lord.

Joni Eareckson Tada

PATH TO PRAYER

How I praise you, Lord, that you desire a two-way communication with me. Forgive me when I talk at you . . . and fail to speak to you and then listen. May my prayer life grow in this way.

SEEK HIS FACE

Read: 2 Chronicles 7:11–16

"If my people, who are called by my name, will humble themselves and pray and seek my face and turn from their wicked ways, then will I hear from heaven and will forgive their sin and will heal their land."—2 Chronicles 7:14

We tend to think that prayer should come easily to us, and many times it does. But prayer in the face of suffering can be a different story. We are often surprised when prayer becomes difficult, when it seems fruitless, when the needs of the moment are so overwhelming that we don't know where to begin. During these times it's easy to lose confidence in our ability to pray or in God's willingness to respond.

God wants us to come to him, even with fumbling words and an unsure heart. He's given us the cries, the prayers of others in the Bible and his Son's guiding words on prayer to help us when prayer becomes difficult—as he knew it would. How greatly he desires our presence. How much he longs to be a father to his children, especially when they are hurting.

If you are struggling with prayer, ask God for help! We have no power to maintain our spiritual life on our own. We need God's help . . . even to pray. And it's okay to ask him for help.

Dave and Jan Dravecky

POINTS TO PONDER

Look carefully at the verse of the day. What do you think is the significance of the "if...then" structure of the sentence? What verbs (action words) does the verse list as necessary for prayer? What verbs are used in God promise in return?

HE'S WAITING, AND HE WILL HEAR

Read: 2 Chronicles 30:1–21

"May the LORD, who is good, pardon everyone who sets his heart on seeking God— the LORD, the God of his fathers."— 2 Chronicles 30:18–19

Sometimes we fear that we cannot come to the Lord in prayer because we don't know the "right" way to do it. Or we worry that he will not hear us if we pour out our hearts because of some past transgression that long ago we confessed. Or we think we must reach some level of advanced spirituality before we can gain a heavenly hearing.

But this is all wrong. It was wrong even in Old Testament days, before Resurrection Sunday and the arrival of the age of grace.

When King Hezekiah invited worshipers from both Israel and Judah to celebrate the Passover, many came to Jerusalem without consecrating themselves. So would they be excluded? A strict application of the law would certainly do so. "But Hezekiah prayed for them, saying, 'May the LORD, who is good, pardon everyone who sets his heart on seeking God—the LORD, the God of his fathers—even if he is not clean according to the rules of the sanctuary." So what happened? "And the LORD heard Hezekiah and healed the people."

Come to God today, just as you are. He's waiting, and he will hear.

Joni Eareckson Tada

WHAT OTHERS HAVE SAID

Great talent is a gift of God, but it is a gift which is by no means necessary in order to pray well. This gift is required in order to converse well with men; but it is not necessary in order to speak well with God. For that, one needs good desires, and nothing more. —St. John of the Cross

Even the Shortest Prayer

Read: Nehemiah 1:3—2:9

The king said to me, "What is it you want?" Then I prayed to the God of heaven, and I answered the king. —Nehemiah 2:4–5

This may be the shortest prayer in the Bible. It's so short it has no words.

Nehemiah knew the king's cupbearer was not permitted to appear before the throne with a sad face, yet he couldn't hide his grief that Jerusalem had been laid in ruins. The king noticed his deep sorrow and asked, "Why does your face look so sad when you are not ill? This can be nothing but sadness of heart."

Nehemiah admits that he grew "very much afraid" at this point, but he suppressed his fear and told the king of his devastated homeland. The king then asked what he really wanted—and here's when Nehemiah addressed his short prayer to heaven. Between gulps, this frightened man of God prayed . . . and God heard his fleeting prayer. Just as he does our own!

Dave and Jan Dravecky

What Others Have Said

Brief prayer has this advantage: it flies up to heaven before the devil can get a shot at it. —Rowland Hill

STARTING OVER

Read: Nehemiah 2:11–18

"Come, let us rebuild the wall of Jerusalem, and we will no longer be in disgrace."—Nehemiah 2:17

With the hand of God upon him, Nehemiah called God's people to take on a great challenge, to rebuild the wall of Jerusalem, certain that God would give them success.

Life is filled with challenges. It was a challenge for me to become a professional baseball player. It was a challenge to try to make a comeback after cancer first attacked my arm. It was a greater challenge when I had to decide about what to do with my life after the amputation. And the challenges just keep on coming.

I am still learning what this life is all about, but I know one thing: no matter what the challenge, *it's better to start over than to give up.* There is great value in starting over—no matter how old you are, what you have lost, or how long you have been dependent on other people. The process of taking responsibility for my own life and decisions has presented any number of challenges to my worth as a man, but by working through the challenges, with God's help, I have gained a greater sense of that worth than I ever enjoyed as a whole-bodied professional athlete.

Dave Dravecky

PATH TO PRAYER

What challenges are you facing? Do you need to start over in some area of your life? Pray that God will give you strength and hope as you take up your challenges. You might like to use Isaiah 40:28–31 as a starting point for your prayer.

WHERE IS JOY?

Read: Nehemiah 8:1–12

"This day is sacred to our Lord. Do not grieve, for the joy of the LORD is your strength."—Nehemiah 8:10

*I*f you're looking for joy, it can only be found in one place—that is, in one Person. "For the joy of the Lord is your strength," said wise Nehemiah to his fellow countrymen.

It is not possible to always be happy. But it *is* possible to always have the joy of the Lord. Some have described it as a calm-centeredness that tickles at the edges. It's a solid assurance that laughs, if given the chance. It is unwavering confidence that can't help but look on the bright side. My friend Tim Hansel once said that joy is peace dancing.

Think of all the things that make up the joy of the Lord, and your smile can't help but last. And when you meditate on God's smile, his joy will be yours.

Joni Eareckson Tada

WHAT OTHERS HAVE SAID

When I think upon my God, my heart is so full of joy that the notes dance and leap from my pen; and since God has given me a cheerful heart, it will be pardoned me that I serve him with a cheerful spirit
— Franz Joseph Haydn

TURNING THINGS AROUND

For the Jews it was a time of happiness and joy, gladness and honor. —Esther 8:16

God can turn things around in amazing ways. Perhaps more than any other book in the Bible, Esther shows how God can use awful setbacks to glorify himself and bless his people. What looked to be one of the darkest days in Israel's history was divinely turned inside out into one of the nation's greatest victories. And a day that began in fear and trembling ended in joy and loud praises.

God loves to turn things around. For you, too.

Are you in the middle of some setback? Has God seemed to open a door only to slam it shut? Remember these words from an old hymn: "Judge not the Lord by what you sense, but trust him for his grace; behind his frowning providence, he hides a smiling face." May God help us to believe that behind his seeming frown is a heavenly smile of blessing!

Joni Eareckson Tada

PATH TO PRAYER

Lord Jesus, my Savior, when my days are dark and it seems that doors have been slammed shut on my hopes and dreams, help me to believe that you are still smiling on me. Help me to trust that, in your grace, you will turn my fear into joy and my trembling into praise. Amen.

TESTING

Read: Job 2:1–10

"Shall we accept good from God, and not trouble?" In all this, Job did not sin in what he said. —Job 2:10

Satan has power to bring suffering to people, and he uses it. Still, we can take comfort that it is limited by God and will one day be done away with forever.

The story of Job is about a righteous and good man who suffered terribly at the hand of Satan. We read that Satan "afflicted Job with painful sores from the soles of his feet to the top of his head" (v. 7). Before Satan was allowed to inflict evil on Job, however, he had to get permission from God (v. 6). And God allowed this injustice only to prove a cosmic point. Satan had challenged God's character by claiming that Job served God only because the Lord had blessed Job's life. But Job clung faithfully to God despite the worst Satan could throw at him. And by the end of the story—after Job had proven God's point—God restored Job's blessings to him. In fact, "the LORD blessed the latter part of Job's life more than the first" (42:12).

Dave and Jan Dravecky

WHAT OTHERS HAVE SAID

God will never permit any troubles to come upon us unless he has a specific plan by which great blessing can come out of the difficulty.
—Peter Marshall

March 9

KEEP YOUR GUILT!

Read: Job 5:17,27—Job 6:1–30

"Relent, do not be unjust; reconsider, for my integrity is at stake."—Job 6:29

Those who suffer can take heart in Job's courageous response to his accusing comforters. He tells it like it is. He says, in effect, "Wait a minute! What you are offering is not comfort. It is not encouragement. Keep your guilt and let me show you what real comfort is!"

Many people who suffer today hear the message, "You are guilty! Otherwise, you wouldn't be in such a situation." The message may be couched in a variety of terms—if only you hadn't done that, if only you had more faith, if only you would confess your secret sins, if only, if only, if only. Whatever the terminology, it is the same message of guilt. Rather than bringing peace and comfort to the individual who is suffering, the condemnation of guilt only adds to the burden.

The fact is that suffering is not only difficult to endure, it is difficult to understand. We rarely know the reasons for suffering in our own lives—let alone the lives of others. Authentic encouragement doesn't come from the person who says, "I have the answer to why you are suffering." Those words often produce guilt. Encouragement most often comes from the person who lovingly says, "I don't have the answer. I don't understand why you are suffering, but I care about you. I want to stand by you as you go through this."

Dave Dravecky

PATH TO PRAYER

Dear Lord, I am amazed at how you work. I may not fully understand, but I am left with only one thing to do: thank you for whatever you are doing in my life. Although I now see only dimly, nevertheless I see that you are preparing for me a far better place than this. Father, help me to keep my eyes fixed on this truth; give me the strength to stay focused on you and undistracted by the circumstances around me. Amen.

YET I WILL HOPE

Read: Job 13:1–22

"Though he slay me, yet will I hope in him." —Job 13:15

*P*erhaps the most remarkable statement in the book of Job is this, where the beleaguered patriarch says of God, "Though he slay me, yet will I hope in him." A statement like this speaks highly of Job. But it speaks more highly of God. Nothing wounds the devil more—and you and I can have a part in rubbing salt in those wounds. The life of the most "insignificant" person is a battlefield on which the mightiest forces of the universe converge in warfare. This elevates the status of the lowliest and least person on earth!

I picture the day when we will depart earth and head for heaven. When our spirits rise out of these shells, the entire universe of angelic hosts will no doubt stand erect, holding their breath in respect. Maybe they will salute in amazement, watching our spirits ascend as a sweet-smelling savor to God. And then—watch out! The party will really break loose!

Each day we go on living means something. God is up to something good when it comes to our trials.

Joni Eareckson Tada

POINTS TO PONDER

* In what respect are you being "slain"?

* What is being "put to death" in you? Pride? Dependence on your "stuff"? Your appetite? Your tendency to overindulge yourself?

* In what way is that "little death" a spiritual battle for you?

* How can you praise God in the midst of the battle?

* Can you imagine angels giving you a nod of respect for having won the battle?

PATIENCE?

Read: Job 16:1–21

"Surely, O God, you have worn me out; you have devastated my entire household."—Job 16:7

Y ou've heard of the patience of Job? To me that never made sense because the book of Job is one long list of complaints. Not one to take suffering meekly, Job cried out in protest against God. Even his friends were shocked at his anger. Goodness, most of us would bite our nails in fear and trembling if we ever talked to God that way.

God, however, does not get offended. He doesn't get insulted or intimidated. In fact, in a supreme touch of irony, in the end God orders Job's pious comforters to seek repentance from the man himself.

I love that about God. Yes, Job's patience was gloriously played out in that he refused to curse God and die. It was the Lord who demonstrated the very best of what it means to be patient. The patience of Job? It should be the patience of God. The God of Job—your God—listens to the complaints of the suffering. He may not respond to your questions with neat, pat answers, but he will *always* answer your questions with his own patience.

Joni Eareckson Tada

FOR FURTHER REFLECTION

Read Exodus 2:24 and 6:5 for more on God's attitude toward suffering; read Psalms 64:1 and 142:1–2 to see how the psalmist poured out his troubles to God.

GOD'S ORDER

Read: Job 36:22—37:24

"The breath of God produces ice, and the broad waters become frozen. . . . He brings the clouds to punish men, or to water his earth and show his love."
—Job 37:10, 13

*M*idwest winters are notorious for their freezing cold. The deepest lakes thicken their icy crust, and the wind's biting fury finds the tiniest crack in your down-filled armor. It can feel like God's cold shoulder, a sort of punishment for living.

We can easily interpret the harshness of such winters, or any difficult circumstance, as God's punishment. And pleasant skies—or pleasant living—are seen as God's favor. Elihu rightly observed that God's breath and hands, as well as his purposes, are varied. He does not order the events of the universe to fulfill the desires of a single soul without considering a world of souls. What seems like hardship for one is blessing for another; the same snow that extends the morning commute by an hour keeps the earth insulated and moist for next year's planting.

Have no doubt that your circumstances are ordered by God. When we accept, endure, and even embrace the seeming frigidness of God's breath, we see his larger purposes, his broader love. He has not turned his back on creation (or you) at all. He's simply loving the work he did as only a Creator could.

Joni Eareckson Tada

POINTS TO PONDER

* What kinds of hard circumstances that are common to all people (like a bad cold or a winter storm) seem like punishment to you? How might each of these things be for your good or for the good of someone else?

* What kinds of circumstances seem like a blessing to you? How might those same things be a hardship for someone else?

* How do these questions encourage you to develop a larger view of God's love?

A Symbol for Growing Christians

Read: Psalm 1

He is like a tree planted by streams of water, which yields its fruit in season and whose leaf does not wither. Whatever he does prospers. —Psalm 1:3

God had a great idea when he chose a tree as a symbol for growing Christians. Just consider: It's a fact that the branches of growing trees not only reach higher, but their roots grow deeper. It's impossible for a strong tree to have high branches without having deep roots. It would become top-heavy and topple over in the wind. The same is true with Christians. It's impossible to grow in the Lord without entwining our roots around his Word and deepening our life in his commands.

A growing tree will always provide shade and comfort for others. A growing tree takes in light and processes it for food. Such a tree is always able to reproduce itself. Sometimes the best trees give their lives for others as branches are lopped off for firewood or lumber.

Joni Eareckson Tada

Path to Prayer

May my roots grow deep in your Word, Lord, may my branches grow high and reach toward you. Then, when winds of adversity come, then I will remain strong.

SLEEP, BLESSED SLEEP

Read: Psalm 4

I will lie down and sleep in peace, for you alone, O LORD, make me dwell in safety.
— Psalm 4:8

Sleep is one of the first areas affected when we face severe trials. It often flees from us like a wildebeest before a lion, like a scrap of paper before a windstorm. Yet God tells us in Psalm 4 that sleep *is* possible, even in the most difficult of circumstances.

During our three-year ordeal in the wilderness, circumstances continually went from bad to worse. But while events around me seemed ominous, it gave me hope to know that God promises we *can* enjoy peaceful sleep—not because our circumstances will change during the night, but because "you alone, O LORD, make me dwell in safety."

I still use the quality of my sleep as a litmus test. If my sleep is troubled, I consider that a sign that I am trying to sustain myself rather than trusting God. The remedy? Return to the wisdom of Psalm 4, ask God to relieve my distress, and trust in the Lord. *Then* "I will lie down and sleep in peace."

Jan Dravecky

PATH TO PRAYER

Jesus, Lover of my Soul, I am confused and anxious, and my sleep is often troubled. But I know that you will keep me safe in your loving care. So I offer up my troubles to your care tonight and every night. Bring me to a quiet place of rest in you, I pray. Amen.

When Sighs Are All There Are

Read: Psalm 5

Give ear to my words, O LORD, consider my sighing. —Psalm 5:1

When we find ourselves in deep distress, our words often vanish like smoke. We find our desperate longings cannot be formed into sentences with subject, verb, and object. We are like the mute: wordless, with nothing on our lips but sighs.

And yet the Lord hears us!

In Psalm 5 David asks not only that the Lord might hear his words, but that God would consider his "sighing" as well. What else can this mean but that David's pain had grown too great for words? What words he had, he offered in prayer; but this was not enough. David therefore asked the Lord that he might accept even his sighs!

What an amazing God we serve; he hears not only our spoken prayers, but also our speechless sighs. Even when we do not know what to pray for, God's Word tells us, "the Spirit himself intercedes for us with groans that words cannot express" (Romans 8:26). And so God meets sigh with sigh—and thus works for our benefit!

Dave Dravecky

Points to Ponder

* When have you found yourself so troubled that you were speechless?

* What kinds of emotions were (or are) you experiencing?

* What comfort do you get from knowing that God meets your sigh with his own?

* Imagine God's sighs echoing your own.

EVEN KINGS GET DEPRESSED

Read: Psalm 6

My soul is in anguish. How long, O LORD, how long? —Psalm 6:3

*I*f you've ever been depressed, you know the symptoms: faintness of heart, agony of body, anguish of soul, weariness from groaning, a pillow stained with tears, eyes weak from sorrow (but which are yet strong enough to notice all their enemies).

Have you ever been there? I have. I have felt many of the same symptoms that David describes in Psalm 6. Here was "a man after [God's] own heart" (Acts 13:22). Israel's most illustrious king, a giant-killer from his youth—and yet also here was a man given to depression. More amazing yet, David's battle with depression was recorded for all time in God's Word, demonstrating that our Lord understands our weakness. He wants us to know we can come out all right!

David shows us not only that difficult times come to us all, but that we can approach God boldly and tell him just how difficult things are.

Jan Dravecky

WHAT OTHERS HAVE SAID

God accepts our prayers just as they are. In the same way that a small child cannot draw a bad picture, so a child of God cannot offer a bad prayer.
—Richard Foster

A RADIO AT FULL VOLUME

Read: Psalm 10

But you, O God, do see trouble and grief; you consider it to take it in hand.
—Psalm 10:14

*I*t's a great comfort to know that God sees my pain and that he promises to help the weak. This is good to remember, for when our emotions are raw from the onslaught of pain, they can become like an open wound, reacting to the slightest touch or the least movement. They are like a radio turned to full volume; the overwhelming noise can make it impossible to distinguish a single, still, small voice. No wonder we question where God is when pain overtakes us! We can't hear him or feel his warmth or his presence. We hear only noise; we feel only pain.

But he is there all the time, ever speaking, never silent. Our challenge is to be still, and to offer him our wounds to heal so we can feel his touch again. As the suffering psalmist also said to the Lord, "The victim commits himself to you." This is the wisest course of action when suffering comes calling.

Jan Dravecky

PATH TO PRAYER

Lord, my emotions are so raw; my spirit is uneasy. Take my trouble and grief into your hand. Quiet my soul and let me hear your voice within my heart. Amen.

No Good Thing but in Him

Read: Psalm 16:1–6

Apart from you I have no good thing. —Psalm 16:2

*H*appiest are those who can make this statement when life is cruising along and the skies are bright and sunny; but happy are those, too, who make this discovery when the dark clouds roll in and darkness covers their personal landscape.

It's a sad truth that many of us never discover the priceless value of the Lord until we are stripped of everything else. But it is an expression of his limitless grace and mercy that when we arrive in the land of utter desolation, our eyes can at last be opened to our true treasure: God himself.

Oh, that we would train our lips to proclaim to the Lord, "Apart from you I have no good thing," that we would train our minds to believe it and that we would train our hearts to feel it! Then when suffering comes, we could endure its hardships with hope, knowing that we can never lose that which is most precious of all.

Dave Dravecky

What Others Have Said

"Without Thee, I cannot live!" Whatever our small practice, belief, or experience may be, nothing can alter the plain fact that God, the spirit of spirits, the Life-giving Life, has made, or rather, is making each person . . . for Himself; and that our lives will not achieve stability until they are ruled by that truth. —Evelyn Underhill

ETERNAL PLEASURES

Read: Psalm 16:7–11

You have made known to me the path of life; you will fill me with joy in your presence, with eternal pleasures at your right hand. —Psalm 16:11

O ur souls are restless, raging, and thirsting for fulfillment, for delight, for . . . pleasure. Someone has said, "The worth and excellency of a soul is to be measured by the object of its love." Who we are in our innermost being is revealed by those things we passionately desire.

Because God has created your need for pleasure, it stands to reason that he must be the consummation of that need. He directs our pleasure-seeking souls when he commands, "Love the Lord your God with all your heart" (Luke 10:27). God is not only the one who gives pleasure, but is himself all pleasure.

Eternal pleasures are found at God's right hand. You don't have to look any further. God places passions within you so that you'll keep searching until you find utter delight in him. So don't deny your desire for delight. Look for it, however, in the only place it can be found. Gorge yourself on God and discover real and deep delight.

Joni Eareckson Tada

PATH TO PRAYER

In your own words, tell God that your greatest passion is in seeking him; that you want to find your greatest and most real delight in him. Ask him to lead you on the path of joyful discovery of his presence. Praise him for being your all-in-all. Sing a hymn or song as a love song to him.

I WILL SEE YOUR FACE

Read: Psalm 17

And I—in righteousness I will see your face; when I awake, I will be satisfied with seeing your likeness. —Psalm 17:15

I have to confess. I have often wished that I could just die. To close my eyes and wake to the sight of my Lord and the sound of angels has consumed my thinking on numerous occasions, especially when I get fatigued or forced to bed with pressure sores.

David, the psalmist, was no stranger to the desire to die. But his words, unlike those who promote euthanasia, are guarded. They are carefully crafted to delete all thoughts of death for the sake of escape: "And I—in righteousness I will see your face." There is no way I'm going to end my life sinfully just so I can behold God. Such a thing is contradictory. I must be righteous in my death as I am in my life.

Joni Eareckson Tada

PATH TO PRAYER

Lord, I want to be with you. Now. I confess it. And I confess my reasons are not always righteous. Too often they are because life here is hard. Make my desire for heaven conform to the face of your will.

THE FATHER'S ANSWER

Read: Psalm 18

In my distress I called to the LORD; I cried to my God for help. From his temple he heard my voice; my cry came before him, into his ears. —Psalm 18:6

D on't ever think that when you pray for God's support, he remains uncaring or unfeeling about your plea. God is not off somewhere on a mountaintop, at arm's length from your cry. When you pray for help, he does not lean over the wall of his ivory tower to tell you to beg louder.

God is as attentive to your needs as a caring father is to his dearest son. Pain stirs the heart of a father like nothing else. My friend Jim knows all about this. He often has to leave his three little boys when he flies away on business. On a recent trip, as the family drove together to the airport, the seven-year-old gladly took last-minute instructions on how to help Mommy while Daddy was away. The five-year-old bravely tucked in his chin and promised he would do his chores. As they turned into the airport, the two-year-old, all smiles and jabber up until then, spotted an airplane on the runway. Suddenly, wailing and sobbing!

"It tore my heart out!" Jim exclaimed. "I almost canceled the trip right then. I just kept hugging that little boy." As I saw Jim's eyes well up with tears, I thought, *If that boy's cries tug at Jim's heart, how much more must our tears move our heavenly Father.* Nothing grips God's heart like the tortured cry of one of his children.

He reaches down. He takes hold. He hears our cry!

Joni Eareckson Tada

TAKE ACTION!

In your own words, write a psalm of your own. Be honest about your heartaches and troubles. Don't mince words with God. He can handle your honest emotions. If you need to, skim through some of the psalms to see how the psalmists have spoken to God and about God.

GLORY!

Read: Psalm 19

The heavens declare the glory of God; the skies proclaim the work of his hands.
—Psalm 19:1–6

Our solar system, as immense as it is, is just one small speck in the Milky Way galaxy. How small? Let's say the Milky Way galaxy were the size of North America. Using that scale, our sun and its planets would fit into a coffee cup somewhere in a little corner of that continent. What's more amazing is that the Milky Way is just an average galaxy among billions of others far bigger. The number of stars, trillions upon trillions, is incomprehensible. Astronomers are now convinced there are more stars in the universe than there are grains of sand on the beaches of the world. This doesn't mean that Earth is a grain of sand; no, our sun—the star—would be the grain of sand. And on this teensy speck of earth, out of billions of people, the Lord of the universe came to earth to save *you.*

Praise God, you are no bother to him. Jesus, the Lord of the heavens, has paid attention to you. He came to earth for you. Awesome! Go outside tonight, look at the stars and give him praise.

Joni Eareckson Tada

WHAT OTHERS HAVE SAID

We know that God is everywhere; but certainly we feel his presence most when his works are on the grandest scale spread before us; and it is in the unclouded night-sky, where his worlds wheel their silent course, that we sense clearest his infinitude, his omnipotence, his omnipresence.
—Charlotte Brontë

WHERE DID YOU GO?

Read: Psalm 22

My God, my God, why have you forsaken me? Why are you so far from saving me, so far from the words of my groaning?—Psalm 22:1

*M*ost of us can identify with David and his cry. We cry out . . . and God seems silent. He seems so far away. The key word is "seems." While our feelings tell us he has abandoned us, our faith insists that he would never do any such thing.

A. W. Tozer helped me understand the roles of feelings and faith. He describes feelings as "the play of emotion over the will, a kind of musical accompaniment to the business of living, and while it is indeed most enjoyable to have the band play as we march . . . it is by no means indispensable. We can work and walk without music and if we have true faith we can walk with God without feeling."

God didn't forsake me in the silence. He was teaching me . . . to have a "true faith" that's unswayed by emotion. At times I have to walk with him without the pleasure of music so that my faith will deepen. And when the music returns, its melody sounds all the more sweet.

Jan Dravecky

POINTS TO PONDER

* Can you relate to the feeling that God often seems far away? That God has "forsaken you"? What was Jesus' experience with those feelings (see Matthew 27:46)?

* What is your response to A.W. Tozer's idea that we can "walk with God without feeling"?

* What do *you* think it would be like to have a faith that is not subject to fluctuations of your mood?

* What is your own experience with the balance between faith and feelings?

A Smile on the Other Side

Read: Psalm 23

Even though I walk through the valley of the shadow of death, I will fear no evil, for you are with me. —Psalm 23:4

Who among us hasn't faced fright and fear head-on by softly quoting the twenty-third Psalm? We repeat those old familiar verses time and again to soothe our souls and break the suffocating grip of fear.

I'm particularly fond of the fourth verse: "Even though I walk through the valley of the shadow of death, I will fear no evil, for you are with me." The psalmist doesn't focus his attention on the dark valley, and he's not distracted by the shadows. He sees through the valley, past the darkness, and looks with confidence toward the other side. He knows the dark valley is a place to go through, not a place to stay in.

Are you in the middle of a dark valley? It may look dark and gloomy right now, but please remember that God does not intend for you to stay in those shadows. The valley he has led you into is the same valley out of which he will lead you. You will, by his grace, go through it. There is, thanks to our Shepherd, a smile on the other side.

Joni Eareckson Tada

Take Action!

If you have not already done so, memorize Psalm 23. Or write it out longhand and decorate the paper with your own illustrations or pictures from a magazine. Post it in a prominent place to remind you that your Good Shepherd is with you.

GET RID OF THE GUILT

Read: Psalm 25

Show me your ways, O LORD, teach me your paths; guide me in your truth and teach me, for you are God my Savior, and my hope is in you all day long.
— *Psalm 25:4–5*

*I*t wasn't easy to break free from the guilt burden I had grown accustomed to lugging around most of my adult life. How such a thing could be habit-forming, I can't imagine. Yet . . . it seemed so difficult to let it go! Even today, I will occasionally fall into the guilt-producing trap of people pleasing. How does it happen? I know that God does not want my heart and life to be burdened down! In Matthew 11:30, Jesus tells us, "My yoke is easy and my burden is light."

So if you find the weight of a guilt burden biting into your shoulders, it is appropriate to consider the source. Very likely you're carrying a burden that doesn't belong on your back at all! When our hearts are troubled or burdened by guilt, we can bring it all before our Father. We can ask him to shine the light of truth on our guilt, so that we can discern what is true and what is false. In this way, one day at a time, we can be set free from the terrible, life-sapping burden of false guilt.

Jan Dravecky

PATH TO PRAYER

Dear Lord, thank you for loving me and caring about every part of me— even my emotions. Please protect me from false guilt and those crushing expectations that don't really come from you. Grant me your wisdom, discernment, and truth, so that I don't take on the burden of responsibilities that belong to others. Help me avoid the trap of seeking to prove that I am acceptable. Make my heart sensitive to your leading, so that I will walk confidently on a firm path through this difficult time. Amen.

ALL IS WELL

Read: Psalm 27

My heart says of you, "Seek his face!" Your face, Lord, I will seek. —Psalm 27:8

Robert Louis Stevenson tells a story about passengers on a ship who became alarmed when a storm sent angry waves crashing over the bow. Many of them thought for certain the end had come.

Finally, one passenger—against orders—crept up on deck where the pilot, strapped tightly to the wheel, was steering the churning vessel. The pilot caught sight of the terror-stricken man and gave him a reassuring smile. The passenger immediately backed down the steps, entered the hold of the ship and announced to the others, "I have seen the face of the pilot and he smiled at me. All is well."

This story perfectly captures what our Pilot is doing when powerful waves of trials crash around us. Oh, if we would only seek the reassuring smile of God, we would be calmed. He knows the way through the waves! And all is well.

Joni Eareckson Tada

WHAT OTHERS HAVE SAID

No soul can have rest until it finds created things are empty. When the soul gives up all for love, so that it can have Him that is all, then it finds true rest. —Julian of Norwich

JOY OF THE LORD

Read: Psalm 30

You turned my wailing into dancing; you removed my sackcloth and clothed me with joy. — Psalm 30:11

*B*ecause of God's promise of ultimate joy, it is possible to see glimpses of joy even when we suffer. I don't mean that this is an easy thing to accomplish. But even in my days of acute suffering, I did experience a sense of joy, usually through the loving care and comfort of others. Precious glimpses of joy came through friends who allowed me to say whatever I needed to say. It came through the faces of those who loved me and didn't beat around the bush but helped me deal with reality. Joy came through the words of the Bible that were shared with me when I didn't have the energy to seek them out myself.

And what about those days when no flash of joy—not even a fleeting glimpse—can be found? In those times, as hard as it can be, Jan and I try to remember the one promise of joy that will never fail: our salvation in Jesus Christ. True joy comes in knowing that God cares enough about us that he has opened wide the doors of heaven.

Dave Dravecky

FOR FURTHER REFLECTION

Read Isaiah 34:16 through Isaiah 35. Reflect on the picture of joyful abundance you find there. If you wish, go on to read John 16:24; Romans 15:13; and Galatians 5:22. What or who is the source of joy? Why do you think one can find joy even in suffering?

JOY IN THE MUD

Read: Psalm 34

I will extol the LORD at all times; his praise will always be on my lips. My soul will boast in the LORD; let the afflicted hear and rejoice. —Psalm 34:1–2

On a particularly damp and windy day, hundreds of calves were huddled outside, shoulder to hindquarter, tucked between the fence and the barn. The rain had created a mess of mud and the calves looked dirty brown instead of the usual black and white. They looked miserable.

All except one calf. In the face of the wind he skipped and jumped like a child, oblivious to the downpour. That mud-caked calf looked happy.

Like that calf, David chose an unusual moment to declare the joy of being a child of God. Huddled around him in the cave of Adulam were 400 smelly, dirty renegades fleeing from Saul. But David had the audacity to declare: "Those who look to him are radiant; their faces are never covered with shame." David submitted his fears to God and was enabled to declare a calf-like joy.

Are you gripped with a spirit of fear? Then take each fear by the horn and lead it to the face of God. Let your fears see the light of eternal day and you, too, can skip, laugh, dance and sing.

Joni Eareckson Tada

PATH TO PRAYER

Lord, today I want to be able to sing and dance with joy. I want my soul to skip and jump like a young calf. So I give my fears to you, my fear of _____ _____ and_____ and_____. I praise you Father, that you are Strength and Peace and Holiness and that you have the power to banish my fears and replace them with faith. Amen and amen.

WHERE DID EVERYONE GO?

Read: Psalm 38

O LORD, do not forsake me; be not far from me, O my God. Come quickly to help me, O Lord my Savior. —Psalm 38:21–22

There are many reasons why people sometimes avoid us in our suffering. Some don't know what to say. Others don't want to be around a person who's "down." Some think our troubles are our own fault, that we should bear the full weight of our guilt. And still others are too preoccupied with their own pain to worry about that of someone else.

When people avoid us in our days of suffering, it is good to remember that they did the same thing to King David. "My friends and companions avoid me because of my wounds," he complained, "my neighbors stay far away" (v.11).

For many, this is the most painful part of suffering—doing it alone. They find out how weak and frail their body is, how easily swayed their faith can be, and how few true friends they really have. So what's the answer? David gives it to us in verses 21 and 22: "O LORD, do not forsake me; be not far from me, O my God. Come quickly to help me, O Lord my Savior."

Jan Dravecky

POINTS TO PONDER

✳ When have you felt as though others had abandoned you and that you were suffering alone?

✳ When have you experienced the most support and concern of others?

✳ In what ways are we *meant* to be supported and comforted by other people? (see 2 Corinthians 1:3; Philippians 2:4; James 5:13–16)

✳ In what ways might we take advantage of "abandoned" times so that we can be alone with God?

STILL WAITING

Read: Psalm 40

I waited patiently for the LORD; he turned to me and heard my cry. —Psalm 40:1

We live in a time when waiting is synonymous with waste. When we wait, we feel we are wasting precious time. Yet for so many people in pain, waiting is the one thing they do—a lot. They wait for the doctor. They wait for test results. They wait for the medicine to work. They wait for the world to take notice that they have needs. They wait in line at the pharmacy. They wait for life to return to "normal." Their days are filled with waiting.

Something amazing often happens, however, to those whose days are filled with waiting. They discover that life is best observed and cherished in the wait. Our waiting gives God time—time to speak to us, to bring us to reflection, surrender, and peace. Waiting allows us to gather the strength and courage we need to face whatever comes.

Dave and Jan Dravecky

POINTS TO PONDER

* What does "waiting for the Lord," mean to you?

* How is just waiting for things to happen (like waiting for test results) like waiting for the Lord? How is it different?

* How can you use the time you spend waiting wisely? What can you do in that time to grow spiritually?

WHY ARE YOU DOWNCAST?

Read: Psalm 42

Why are you downcast, O my soul? Why so disturbed within me? Put your hope in God, for I will yet praise him, my Savior. —Psalm 42:5

Have you ever started out your day feeling downhearted, a little blue—for no discernible reason? The psalmist asks a good question, "Why are you downcast, O my soul?".

Is it the weather? What you ate last night for supper? Some annoyance that's been building, or just a vague, hazy dullness of soul that can't be explained? Often there's simply no reason for being downhearted.

That's why the psalmist quickly advises to put our hope in God and to do it by praising him. Nothing lifts our spirits quicker or higher than to place our praise at the feet of the Lord Jesus.

Joni Eareckson Tada

PATH TO PRAYER

Lord of Hope, I place my trust in you and I praise you for making all things well with my soul. Please receive glory as I magnify and adore your name, lifting my soul before you. With you, there is no reason to be downhearted.

April

April 1

The Blessing of Silence

"Be still, and know that I am God."—Psalm 46:10

*I*t happens all the time. You get together with a friend, or someone you haven't seen in a while, and before you know it, you've filled the air with a lot of talk about . . . you. You realize in embarrassment that you're rambling on about yourself and have nearly forgotten to include your friend—or even God—in the conversation. Oh, to be able to use words with restraint.

That's why I love traveling with my husband or my best friends. We are able to relax and be silent in each other's presence. No filling the air with empty words. What a blessing it is to be able to sit with someone you love . . . and enjoy the quiet together. Friendships, whether with others or with God, will deepen in silence.

When you stop talking long enough to listen, you learn something—only in silence can what you hear filter from your head into your heart. Only in silence can you hear the heartbeat of God and his still, small voice. In quiet, you realize spiritual insights that reach far beyond words.

Joni Eareckson Tada

What Others Have Said

I don't say anything to God. I just sit and look at him and he looks at me.
—Old peasant of Ars

GOD IN THE BLACK

Read: Psalm 50

I have no need of a bull from your stall or of goats from your pens, for every animal of the forest is mine, and the cattle on a thousand hills. —Psalm 50:9–10

God is completely and utterly self-sufficient. But how many times do we entertain the thought that he needs a "little help from his friends," as though he were low on cash, short on reserves, or in need of extra resources? *Can God help me?* We think: *Is he able? Does he have enough "oomph" to make a difference?*

God has everything he needs and more. Much, much more. He is not behind schedule, low on energy, short of clout, thin on reserves, nervous about the stock market, or hoping people will follow through on their pledges. He's not short on donors or awaiting bank approval and a zoning permit to fulfill his plans, because he has "no need of a bull from your stall or of goats from your pens, for every animal of the forest" is his, as are the creatures of the field.

God does not operate in the red. He's in the black. And he has more than enough resources to meet each and every one of your needs.

Joni Eareckson Tada

POINTS TO PONDER

* When you think about God's resources, what comes to mind?
* What resources are you in need of?
* What resources do you have that you could share with others?

A BROKEN SPIRIT

Read: Psalm 51

The sacrifices of God are a broken spirit; a broken and contrite heart, O God, you will not despise. —Psalm 51:17

Those who are suffering take great comfort in Psalm 51:17. Why? Because most of them *know* they are broken in spirit. During my depression I leaned hard on this verse. I knew I had a broken spirit, but I also knew this was a good thing before God. A broken spirit brings us to a place where God can mold us and shape us.

We tend to think that our sacrifices, our offerings to God, are what please him. We think he wants us to perform for him and bring him our good deeds. We think we must have something in our hands to show and please God, like the animal sacrifices the ancient Israelites brought to the temple.

The sweet message of this verse is that the sacrifice God wants is not the work of our hands to please him, but our open hands to receive him. He wants *us*.

Jan Dravecky

POINTS TO PONDER

* What do you think it means to have a broken spirit?
* In what way is a broken spirit a sacrifice before God?
* Why does suffering tend to "break" one's spirit?
* Why does suffering cause one's spirit to be more open to repentance?

TROUBLING THOUGHTS

Read: Psalm 55:1–17

Listen to my prayer, O God, do not ignore my plea; hear me and answer me. My thoughts trouble me and I am distraught. —Psalm 55:1–2

During my time of depression, I had problems with strange, awful thoughts. My thoughts frightened me; it scared me that I was even capable of thinking such terrible things.

I later learned that obsessive-compulsive thoughts are often a symptom of depression. I was so relieved when I read that King David also was troubled by his thoughts. Today I point to Psalm 55:2 when I work with people who are experiencing depression and who have obsessive-compulsive thoughts. Many will not even admit to such thoughts because they, too, are horrified that they could think such things.

David gives us a wonderful example of what to do about this problem. "Tell God about them," he counsels us. Bringing them out in the open takes away their secret power of shame and guilt. And it gives us the opportunity to ask God to help us overcome them.

Jan Dravecky

PATH TO PRAYER

What thoughts consistently and persistently trouble you? What or who are the enemies that threaten you? Identify them before God, writing them down if you need to clarify them. Ask God to remove them from your mind and give you peace. (If you are troubled by persistent depression or obsessive thoughts, seek guidance from a pastor, doctor, or mental health professional.)

April 5

NOT JUST ONCE

Read: Psalm 55:17–23

But I call to God, and the LORD saves me. Evening, morning and noon I cry out in distress, and he hears my voice. —Psalm 55:16–17

*I*t's hard for many of us to pray when things aren't going so well. Sometimes we say to ourselves, "Well, what good does prayer do anyway? I've been praying, and things aren't getting any better. I just don't have the energy to do this anymore."

King David encountered as many difficulties as we do, and yet he determined that he would not give up the one thing that gave him hope. "Evening, morning and noon I cry out in distress," he admits, "and [God] hears my voice."

David refused to give up his lifeline. He continued to pour out his heart, whether he saw any immediate improvement in his circumstances or not. He didn't pray just once. He didn't wait until Sunday. He didn't give up. Like a hurt child tugging on his mother's apron, he knew that God would respond because he knew God's loving heart

Dave and Jan Dravecky

FOR FURTHER REFLECTION

Read Luke 18:1; Romans 12:12; and 1Thessalonians 5:17–18 to discover more about persistence in prayer.

A Rock in a High Place

Psalm 61

From the ends of the earth I call to you, I call as my heart grows faint; lead me to the rock that is higher than I. —Psalm 61:2

My family spent the summer of 1959 near a little cow town just north of Phoenix, Arizona. We were helping my Uncle Ted separate his herds of cattle. Each day my sisters and I headed out on the best cow ponies to round up the herds before morning melted into the desert afternoon.

Uncle Ted had told us to head for "the big red boulder up on that yonder ridge" if we ever got lost. One sizzling day I did. I kicked my pony in the boulder's direction and found shelter in the boulder's shadow. It was, for me, a place of refuge.

Within an hour I heard galloping hooves coming up the ridge. I knew I would be found. I knew the high rock had been my certain and only hope.

The same is true for you. No matter how lost you feel God is with you. If you are resting in him, you are exactly where you're supposed to be. You'll be found. You are safe. Sanctuary in him is only a prayer away.

Joni Eareckson Tada

PATH TO PRAYER

Lord God, My Rock, my certainty and my hope, lead me into your presence and lift me up, I pray. Thank you for being a solid presence in my life, when everything seems to be shifting and changing. Even though I sometimes feel lost and alone, I know that you are with me. Thank you for always drawing my eyes back to you. Amen.

THIRST

Read: Psalm 63

O God, you are my God, earnestly I seek you; my soul thirsts for you, my body longs for you, in a dry and weary land where there is no water. —Psalm 63:1

When we get thirsty, we simply throw cold liquid down the hatch and presto! We're not thirsty anymore. The body, however, thinks of thirst in a much different way. The hypothalamus is the region of the brain primarily responsible for monitoring the body's level of water, sensing an increased concentration of salt in the bloodstream.

Our soul experiences its own kind of thirst. Those deep, inner longings we feel are simply the soul signaling to us that it needs something—comfort, affirmation, and love. Our soul was designed to consume one thing, and one thing only: God. All other earthly pursuits to quench our thirst do just the opposite. The things we think will quench our thirst are simply laden with more "salt" of self-doubt, covetousness, and pride. Only God is pure, clean, and deeply satisfying to our soul. Only God meets every need. Only God ends the hopeless search for the soul's true comfort, affirmation, and love.

Only God. Let those two words echo in your mind today.

Joni Eareckson Tada

TAKE ACTION!

Pour a tall glass of water. Hold it in your hand and reflect on how you thirst for God's presence. Drink the glass of water and think about how satisfying it is. Reflect on Jesus as the Living Water, poured out that you need never thirst.

A HEART OF SILVER

Read: Psalm 66:1–12

For you, O God, tested us; you refined us like silver . . . but you brought us to a place of abundance. —Psalm 66:9,12

*L*ove says, "I'd do anything for you, God, follow you anywhere." Obedience says, ". . . and let me prove it."

Obedience is not so much for God's sake as for ours. God wants us to realize the depth of our love for him.

So he tests us. He is the one who brings us into prisons and lays burdens on our backs. All the while, he never withholds his love from us. His love drives him to test us in order to refine us like silver. When gold is put through a refining process, it involves heat, as in a furnace. But when silver is refined, it involves pressure, as when one crushes a metal in a crucible. When a test heats up, we want to escape; when a trial is pressuring, we want to collapse. If we hold on, remain faithful and rigorously obey, our hearts become refined. Obedience melts away pride and prejudice. Obedience crushes into dust self-centeredness, revealing a heart pure and at peace.

Joni Eareckson Tada

WHAT OTHERS HAVE SAID

The best measure of a spiritual life is not its ecstasies but its obedience. —Oswald Chambers

WHINING AND DINING

Read: Psalm 66:13–20

If I had cherished sin in my heart, the Lord would not have listened; but God has surely listened and heard my voice in prayer. —Psalm 66:18–19

Whenever we're tempted to pitch a fit or throw a tantrum because of something gone awry in our world, we need to remember the principle *stop whining and dining.*

Stop whining: God's voice can't be heard above my complaints. No matter that his voice has shaken mountains; it's no match for my whining, negative spirit. I won't hear his comfort or his solution to my problem above the din of my self-pity.

Stop dining: Our solutions to crises sometimes come in the form of indulgences. I might indulge in food or fantasy. I'll work feverishly or play dangerously—anything to stop the pain. But the pain will not stop and the crisis will not pass until I stop trying to consume everything I desire. God's hand will not be felt while I grasp at pleasure.

What are you whining and dining on? When you end it, that's when God intervenes in quietness and strength. The crisis will pass. All things will work together for good. He will have his way. See it for yourself today.

Joni Eareckson Tada

POINTS TO PONDER

* When is complaining a negative thing? When might complaint be legitimate?

* Why does complaining keep us from hearing God's voice?

* Why do you think that indulging as an escape from pain obscures our sense of God's working in our lives?

COMFORT FOR THE CORNERED

Read: Psalm 69:1–15

Save me, O God, for the waters have come up to my neck . . . I am worn out calling for help; my throat is parched. My eyes fail, looking for my God. —Psalm 69:1,3

 *T*he waters have risen to your neck, you're sinking fast, and your throat is cracked and dry from yelling for help. You scan the horizon for any faint hope of rescue—and your eyes come up empty.

Are you among the cornered, the desperate? If you are, you're in good company. Many of God's children have felt the same noose around their necks—and yet they made it through to sing of their salvation.

One comfort for the cornered is the knowledge that they are not the first (nor will they be the last) to endure such desperate hours. To build our trust in him, God often waits until the last moment, the final second, to accomplish our rescue. And then it becomes plain that our predicament turns out to be both a test (will we trust him?) and an opportunity (how can we gain strength from this?). It helps to know that others, like the psalmist (vv. 1–3), have been there before us.

Dave and Jan Dravecky

PATH TO PRAYER

Jesus, Lover of my soul, I don't know where to turn but to you. Help now, I pray in these dark times. Heal my hurting heart and let me know that you are near to me. Amen.

WRITTEN YESTERDAY?

Read: Psalm 69:19–36

"I looked for sympathy, but there was none, for comforters, but I found none.
—Psalm 69:20

*I*t sounds as if it were written yesterday. Yet this lament didn't come out of a recent news report, but from a complaint written thousands of years ago by a disheartened sufferer. And in the providence of God, it became not only a true reflection of the tormented human heart, but also a prophecy about the broken heart of God's Son.

Don't believe it? Then look at the next verse: "They put gall in my food and gave me vinegar for my thirst"—a clear reference to the bitter drink Roman soldiers gave to Jesus Christ as he hung on the cross for you and me (Luke 23:36; John 19:29).

Jesus knew what it was like to look for sympathy and not find it, to seek comforters and discover none. All his disciples fled when he needed them most (Matthew 26:56). So never think God doesn't understand your loneliness. He knows—better than you can possibly imagine.

Dave and Jan Dravecky

PATH TO PRAYER

Jesus, you suffered the worst loneliness and sorrow and pain that anyone ever has felt. So how can I not turn to you when I am alone now and suffering? In your loving and sympathetic eyes may I find peace and comfort.

When Deliverance Comes

Read: Psalm 72

For [the king] will deliver the needy who cry out, the afflicted who have no one to help. He will take pity on the weak and the needy and save the needy from death.
—Psalm 72:12–13

I have a widowed friend who desperately tries to be self-sufficient. I have to pry prayer needs out of her and dig to uncover how she really feels. She seldom admits she is in over her head—although it's obvious to everyone around her. It's hard to help her because her hands don't reach out for help; they cover up her wounds instead.

The message of Psalm 72:12–14 is for my friend. God longs to bring her the deliverance only his love can bring, but she won't "cry out" for help; she thinks it's a sign of weakness. God brings helpers to her door, but she turns them away; she doesn't want to be a burden. God wants her to know how precious and valuable her life is to him, that he paid an unbelievable price to ransom her soul; but she thinks she isn't worthy of his love. . . . How I wish I could convince her to take her hands off her wounds and lift them to God! "He will deliver the needy who cry out"—but they have to let him.

Jan Dravecky

Points to Ponder

* Why is it so hard for some people to accept help from others?
* How could letting others help be a blessing to both parties?
* How might rejecting the help of others be the same as rejecting God's help?

April 13

THE CURE FOR ENVY

Read: Psalm 73

But as for me, my feet had almost slipped; I had nearly lost my foothold. For I envied the arrogant when I saw the prosperity of the wicked. —Psalm 73:2–3

*P*erhaps it has happened to you. Although you gave the best years of your life in faithful service to God, some illness or misfortune invaded your home through no fault of your own. To make matters worse, you look outside from your sick bed . . . and see your healthy neighbors whooping it up to all hours of the night in all kinds of gross sin.

And you seethe: It isn't fair! What use was my faithfulness to God? They have it better than I do! IT JUST ISN'T FAIR!

That's envy, and it's pretty common among believers who are going through trials. They find themselves saying, along with the psalmist, "Surely in vain have I kept my heart pure."

The only cure is the one the psalmist found. He entered the house of God and looked beyond current, transient circumstances. What he saw instantly sobered him, for he realized the final destiny of the godless: ruin, destruction, terror, and judgment. And that is nothing to envy. To be avoided, yes. To be envied, never.

Dave and Jan Dravecky

POINTS TO PONDER

* When have you experienced the kind of envy the psalmist speaks of?
* Are you experiencing that kind of envy right now?
* How do you cope when confronted with the unfairness of life?

THE DARK NIGHT OF THE SOUL

Read: Psalm 77

*I cried out to God for help; I cried out to God to hear me. When I was in distress,
I sought the Lord; at night I stretched out untiring hands and my soul refused to be
comforted. —Psalm 77:1–2*

S aint John of the Cross, a sixteenth-century Spanish mystic, described in a famous poem the experience of a believer who draws
close to God through the agonies of desolation and despair. He teaches
that one who patiently accepts trials can attain a communion with God
unavailable in any other way.

Those who find themselves in such a dark night of the soul often become convinced that God has abandoned them and cast them into darkness—to wander alone in the blackness for weeks, months, even years.
But John testifies that such a dark night may lead to brilliant light in the
very bosom of God.

Psalm 77 appears to picture just such a dark night of the soul. The psalmist cries out to God—and hears nothing. His soul refuses to be comforted. He wonders when God will again show him favor. Finally he makes
a decision: to recall the Lord's mighty works of the past. He dares to
believe that God will again work in his life. And that thought begins to
bring him hope. Not light, perhaps, not yet—but hope. And hope works
even in the dark.

Dave and Jan Dravecky

WHAT OTHERS HAVE SAID

Live in faith and hope, though it be in darkness, for in this darkness God
protects the soul. Cast your care upon God, for you are his and he will not
forget you. —St. John of the Cross

THE SHEPHERD OF ISRAEL

Read: Psalm 80:1–7

Hear us, O Shepherd of Israel, you who lead Joseph like a flock. . . . Awaken your might; come and save us. —Psalm 80:1,2

Y ou know you've come to a God unlike any other when you bump into Psalm 80:1. In that text the God of Israel is delighted to reveal himself as . . . a shepherd!

A king, we can understand. A warrior, we could expect. A counselor, we might anticipate. But a shepherd? What ancient religion would ever think to boast that its god tended sheep? What primitive faith would glory in a deity eager to identify with lambs and ewes? The gods of the ancients—these were vindictive beings of cunning and arrogance, best symbolized by lions, griffins, dragons and other monsters of claw and fang.

Yet the God of Israel reveals himself as a loving Lord who leads Joseph "like a flock." Oh yes, he sits enthroned between the cherubim—he is a King! He wields saving might—he is a Warrior! He guides his people— he is a Counselor!

But he loves to be called "Shepherd." And even more, he loves his sheep.

So keep your griffins. Cling to your dragons. Stick with your monsters. As for me, I'll stay close by my Shepherd. Because he stays close to me.

Dave Dravecky

TAKE ACTION!

In our culture, we might have difficulty understanding just how much sheep depend on their Shepherd. Some night, go out into a dark (and safe) spot and sit in the darkness for fifteen minutes or so. Imagine what it be like to be left in the dark. What would it be like to have someone come along with a lantern? Imagine what would it be like to be totally dependent on someone for food and shelter.

STRENGTH TO STRENGTH

Read: Psalm 84

Blessed are those who dwell in your house; they are ever praising you. Blessed are those whose strength is in you. — Psalm 84:4

*I*f you were to serve as "my hands" for a day, I'd keep you plenty busy. I would need you to sit next to me at my computer and type as I speak. Can you do a hundred words a minute? That's how fast I talk, once I get rolling.

Later on you could help me organize my books, photocopy pages, brew coffee, take dictation, type letters, cook lunch, empty my leg bag, dial phone numbers, run a few errands and, if I need an adjustment with my corset or catheter, help me lie down on the office sofa. And we're only halfway through the day!

How would we accomplish so much work? Spirit-inspired energy! My secretary and I go "from strength to strength." That means pausing in between projects to pray. Pulling a hymnal off the shelf to sing praise songs before lunch. Praying over the phone with someone who happens to call. Stopping for tea at four o'clock and reading a line or two of Scripture. Going from strength to strength in God's Spirit is the pause that refreshes.

It's the only way to work. It's the only way to live.

Joni Eareckson Tada

POINTS TO PONDER

* How do you manage your day?
* Could you borrow some of Joni's "working in the Spirit" habits?
* What could you do to establish some of your own "strength to strength" habits?

A SIGN OF HIS GOODNESS

Read: Psalm 86:14–17

Give me a sign of your goodness, that my enemies may see it and be put to shame, for you, O LORD, have helped me and comforted me. —Psalm 86:17

What's the difference between bold prayers and presumptuous prayers, between fragile faith and unbelief? Psalm 86:17 gives us a clue when the psalmist asks the Lord to "Give me a sign of your goodness."

The Bible contains many examples of people asking for signs, and not all are laudable. We think of Gideon, who out of unbelief asked for a sign (Judges 6). Or we recall the opponents of Jesus, who arrogantly demanded a sign (Luke 11:16).

On the other hand, in Isaiah 7:11 the Lord himself directs King Ahaz to "ask the LORD your God for a sign, whether in the deepest depths or in the highest heights." So when is asking for a sign good, and when is it evil? It appears the psalmist's desperate prayer is both legitimate and good, for he makes his request out of a deep desire to see God at work in his life, not out of a demand for God to do his bidding. God is at the center of this prayer, not the sign. And that makes all the difference.

Dave and Jan Dravecky

PATH TO PRAYER

Putting God at the center of your prayer, ask him with humility to give you a sign of his goodness, his mercy, his forgiveness, and his guidance so that you can see his presence in your life.

My Friend, the Darkness

Read: Psalm 88

Why, O LORD, do you reject me and hide your face from me?—Psalm 88:14

When someone has battled a life-threatening illness for years, he or she often feels utterly alone, as though no one else has ever sunk so low in the pit of despair. Psalm 88 is a comfort for such men and women because it shows they are not breaking ground in the field of human suffering.

Perhaps the most painful part of suffering is the perceived absence of God. So the psalmist cries out, "Why, O LORD, do you reject me and hide your face from me?" In an odd sort of way, it helps us to know that we have not been personally singled out by God to endure some wrenching trial. Others have passed this way before us.

Psalm 88 brings another peculiar comfort in that it ends in a minor key; clouds still obscure the sun when the writer puts down his pen: "The darkness is my closest friend." He shows us that others have passed this way before . . . and God honored their journey by enshrining it in his Word. Odd comfort, perhaps—but real nonetheless.

Dave and Jan Dravecky

Points to Ponder

* Have you ever felt as though God had rejected you and hidden his face?

* Can you relate to the psalmist when he writes, "The darkness is my closest friend"? What do you think he means by that?

* Does it comfort you to know that others have felt this way before? Why or why not?

April 19

NUMBER YOUR DAYS

Teach us to number our days aright, that we may gain a heart of wisdom.
—Psalm 90:12

W e count a lot of things, but the one thing we ought to count the most is probably the one thing we count the least. How many of us number our days, as we're directed in verse 12?

We number everything else so easily. We know how much money we have in the bank. Farmers number their sheep and cattle. Restaurants number meals served in a week. Gardeners can tell you how many tomato plants are in the backyard.

Yet we find it hard to number something so precious as our days. Perhaps that's because we see our days stretching on and on. They seem infinite, so there is no need, we think, to number them.

But things we fail to account for, we waste. That's why it is wise to ask God to teach us to consider each day separate from the next—distinct in its purpose, unique in the way it is to be lived. When we finally arrive in heaven, many things will be surprise us—but nothing will amaze us more than how short life on earth really was.

Joni Eareckson Tada

PATH TO PRAYER

Ask God to teach you to number your days and to live each day to its full measure. Ask God to show you what he requires of you this day, and to give you wisdom and joy in doing it.

LOOK TO THE MOUNTAIN

Read: Psalm 95

For the LORD is the great God, the great King above all gods. In his hand are the depths of the earth, and the mountain peaks belong to him. The sea is his, for he made it, and his hands formed the dry land. —Psalm 95:3–5

S ue had fired her doctor, was served divorce papers by her husband, alienated her friends and lost her leg below the knee to the aggressive cancer. And she asked me, "Where is God?"

I didn't know how to answer, but sensed the Lord taking our conversation in a different direction. Sue lived at the foot of the massive Mount Rainier and the day we spoke, the mountain wasn't obscured by clouds for the first time in weeks. With an authority and conviction I knew to be from God, I told Sue to go outside and take a good look at the mountain. "If God can create something that beautiful and breathtaking in less than one week, surely he can create something just as beautiful and breathtaking out of the crumbled pieces of your life," I said.

Psalm 95 teaches us that God is the God of creation both in the physical world and in the spiritual world, where broken hearts reside. Sue recently told me that now when she feels overwhelmed with her circumstances, she stands on her back porch and looks to the mountain.

Dave Dravecky

TAKE ACTION!

Go out for a walk and find some evidence of God's beauty and power. Take a photo of it and put it in your Bible with this verse on the back. Or make a collage of magazines pictures that show the beauty of God's creation and label it with today's verse.

LIKE GRASS?

Read: Psalm 103

As for man, his days are like grass, he flourishes like a flower of the field; the wind blows over it and it is gone, and its place remembers it no more.
—Psalm 103:15–16

*A*ccording to Psalm 103, we're all like grass that fades away. And that's not such a bad thing.

Just think what life would be like if we lasted forever in the flesh and never faded. First, you'd have to live with yourself forever. Many people are afraid to die, but I'm not so sure that living forever in these present bodies is such a hot idea. I can't imagine living in this sinful body with all of its frailties and leanings toward sin. When my deadline arrives, I'm not filing for an extension.

Second, not only would you live forever, but those who persecute you and who hate God would also live forever. Living forever would not help us escape their influence and actions. Oh, what a disaster that would be!

So feel a little more encouraged about your latest medical problem, your latest fight with the boss, or your latest battle with sin! Cheer up. It won't last. It's grass.

Joni Eareckson Tada

PATH TO PRAYER

Lord, my life is passing so rapidly—I really do feel like grass. You have given me life, and I thank you for that and value it. But I also look forward to the day when I will be united with you for eternity. Amen.

CLOTHED WITH SPLENDOR

Read: Psalm 104:1–9

O Lord my God, you are very great; you are clothed with splendor and majesty.
—Psalm 104:1

*M*ark Twain once said, "Clothes make the man. Naked people have little to no influence on society." Right or wrong, clothes certainly do influence the way we regard others. We *notice* clothes. We admire some outfits, detest others and ignore still others. Clothes may not "make" the person, as Twain claimed, but at least they get our attention.

So why do God's clothes seem to grab our fancy so little? No one is attired like him—"O Lord my God, you are very great; you are clothed with splendor and majesty"—yet how often do we "ooh" and "aah" over his apparel? Nothing so cheap as spun gold or rare silk for him! His clothes come straight from the looms of Splendor & Majesty, Ltd. —a shop that caters to an exclusive clientele of One.

And what finery he wears! "He wraps himself in light," the psalmist says. Talk about shimmering garments! He hangs light itself in his wardrobe. No need for a lamp in his closet, for even his duds dispel the darkness! And *those* are his work clothes!

Dave and Jan Dravecky

PATH TO PRAYER

Sit in silence, close your eyes and meditate on God's splendor and majesty. Think of the way God is described in Psalm 104. Respond to God in praise.

WINTER STORMS

Read: Psalm 107

[The Lord] stilled the storm to a whisper; the waves of the sea were hushed. They were glad when it grew calm, and he guided them to their desired haven.
—*Psalm 107:29–30*

Roaring winds, the spray of sleet and snow. Do you remember winter storms as a child? I sure do. I'd shiver under my quilt, listening to the creaking branches outside my bedroom window. Moaning winds made me feel lonesome. I hoped sleep would let me escape the night, but every time I'd nod off, rattling windows would shake me awake. I watched the twisted shadows of branches jerk madly across the bedroom wall. Would morning ever come?

Yes, but with it, a different picture. I awoke to soft rays of sun warming my bed covers. The howling had ceased. Quiet called me out of bed and to the window where I gasped at the dazzling white landscape. It was . . . beautiful.

There are days when my soul feels windblown, raw, and exposed—times when I'm tossed in a blustery tempest with everything breaking loose. But the God who brings beauty out of blizzards promises to bring peace after the storm. And when the beauty dawns, I hardly remember the fright of that stormy trial.

Joni Eareckson Tada

PATH TO PRAYER

If you are in the midst of a physical, emotional, or circumstantial "storm," pray that God will not only quiet the storm, but also give you peace in the midst of it. Pray for eyes to see the beauty that God will bring out of it. If you are in a time of peace, thank God for it.

NO OTHER HOPE

Read: Psalm 109:21–31

Out of the goodness of your love, deliver me. For I am poor and needy, and my heart is wounded within me. —Psalm 109:21–22

S everal years ago I traveled to Ghana, West Africa, to give wheelchairs and Bibles to homeless disabled people living in the filthy slums. A disabled boy who lived in a box by a trash heap said, "God has blessed people in your country so much; why are so many unhappy?" Another said, "Welcome to our country, where our God is bigger than your God." I heard it time and again in Ghana: "We have to trust God. We have no other hope."

Don't think I'm glorifying the poor and needy of Africa; they are more like us than they realize. They, too, want what they do not have and have what they do not want. The difference is in the way they look at God.

God always seems bigger to those who need him the most. Spiritual and physical poverty is the tool God uses to help us need him more. Hardships press us up against him. In the words of the psalmist, "Deliver me. For I am poor and needy, and my heart is wounded within me."

Joni Eareckson Tada

WHAT OTHERS HAVE SAID

The poor man, rich in faith, who toils for the love of God and is generous of the little fruit of his labors, is much nearer to Heaven than the rich man who spends a fortune in goods and works from no higher motive than his natural inclination to benevolence. —William Bernard Ullathorne

HE ORDAINED IT

He provided redemption for his people; he ordained his covenant forever—holy and awesome is his name. —Psalm 111:9

God does look down on his world and weep. But its twistedness did not catch him by surprise. He knew that humans would fall into sin. He knew the immeasurable sorrow this would let loose. He knew the suffering it would cost his own Son. But he decreed to permit this fall because he knew how he would resolve it: Jesus would die, his church would eventually triumph through innumerable trials, Satan's fingers would be pried off the planet, justice would be served at the final judgment, that heaven would make up for all, and that God would receive more glory—and we would know more joy—than if the fall had never happened. Can anyone but God see enough of this coming ecstasy to make sense out of our present agony? *God sees this glorious end as clearly as if it were today.*

Joni Eareckson Tada

WHAT OTHERS HAVE SAID

The terms for "salvation" in many languages are derived from roots like *salvus, saos, whole, heil,* which designate health, the opposite of disintegration and disruption. Salvation is healing in the ultimate sense; it is final, cosmic, and individual healing. —Paul Tillich

A CURE

Read: Psalm 116:1–14

Then I called on the name of the LORD: "O LORD, save me!"—Psalm 116:4

There was a time during the early years of my paralysis when I could not even bring myself to talk about the depression that overwhelmed me. I did nothing; I said nothing. The look on my face was one of sullen, numb despair. I felt strangled by the cords of a living death, just as it says in verses 3–4. I didn't even care if there was a cure for my depression.

Thank God, there *was* a cure. Several friends met with my church youth leader every week to pray specifically for me, asking God to push back the darkness. Changes did not happen overnight, but slowly my countenance began to brighten. God was using the prayers of my friends to sever the cords of deathly despair that entangled me. Praise God for friends who are willing to call on the name of the Lord on my behalf!

If you are feeling slump-shouldered today, call on the name of the Lord and ask him to save you. Remember, you may feel overcome by trouble and sorrow, but he who has overcome the world can deliver you.

Joni Eareckson Tada

PATH TO PRAYER

My Lord and Savior, I call on your name. O Lord, save me from despair and push back my darkness. Help me to overcome sadness and depression, so that I will again be able to sing your praise with joy.

A CARPENTER'S STORY

Read: Psalm 116:15–19

Precious in the sight of the LORD is the death of his saints. —Psalm 116:15

*L*ike the Lord he loved, Newell Corliss laid down his carpentry tools to build men's lives instead. Newell found his life's passion in the pastorate. But it was short-lived.

With his wife and three young children by his side, Newell battled valiantly to overcome an aggressive cancer that had cost him his right arm, and a lung—and that now was threatening his very life. How could someone so young, so godly, be called home so soon?

Days before he left this earth, his wife, Stacy, shared this verse with her dying husband. She told him that God loved him so much, that he was anxious to see him—to welcome him home. She understood the intense longing to hold one's child in her arms, for she felt that way about each of the children she had carried in her womb.

Newell's homecoming (*not* his home going) was precious in God's sight because Newell is precious in God's sight. Knowing how much God longed to love and comfort Newell gave Stacy the courage to give him up and Newell the courage to go.

Dave and Jan Dravecky

POINTS TO PONDER

* Meditate on the verse of the day.
* What is your heart's response to this meditation?
* Do you believe that you are precious in God's sight?
* How does it affect your view of your own death?

Hidden in the Heart

Read: Psalm 119:9–16

I have hidden your word in my heart that I might not sin against you.
—Psalm 119:11

As a little girl dressed in her Sunday best, I would turn the beautiful gold-trimmed pages of my prayer book. But I would wince when I read, "Wherefore, fulfill now, O Lord, the desires and petitions of Thy servants as may be most expedient for them." I was a dutiful child, and so I obediently memorized the liturgy—even though the words sounded old and dusty.

Back then I didn't appreciate the treasure of psalms and verses I was storing up. Even if I had been told that God's Word never returns empty (Isaiah 55:11), I would have said, "Huh?"

Years later, the riches I had hidden away in my heart as a child paid a marvelous dividend. During lonely nights in the hospital, chunks of psalms and prayers floated to the surface of my memory. I could almost see page 14 of the Book of Common Prayer and the words, though old, glowed with the soft patina of timeless truth as I repeated them in a whisper.

Hide God's Word in your heart! It's a treasure that never runs out.

Joni Eareckson Tada

Take Action!

Find a beautiful hymn or Scripture song that you love but have not memorized. Look up the words in a hymnal, write them down, and put them on a bathroom mirror until you can sing it by heart.

THE BEAUTY OF FROST

Read: Psalm 119:65–72

It was good for me to be afflicted so that I might learn your decrees.
—Psalm 119:71

The crocuses in my backyard are fragrant and beautiful, even for the dry, warm climate of Southern California. I don't know how to account for such a profusion of flowers except to say that we had a couple weeks of hard frost back in January. I'm only an amateur gardener, but I'm convinced the freezing cold forced a lot of beauty out of my crocuses.

A theologian who also knew something about gardening once said, "The nipping frosts of trial and affliction are often needed if God's trees are to grow. They need the cold to revive and bud." What is true for crocuses is true for people, as verse 71 declares afflictions are God's way of helping to create something beautiful in our life.

Do you feel the nipping frost of loneliness or the biting cold of persecution, the icy sting of rejection or the numbing chill of heartache? Just as flower bulbs need the nipping frost to revive and blossom, hardships have a way of helping peace and joy blossom in your life. Patience can flower out of failure, and self-control or kindness can bud out of brokenness.

Joni Eareckson Tada

FOR FURTHER REFLECTION

Consider 1 Peter 1:3–9 and James 1:2–5 and reflect more fully on the relationship between suffering and growth.

I Lift Up My Eyes

Read: Psalm 121

I lift up my eyes to the hills—where does my help come from? My help comes from the Lord, the Maker of heaven and earth. —Psalm 121:1–2

Whether the hills are rolling and dusty like the ones leading up to Jerusalem, jagged and forbidding like the mountains of Sinai, or grand and breathtaking like the Rockies outside my window, they are but a reflection of the majesty of our Lord.

As I look up to these hills and mountains for inspiration, I also look up to him in dependence (and often, desperation). They remind me of several truths. I am on earth; he dwells in the heavens. I am mortal; he is immortal. And when trouble overtakes me and I lose sight of just how awesome and all-powerful he is, I can lift my eyes to the hills and be reminded that my help comes from their Creator—a God who invites me to call him "Father."

Dave Dravecky

Take Action!

Find a picture of mountains in a magazine and cut it out. Label it with this verse and post it where you can look at it often and remember where your help comes from.

May

SURROUNDED FOREVER

Read: Psalm 125

As the mountains surround Jerusalem, so the LORD surrounds his people both now and forevermore. —Psalm 125:2

*I*n the movies it's not usually a good thing to be surrounded. "Come on out, Bugsy—we've got you surrounded! There's no escape!" To be surrounded in film lore means to be outflanked by an enemy, to be in grave danger, to be ready to be wiped out at any moment.

In the Scriptures, however, being surrounded can have infinitely better connotations, especially in a verse like verse 2. Think of it! We are surrounded—encircled, hemmed in, wholly embraced—not by ferocious enemies, but by an almighty God who loves us with infinite tenderness. And to be surrounded in this way "both now and forevermore"—well, if that doesn't bring us great comfort, what will? Some movies *seem* like they'll never end, but God's loving encirclement of his own truly will never cease. He's got us surrounded! And who would *want* to escape from that?

Dave and Jan Dravecky

WHAT OTHERS HAVE SAID

God is above, presiding; beneath, sustaining; within, filling.
—Hildebert of Lavardin

A Great Investment

Read: Psalm 126

Those who sow in tears will reap with songs of joy. He who goes out weeping, carrying seed to sow, will return with songs of joy, carrying sheaves with him.
—Psalm 126:5–6

What a promise! Think of it. When you sow in tears, you will enjoy a marvelous and abundant return on your investment. *But,* you may be thinking, *when have I ever gone out weeping, carrying seed to sow?*

If you have ever reached through an invisible wall of pain to embrace God with willful thanks, you have sown in tears. If you've ever been rejected by a dear one and yet turned the other cheek in love, you have sown in tears. If you have patiently endured physical affliction, or responded in love through a difficult marriage, then Psalm 126:5–6 could be your life verse.

When you hurt physically or emotionally, it's hard to muster a patient or godly response. Pain has a way of screaming for our undivided attention. But when you either offer a sacrifice of praise to God in the midst of your hurt or respond in faith to a heartbreak or hardship, you are sowing in tears. Take heart, for one day God will reward you with sheaves of joy—all because you were faithful through tears.

Joni Eareckson Tada

Path to Prayer

Jesus, you said that those who mourn are blessed and will one day be comforted. Now I mourn and I reach to you for comfort and strength. And I pray that you will give me the grace to respond to my suffering with a patient and loving attitude, so that I will sing songs of praise and joy to you. Amen.

NO LISTS

Read: Psalm 130

If you, O LORD, kept a record of sins, O Lord, who could stand? But with you there is forgiveness; therefore you are feared. —Psalm 130:3–4

S omewhere in the back of my memory, I have a list called "Forgiven Sins That I Can't Forget." The list isn't long, but it contains a handful of personal transgressions that, in my estimation, tend toward the vile and disgusting. In my lower moments, these old sins flash in neon lights in front of my thinking. I cringe, recalling those awful things I am capable of doing.

Thankfully, my conscience does not render the final judgment. Christ does. And oh, how I praise the Lord that he keeps no lists! To be sure, he takes notice of every sin. But does he keep account? No. Verses 3–4 declare, "If you, O LORD, kept a record of sins, O Lord, who could stand? But with you there is forgiveness."

When we confess our sin, we acknowledge that Christ paid the penalty for it on the cross. He wipes the slate clean. He washes away the guilt and cleans our conscience. In other words, he erases the list. When it comes to the sin of his truly repentant children, God forgives and forgets. That's the nature of his grace.

Joni Eareckson Tada

TAKE ACTION!

Make a list of "forgiven sings that you can't forget." Take it outside or hold it over a tin pie plate or other fireproof container. Light a match to it and watch the flames consume those sins. Thank Jesus Christ for erasing your sins and making you clean.

A PICTURE OF UNITY

Read: Psalm 133

How good and pleasant it is when brothers live together in unity! For there the
LORD bestows his blessing, even life forevermore. —Psalm 133:1,3

I grew up with three sisters, and we were the perfect picture of unity at all times. Hah! I wish. Like any other family we had our differences, but there were many times when Psalm 133 seemed like a family motto. It made us regret the times of conflict.

Struggles between you and another brother or sister can create a desert-like feeling in your soul. Everything about your life seems lifeless and dry, but when that moment of agreement in the spirit comes, your body literally feels refreshed.

Perhaps at this moment you're in the midst of a great struggle to resolve conflict in your family or in the family of God. You know the pain and sleepless nights that such conflict causes. If you are trying to resolve a conflict, it's almost worth dropping everything else to bring about peace. Only then can your soul—and the soul of that brother or sister—be at rest. Unity is good. It is pleasant. It is refreshment.

Joni Eareckson Tada

FOR FURTHER REFLECTION

Check out Matthew 18:15–22; Ephesians 4:1–3; and Colossians 3:12–14 to learn more about dealing with conflict.

HE FINISHES WHAT HE STARTS

Read: Psalm 138

The LORD will fulfill his purpose for me; your love, O LORD, endures forever—do not abandon the works of your hands. —Psalm 138:8

God always finishes what he starts. He never begins a project only to leave it half-done. He never walks away from a messy workbench. Unlike us, God never carries over items on his "To Do" list from one eternity to the next. He always completes what he begins. That includes you.

He started working on you years ago, long before you became a Christian. And the blueprint for your life is still spread before him. He won't stop working on you until he reaches his goal.

Read Psalm 138 to see how God accomplishes his work in your life. He fulfills his purpose in you with love and faithfulness. Part of his goal is to make you fearless and stouthearted, humble, and confident in his ability to preserve and protect you. And he won't give up until he's done. He will never abandon or forsake you. His goal is to make you more like Jesus, and he won't stop working on his goal for you until you are complete.

Joni Eareckson Tada

PATH TO PRAYER

Thanks be to you Father, that you are working in me to fulfill your goals. Though your discipline is sometimes painful, I praise you for it. Thank you for working on my heart to make me fearless, humble, and above all, confident that you will protect and preserve me until I am with you in heaven.

THERE IS NO ESCAPE FROM GOD'S LOVE

Read: Psalm 139:1–12

If I go up to the heavens, you are there; if I make my bed in the depths, you are there. If I rise on the wings of the dawn, if I settle on the far side of the sea, even there your hand will guide me, your right hand will hold me fast. —Psalm 139:8–10

There's hardly a soul who hasn't wrestled with the overwhelming urge to flee when faced with suffering. Whether it be from bad health, bad finances or bad relationships, people—even Christians—search for an escape. Escape into daydreams. Escape into sleep. Escape into television. And a few even escape into suicide. Sometimes the strongest, the most stalwart of saints, are the most likely candidates.

Circumstances may vary from person to person, but we can draw comfort from the fact that all of us are vulnerable. And if you look closely at how David surfaced out of his despair, you'll see that God himself took the king in his arms and wiped away his tears.

Joni Eareckson Tada

PATH TO PRAYER

Lord, if I go up to the heavens, you are there. If I rise on the wings of the dawn and settle on the far side of the sea, even there your hand will guide me and your right hand will hold me fast. There's no way I can escape your love . . . I praise you for that!

A PRAYER FOR ANXIOUS DAYS

Read: Psalm 139:13–24

*Search me, O God, and know my heart; test me and know my anxious thoughts. See
if there is any offensive way in me, and lead me in the way everlasting.*
—Psalm 139:23–24

What a relief it is to be able to pour out your heart to God and
know that he will listen to your prayer—no matter how composed or irrational, giddy or angry, direct or confused—as the cry of one
of his best-loved children.

In verses 23–24 the writer invites his Lord to "Search me, O God, and
know my heart; test me and know my anxious thoughts. See if there is
any offensive way in me, and lead me in the way everlasting."

When I can't feel his presence, when I don't know what he is trying to
teach me, when the way before me is shrouded in fog and I can't see
the path ahead, when my motives and actions come under question and
truth is elusive, when my soul is desperate for God's direction and guidance—I can throw my soul down before God and utter this psalm, this
heart cry of a soul longing for his Father's help.

Jan Dravecky

PATH TO PRAYER

Pray through Psalm 139 today, inserting the details of your own situation
and thoughts where appropriate.

WHAT IS MAN?

Read: Psalm 144:1–10

O LORD, what is man that you care for him, the son of man that you think of him?
—Psalm 144:3

*T*he psalmist's question arises out of wonder, out of a long and astonished meditation on the miracle of it all.

David has been pondering the awesome nature of God, and he just can't help asking, "Why, God, do you pay us any attention at all? You are so big; we are so small. You are so holy; we are so filthy with sin. You are so majestic; we are so petty. Why do you bother?"

There is only one answer: love. He loves us because he is love, not because we are lovely. When we truly experience God's love, humility and praise are the natural results. Experiencing God's presence and his love for us should be our soul's greatest longing and passion. If it isn't, we are robbing ourselves of the greatest blessing we will ever know—and we will fall short of the purpose of our very existence: to know him.

Dave Dravecky

WHAT OTHERS HAVE SAID

God does not love us because we are valuable. We are valuable because God loves us. —Fulton John Sheen

HANG-UPS NOTWITHSTANDING

Read: Psalm 144:11–15

Blessed are the people whose God is the LORD. —Psalm 144:15

Whether you are weak or strong, saintly or struggling, Jesus cares for you. If your God is the Lord, as Psalm 144:15 says, then you are truly blessed. I realize you may be thinking, *Sure, Jesus cares for me in the general sense, as for the whole world, but when it comes to specifics, surely there must be others he is more interested in. After all, I can't pray out loud. . . . I have a hard time understanding the Bible. . . . I can't seem to shake bad habits. Yes, I know he cares—but not as much as he does for more obedient types.*

Not so! The Lord's care for you does not hinge on your hang-ups. His care for you has nothing to do with your baggage of personal problems. You could be a wimp when it comes to standing for the Lord; it doesn't matter. As a child of God, you have the full force and undivided attention of eternal Love. Love that cares with no strings attached. As 1 Peter 5:7 says, "Cast all your anxiety on him because he cares for you."

Joni Eareckson Tada

POINTS TO PONDER

* Do you believe that Jesus cares for you personally and individually?

* What gets in the way of believing that?

* How might you change your expectations and beliefs about God's love for you?

* How might you cast your anxieties on Jesus, even your deepest anxieties about his love for you?

May 10

LIKE NO ONE ELSE

Read: Psalm 145

You open your hand and satisfy the desires of every living thing. —Psalm 145:16

There's nothing quite like the satisfaction of a glass of cold spring water on a hot August afternoon. A cold shower after mowing the lawn. A dive into a stream after a long, tiring hike. A glass of lemonade fresh out of the refrigerator. Being satisfied means you've been filled, you want nothing more, and the thirsty longing has been quenched.

That's exactly how Jesus satisfies. To have Jesus means that you have it all. To trust him means that your needs are met. To know him is to realize that he is your dearest, most faithful companion.

The next time you pour a cold drink on a hot afternoon, pause and praise the Lord for the way he quenches your thirst. He, the wellspring of water, overcomes, subdues, fulfills and satisfies like nothing and no one else.

Joni Eareckson Tada

FOR FURTHER REFLECTION

Refresh yourself with a look at Zechariah 14:8; John 7:37–38; and Revelation 21:6, 22:1,17.

GOD SHARES HIS JOY

Read: Psalm 149

For the LORD takes delight in his people; he crowns the humble with salvation. Let the saints rejoice in this honor and sing for joy on their beds. —Psalm 149:4–5

God, we might say, is in a good mood. He's not depressed. He's not misery seeking company. He's not some bitter, cosmic Neanderthal with his finger on a nuclear weapon. *God is joy spilling over.*

This is where his mercy comes from. The full tank of love he enjoys is splashing out over heaven's walls. He swims in elation and is driven to share it with us.

But God is nobody's water boy. As the solemn Monarch of all, he shares his gladness on his own terms. And those terms call for us to suffer—to suffer, in some measure, as his beloved Son did while on earth. We may not understand his reasons, but we are insane to fight him on this.

He is in ecstasy beyond words.

It is worth *anything* to be his friend.

Joni Eareckson Tada

WHAT OTHERS HAVE SAID

A joyful heart is the normal result of a heart burning with love.
—Mother Teresa

GUARD YOUR HEART

Read: Proverbs 4:10–27

Above all else, guard your heart, for it is the wellspring of life. —Proverbs 4:23

Thankfully, our hearts are always a beat ahead of our minds and bodies. Proverbs 4:23 is not off base when it says the heart goes deeper than the mind: "Above all else, guard your heart, for it is the well-spring of life." True, the Bible also says the heart is desperately wicked, but that still demonstrates that it is the seat of deep passions. Important things happen in the heart. Out of it "flow the issues of life."

We may have one foot here and the other in the hereafter, but our heart is often that part of us that tugs and pulls at that one foot stuck in the mud of earth, saying, "Get off of the earthly images, would you? Look, here's your other foot anyway. Up here is what you're longing for."

Joni Eareckson Tada

WHAT OTHERS HAVE SAID

The "heart" in the biblical sense is not the inward life, but the whole man in relation to God. —Dietrich Bonhoeffer

FIND WISDOM

Read: Proverbs 8

For whoever finds [wisdom] finds life and receives favor from the LORD. But whoever fails to find me harms himself; all who hate me love death.
—Proverbs 8:35–36

I know this to be true by personal experience. There was a time when I thought I had to put on a good show, despite how I really felt inside. The result? I was wearing myself out and felt used by people. I felt sucked out until there was nothing left to suck out anymore.

When I finally listened to some godly wisdom and let my real self show, I found acceptance instead of rejection. I began to see that I didn't have to pretend. While I was spilling out the truth about how drained I felt, God started filling me up with the acceptance of friends and acquaintances. Then I could move forward, charged up instead of wiped out.

Dave Dravecky

TAKE ACTION!

Memorize Proverbs 9:10–11: The fear of the LORD is the beginning of wisdom, and knowledge of the Holy One is understanding. For through me your days will be many, and years will be added to your life.

PRACTICAL LOVE

Read: Proverbs 11:16–31

A kindhearted woman gains respect, but ruthless men gain only wealth. A kind man benefits himself, but a cruel man brings trouble on himself. —Proverbs 11:16–17

When you feel abandoned by a friend who says he cares but doesn't back you up, the bond between you and your friend is stripped away, tempting you to withdraw. Of course, when people fail to back us up, God will come through for us in some way; but that's not his ideal plan.

God commands us to love each other. The words of passages like Proverbs 11:16,17 and 25—"A kindhearted woman gains respect, but ruthless men gain only wealth. A kind man benefits himself, but a cruel man brings trouble on himself"—are not just sweet sentiments. True love is practical. A big part of loving each other is being there to back each other up when we are in trouble. We are not to withdraw from others just because no one was there to back *us* up when we needed *them*.

Dave Dravecky

WHAT OTHERS HAVE SAID

Kindness is the golden chain by which society is bound together.
—Johann Wolfgang von Goethe

ESSENTIAL HOPE

Read: Proverbs 13:12–25

Hope deferred makes the heart sick, but a longing fulfilled is a tree of life.
—Proverbs 13:12

Hope is as essential to life as food, as the very air. And when it seems far from us, we grow frantic.

Jesus knew "hope deferred." That's why he cried out on the cross, "My God, my God, why have you forsaken me?" (Matthew 27:46). So can God the Father turn a deaf ear to the plea of his own Son? The answer resounds from an empty tomb three days after the crucifixion: No, may it never be! And because the Father raised Jesus from the dead, there is hope for us all. Jesus felt God's slap so that we could feel God's caress. Oh, we may *feel* forsaken in the midst of our suffering, but the fact remains, we're *not*. "My God, my God, why have your forsaken me" was the cry of Christ on behalf of all humanity so that, in contrast, he could tenderly say to us, "Never will I forsake you" (Hebrews 13:5). Despair may be bound to God, but so is all hope.

Joni Eareckson Tada

FOR FURTHER REFLECTION

Think about Ephesians 1:15–20; 1 Thessalonians 4:13; and Hebrews 6:16–19 to find deeper understanding of the hope that God offers you.

THE CRUSHED SPIRIT

Read: Proverbs 15:1–15

A happy heart makes the face cheerful, but heartache crushes the spirit.
—Proverbs 15:13

W hich pain is worse, emotional or physical? Like you, I've faced both kinds: crushing physical pain with no position in which I can get comfortable; crushing heartache in which my head spins with grief and I can't stop the tears. As Proverbs says, "Heartache crushes the spirit."

You can almost distract yourself from physical pain. Even in a wheelchair, I've devised clever ways to forget about my paralysis. But inside suffering—that's another matter. You can't put mental anguish or heartache behind you. Those hurts create an emptiness that refuses to be pushed or crowded out of your thoughts. It bites. Gnaws. Grinds away at your spirit.

I'm convinced emotional pain is much worse than physical pain. But I'm also convinced it does something to our heart that physical pain often can't. Inner anguish melts the heart, making our souls pliable and bendable. Because we can't drive it from our thoughts, it forces us to embrace God out of desperate, urgent need. God is never closer than when your heart is aching.

Joni Eareckson Tada

PATH TO PRAYER

Lord, my heart is aching, and my spirit feels as though it is in a vice. I call out to you; help me I pray. Come close to me and hold me in your loving arms.

ONE CHOICE AT A TIME

Read: Proverbs 21:1–5,21

He who pursues righteousness and love finds life, prosperity and honor.
—Proverbs 21:21

*L*ove is lived out one choice at a time: quick decisions to lay aside differences and cheer someone on; skin-of-the-teeth, under-the-wire bits of love that say, "You mean a lot to me." Always, love is a choice.

We come up against scores of opportunities every day to love or not to love. We encounter hundreds of small chances to please our friends, delight our Lord and encourage our family. That's why love and obedience are intimately linked; we can't have one without the other. And note what they produce: "He who pursues righteousness and love finds life, prosperity and honor."

Let's choose to love and obey our Lord. And may the small things we do today tell others, "Jesus loves you."

Joni Eareckson Tada

TAKE ACTION!

What opportunities do you have today to love someone with a smile, an encouraging word, or a note? What is the Spirit prompting you to do? Don't ignore it or put it off. Do it today. Do it now.

GENEROSITY

Proverbs 22:2,4,9

A generous man will himself be blessed, for he shares his food with the poor.
—Proverbs 22:9

his verse applies to far more than giving away groceries. "A generous man will himself be blessed," Solomon wrote, "for he shares
his food with the poor." Sometimes the "food" a generous man shares is
his time; at other times it's a listening ear; but most of the time, it's he
himself, a caring friend.

When we become men and women like this, we may be astonished at
how quickly (and in what abundance) the "food" comes back to us when
we find ourselves starving. We discover that generosity of spirit is paid
back in full. Generosity is not only a two-way street; it often becomes a
two-way, multiple-lane highway.

We need to give more than lip service to the idea of sharing burdens with
one another. We truly do *need* one another, especially when we are suffering. One way we affirm the value of our friends is to take turns bear-
ing each other's burdens.

Dave Dravecky

TAKE ACTION!

So many people are in need all around us if we take the time to look. Take
one of the following suggestions and act on it, or think of your own action
plan:

* Bake a batch of cookies or cook a meal for someone who is shut in or ill.

* Buy a bag full of toiletry items and drop them off at a homeless shelter
or a domestic abuse shelter.

* Volunteer at an after-school childcare program. Bring some art supplies
or books.

* Ask a single mother or elderly neighbor if there is anything you can do
to help around their house or yard.

THE DESIRE FOR GOD

Read: Ecclesiastes 1

All things are wearisome, more than one can say. The eye never has enough of seeing, nor the ear its fill of hearing. What has been will be again, what has been done will be done again; there is nothing new under the sun. —Ecclesiastes 1:8–9

No verses better describe the plight of a person without God in his or her life than these. Such a person is bored and itching for something more. Humans get hungry, and not just for food, but for a whole range of desires and dreams. It's strange how people are bent on mad pursuit, making the same mistakes every day, hoping that life will someday reveal an answer, even though the experiences of most have taught them otherwise. Why do people keep seeking and pushing past the boredom? Because they *have* to.

Our seeking is a response to the stirring of a fundamental need that simply must be satisfied—our need for God. Every desire, longing, aspiration, hunger, and thirst is no less than a desire for God.

God has good reasons for giving us such large appetites. He causes us to hunger so that we might learn to feed on the Bread of Heaven, to live on every word that comes from the mouth of the Lord. To hunger is to be human; to hunger for God is to feed on him in your heart. Hunger and thirst after his righteousness (Matthew 5:6). Taste and see that the Lord is good (Psalm 34:7); it is he who will fill you to satisfaction.

Joni Eareckson Tada

POINTS TO PONDER

What are your hungry for? What are your unfilled appetites? Do you try to fill yourself up with food, with pleasure, with multiple vacations, with shopping or movies, with work? How can you pursue God instead? Be creative and try to find a "menu" of Bible study and prayer that fits your own style a schedule.

Timeless Moments

Read: Ecclesiastes 3:1–14

[God] has made everything beautiful in its time. He has also set eternity in the hearts of men. —Ecclesiastes 3:11

Now and then the God of eternity grants us timeless moments in the here and now, striking that resonate chord in our heart that echoes eternity. He woos us away from this world with that heavenly haunting. It happens when we're enfolded in the arms of the one we love. Or we're gazing at a sunset of such depth and beauty we can't find words to describe it. Or we hear a baby break into a giggle. Or savor some Scripture that suddenly leaps into flame in our hearts. Or feel that lump in our throat when a choir sings some triumphant, soaring anthem.

Timeless moments are those that—however briefly—send our hearts on ahead to heaven. Moments when we demonstrate drastic obedience, choose patience over complaint, or honor God when everything within us screams to please ourselves. Amy Carmichael calls this "winning victories" in the few hours we have before sunset.

Joni Eareckson Tada

Points to Ponder

* How would you define a "timeless moment"?

* In retrospect, what are some of the "timeless moments" you've experienced in the past?

* What circumstances led up to them?

GOOD TIMES, BAD TIMES

Read: Ecclesiastes 7:10–14

*When times are good, be happy; but when times are bad, consider: God has made
the one as well as the other. —Ecclesiastes 7:14*

When the death toll rises from a devastating tornado or a hurricane, people call such tragedies "acts of God." The term is even used in insurance contracts for house damage caused by floods or fires. We are quick to attribute weather calamities to God—but let's also be fair and credit him for beautiful breezes and balmy days. As Solomon wrote, "When times are good, be happy; but when times are bad, consider: God has made the one as well as the other."

Weather calamities and other disasters make us feel as though life is beyond our control. This isn't bad. Larger-than-life insecurities force us to wonder: *My life is so fragile. I'm confused when the props are kicked out from under me. Maybe God is bigger and more awesome than I realized!*

Joni Eareckson Tada

PATH TO PRAYER

Sometimes tragedy and heartache seem worse because we expect that our lives should always be good. Ask God to give you realistic expectations about good times and bad times in your life and for the realization that life is fragile and precious. Ask him to show you his holiness, power, and majesty regardless of the circumstances that might come your way.

May 22

REMEMBER YOUR CREATOR

Read: Ecclesiastes 12:1–8

Remember your Creator in the days of your youth, before the days of trouble come and the years approach when you will say, "I find no pleasure in them."
—Ecclesiastes 12:1

Having come face to face with a life-threatening illness, I have a different perspective on life; I approach my hours and days with a different attitude. I have been personally impacted with the reality that life is short, and what I do with the time I have is important. My illness sounded an alarm that caused me to react and take action, so that I can give the greatest amount of attention to the things that really matter. I'm certainly not perfect (ask anyone!), but my goal is to make every moment count, to learn the lessons that each day brings, and to be conscious of the legacy I leave behind.

Dave Dravecky

WHAT OTHERS HAVE SAID

Only eternal values can give meaning to temporal ones. Time must be the servant of eternity. —Erwin W. Lutzer

THE WINTER IS PAST

Read: Song of Songs 2:1–13

See! The winter is past; the rains are over and gone. Flowers appear on the earth; the season of singing has come. —Song of Songs 2:11–12

I learned for myself that the path out of the valley of depression is slow and laborious. From the time of my first panic attack in 1990, it took me over five years to recover, and I can't tell how long I was depressed before I had to face up to it and find help. Many times storm clouds rolled over the mountains and drenched me in showers of tears. Many times I almost missed the beams of hope gleaming through the black clouds.

But in the mountains, after the storms pass, the air is fresh, the sky a clear translucent blue. Wildflowers that were watered by the rains paint the fields with brilliant colors as far as the eye can see. Like Solomon, I can say, "See! The winter is past; the rains are over and gone. Flowers appear on the earth; the season of singing has come."

That is what I see in my life now: a fresh newness, a spring-like beauty and joy. Through the valleys of depression and the storms of tears, the promises of God have proven true in my life.

Jan Dravecky

TAKE ACTION!

Memorize Song of Songs 2:11–12 as a message of hope and new life.

A WINDOW OF HOPE

Read: Isaiah 4:2–6

Over all the glory will be a canopy. It will be a shelter and shade from the heat of the day, and a refuge and hiding place from the storm and rain. —Isaiah 4:5–6

This passage is an oracle about the day when the Messiah appears as the glory of Israel. It gives Isaiah's readers a glimpse of the coming beauty and majesty of the "Branch of the Lord." Framed within a dark prophecy of judgment and destruction, it offers God's people a window of hope—hope of holiness salvation and protection—a vision of the way in which God would someday be present among them as their protector and shelter. "Over all the glory will be a canopy. It will be a shelter and shade . . . a refuge and hiding place from the storm and rain."

God wants us to anticipate our future with him. So he gives us little glimpses, like that in these verses. Once heaven has our attention, a fervid anticipation for God's ultimate reality—appearing with him in glory—begins to glow, making everything earthly pale in comparison. Earth's pain keeps crushing our hopes, reminding us this world can never satisfy; only heaven can.

Joni Eareckson Tada

POINTS TO PONDER

Recall the last time you found shade on a hot day. Remember how rested you felt from that burning sun? Relieved. Consoled. Comforted. That's the way you can feel in the sheltering shade of the Most High God. Rested. Unburdened. Secure. Take a moment to come before your Place of Refuge in prayer. Picture yourself in his protective shadow. Imagine yourself finding a safe place in the cleft of the Rock. Now, fix your eyes on Jesus and bring to him those circumstances that distract you. Lay each one in his comforting shadow.

GOD WITH US

Read: Isaiah 7:10–17

Therefore the Lord himself will give you a sign: The virgin will be with child and will give birth to a son, and will call him Immanuel. —Isaiah 7:14

"Immanuel"—God with us. What wonderful words these are! They make all the difference.

Remember those tough days at school? What a relief it was when the teacher showed up at just the right moment to make things right. To stop the talking. To halt the fight. The teacher was in the room and all was well. Whew! So, too, God said he would be with us in the person of Jesus Christ. This mighty promise in the book of Isaiah was fulfilled through Jesus' birth (Matthew 1:22–23).

But that's not all. God was not only going to be here, he would be on our side. Just like the teacher who says, "I'm with you, son. The rest of you, run along."

Life doesn't present itself in a pretty package each day. But we can know that God is with us. He's on our side. So how can we fail? He is ours and he is here.

Joni Eareckson Tada

FOR FURTHER REFLECTION

Read John 1:14; Colossians 1:15–20; and Hebrews 2:17–18; 4:15–16 for more insights on Jesus as Immanuel.

PRINCE OF PEACE

Read: Isaiah 9:1–7

For to us a child is born, to us a son is given, and the government will be on his shoulders. And he will be called Wonderful Counselor, Mighty God, Everlasting Father, Prince of Peace. —Isaiah 9:7

Since the days of Eden, people have been haunted by fear of each side of the grave. As the old song goes, "I'm tired of living but scared of dying."

The Prince of Peace is the only one who can rid you of fear, whether it's fear of the here and now or fear of the future. Jesus, through his death, broke the power of the devil and his lies. This same Jesus desires to deliver you of your fears, whether you're frightened of life as a living nightmare or fearing death as a scary unknown. To place your trust in Jesus gives you peace now and peace about the hereafter.

To place your hand in the Prince of Peace's hand does not guarantee you protection from suffering. But it does give you protection from fear, including a steadfast hand to hold onto and the certainty that a loving and all-powerful God who knows everything is standing by your side. Putting your confidence in Christ will free you from living all your life as a slave to dread.

Joni Eareckson Tada

FOR FURTHER REFLECTION

Read John 14:25–27; Hebrews 2:14–15; and 1 John 4:16–18 for more insights on the Wonderful Counselor, who can bring you peace and banish your fears.

PERFECT PEACE

Read: Isaiah 26:1–12

You will keep in perfect peace him whose mind is steadfast, because he trusts in you. —Isaiah 26:3

*M*y mind was a jumble of thoughts and philosophies. Logical, rational, intellectual positions were posed and just as quickly disposed of by opposing concepts, apparently just as valid. What was right? What was wrong? Did God really exist? Or was life meaningless after all? Oh, what a maze of confusion. *Am I losing my mind as well as my body?*

Weary from thinking, my eyelids fells shut. Then, from somewhere, a calm took over. A thought—or memory—"a still, small voice"—reminded my troubled brain. "You will keep in perfect peace him whose mind is steadfast, because he trusts in you."

And I slept.

Joni Eareckson Tada

PATH TO PRAYER

Meditate on today's verse. What does "perfect peace" mean to you? What does it mean to be steadfast? What does it mean to trust the Creator of the universe, the One who made you, the One who created sleep to refresh you body and soul? Respond to God in prayer.

A Sure Foundation

Read: Isaiah 28:16–17

So this is what the Sovereign LORD says: "See, I lay a stone in Zion, a tested stone, a precious cornerstone for a sure foundation; the one who trusts will never be dismayed."—Isaiah 28:16

Isaiah was talking about Jesus when he wrote this. He is the cornerstone on which you can build your hope and trust.

You have a heavenly Father who loves you and cares for you deeply. Ask him to help you find the supportive friendships, the family you need. He may use long-lost relatives, neighbors, a support group, your local church, or friends to provide comfort and encouragement. But the most important friend is Jesus. The Bible elsewhere describes him as "near to the brokenhearted" and the "friend who sticks closer than a brother." So invite him into your home. Allow him to fill your heart with peace, grace, mercy, and love. He has promised to "never leave or forsake" you. If you trust in him, as Isaiah says, you will never be dismayed.

Dave and Jan Dravecky

PATH TO PRAYER

Heavenly Father, thank you that you love me so much; that you care for me in every circumstance of my life. I want to put my trust in you to meet my needs and heal my brokenness. Help me, I pray, to find comfort and support among the people you have sent into my life. Help me to make new connections that will give me the help I need, and that I can help in return. Help me to know you as my close friend, Jesus, I pray.

GODLY COUNSEL

Read: Isaiah 28:23–29

All this also comes from the LORD Almighty, wonderful in counsel and magnificent in wisdom. —Isaiah 28:29

I understand how Christians can be skeptical about the emphasis some people put on using a counselor as a substitute for seeking wisdom from God—the God who is called "wonderful in counsel and magnificent in wisdom." But none of our Christian counselors ever led us away from seeking God's wisdom. Instead, they shared the godly wisdom they had gained with us while they taught us to examine our lives to make sure we were living the balanced life God would have us live. The Bible encourages us to seek out wisdom and search for understanding as one would search for hidden treasure. That's what we were doing in seeking godly counsel. Without the understanding we gained, we would not have made the changes that helped us come out of depression.

Jan Dravecky

POINTS TO PONDER

* When should one seek a professional counselor or pastor for help?

* How can God use godly professionals to help people?

* How can seeking help from a qualified counselor help one to be accountable?

* How can verbalizing anxieties and concerns help heal a person?

THE WAY

Read: Isaiah 30:18–21

Whether you turn to the right or to the left, your ears will hear a voice behind you, saying, "This is the way; walk in it. —Isaiah 30:21

I've always enjoyed maps. I feel good when I have a decent idea of where I'm going and how to get there. A map allows me to mark off progress, to help me see how much farther I have to go.

That's why I enjoy my walk with Jesus. His Word is just like a map. Pick a verse, any verse, and you're on your way. God orders your steps. He points to the narrow road rather than the broad one. He says, "I am the way," and you certainly can't get lost when you tailgate the Lord. And if you're a little unsure of your directions, Isaiah 30:21 reads just like a road sign.

Look at the road ahead today as though it were a journey full of adventure. Remember that heaven is your destination. Just keep your eye on the Way. That's all the direction you need.

Joni Eareckson Tada

WHAT OTHERS HAVE SAID

In me there is darkness, but with thee there is light. I am lonely, but thou leavest me not; I am feeble in heart, but thou leavest me not; I am restless, but with thee there is patience. Thy ways are past understanding, but thou knowest the way for me. —Dietrich Bonhoeffer

Peaceful Landscape

Read: Isaiah 33:15–22

Your eyes will see the king in his beauty and view a land that stretches afar . . .
your eyes will see Jerusalem, a peaceful abode, a tent that will not be moved.
—Isaiah 33:17,20

G od barely gets noticed during "crazy times." Have you noticed that? If we're thinking, we may quickly fire off a prayer for help. But we need more than that. We need to be driven to our knees by the conviction that we have nowhere else to turn.

It takes crazy moments, times when you almost border on mental collapse, to force you to your knees to seek Jesus. Maybe you sing a hymn as tears splatter on the hymnal pages. Maybe you pray Psalm 23 over and over until your nerves quit jangling. Then, oh, the delicious calm that sweeps over you when all you see is the King in his beauty and an uncluttered landscape of peace. When your focus is fixed on the Lord, those crazy moments fade into the background.

Be driven to your knees today by the overwhelming conviction that you have absolutely nowhere else to go.

Joni Eareckson Tada

PATH TO PRAYER

Pray the words of Elizabeth of the Trinit: "O my God, Trinity whom I adore, let me entirely forget myself that I may abide in you, still and peaceful as if my soul were already in eternity; let nothing disturb my peace nor separate me from you, O my unchanging God, but that each moment may take me further into the depths of your mystery."

June

THE JOY OF THE REDEEMED

Read: Isaiah 35

They will enter Zion with singing; everlasting joy will crown their heads. Gladness and joy will overtake them, and sorrow and sighing will flee away. —Isaiah 35:10

This passage gives us a peek at God's gift of heaven. To have my head crowned with everlasting joy is one of those earthly images that looks askew, but I don't mind. People caught up in ecstasy don't worry about such things. Suffice to say, it's a gift, a crowning gift.

Look at the gift with me for a moment. Joy is a fruit of the Spirit, and that means it has in it the essence of eternity. When joy grips us, it always appears new, like a surprise. At the same moment, it seems ancient, as though it had always been there. Joy always has in it a timeless, eternal element. Pleasure and happiness may come and go, but joy seems to remain. Happy feelings have nothing of that air of eternity about them that joy has. That's because joy, in its essence, is of God. He is "the Lord of joy."

Joni Eareckson Tada

PATH TO PRAYER

Holy God, Lord, I praise you and rejoice in you, that you have given your people the gift of joy in your Spirit, the fresh, surprising joy that is both ancient and new, eternal and timeless. Thank you for those glad moments of joy when the window of heaven is opened and I have glimpses of the greatest joy, being with you.

FORGET ABOUT FAIRNESS

Read: Isaiah 40

Whom did the LORD consult to enlighten him, and who taught him the right way? Who was it that taught him knowledge or showed him the path of understanding?
—Isaiah 40:14

Have you ever walked into a room halfway through an argument and been asked for your opinion? It's impossible to respond. You don't have all the facts. You don't fully appreciate both sides of the argument and, therefore, you can't give a just verdict.

Trying to discern whether God is fair in any given situation is much like walking into a room halfway through someone else's argument. For one thing, you don't have all the facts, and you won't have them until you get to the other side of eternity. Besides, "fairness" is impossible to grasp because you are unequipped to appreciate the hidden purposes God has in mind.

The "fairness doctrine" is based on a limited value system and timetable. And God is not "fair"; he is just. He is loving. His values are higher, far exalted above yours. His timetable is different. So bow to his justice, trust in his love, and forget about fairness.

Joni Eareckson Tada

POINTS TO PONDER

* Where did you learn your ideas about fairness? About justice?
* How do *you* decide what is just and fair?
* Why is it important to know all the facts when deciding what is fair?
* How is our human longing for fairness really a desire for justice from God?

"FOR MY OWN SAKE"

Read: Isaiah 43:15–25

"I, even I, am he who blots out your transgressions, for my own sake, and remembers your sins no more."— Isaiah 43:25

*M*ost parents can't remember the sins of their children for very long. In an amazingly short time, little devils get transformed into little angels. How? I think parents forget because their love can't retain those sins for very long. Our love doesn't hold on to that which grieves us.

God's paternal love has a weak memory as well. He tells us that he blots out our transgressions and forgets them on purpose. Why? "For my own sake," he says. So grievous was our sin that God sought an effective and eternal eradication. No sentimental, romantic senility would do. No divine dementia. Only his Son could blot out the trespass forever. Only Jesus could serve as the "forsaken one" so we might be embraced as the "sins-forgiven" ones—for God's sake.

Joni Eareckson Tada

WHAT OTHERS HAVE SAID

The most marvelous ingredient in the forgiveness of God is that he also forgets, the one thing a human being can never do. Forgetting with God is a divine attribute; God's forgiveness forgets. —Oswald Chambers

REFINING FIRE

See, I have refined you, though not as silver; I have tested you in the furnace of affliction. —Isaiah 48:10

G od wants to refine you. Your trial is a refining. Your God is a consuming fire and he sits as the Refiner purging every impurity from your life.

God wants to sift you. Your trial is a sifting. You are God's grain, planted by him and to be gathered by his hand. You are coarse and rough grain and must pass through several processes of sifting. Each sieve is finer, "However, it produces a harvest of righteousness and peace" (Hebrews 12:11).

God wants to prune you. Your trial is a pruning. "Every branch that does bear fruit he prunes clean so that it will be even more fruitful" (John 15:2). The pruning process hurts, but God is a careful gardener, and he prunes you with great skill and love.

Joni Eareckson Tada

POINTS TO PONDER

* In what events or circumstances of your life have you felt God was refining you?

* Did you realize that you were being "pruned" in the midst of those circumstances?

* Can you see the results of God's testing and refining in your life? What are they?

INTIMATE LANGUAGE

Read: Isaiah 49:8–18

For the LORD comforts his people . . . and will have compassion on his afflicted ones. Can a mother forget the baby at her breast and have no compassion on the child she has borne? Though she may forget, I will not forget you!
—Isaiah 49:13,15

God always uses such intimate language when he relates to us. He paints warm images of sheltering us under his wings, holding us in the palm of his hand, or drawing us close to his breast. If you desire to be free of fear, memorize and meditate on portions of Scripture that describe God's love and your need. Read parts of John's Gospel to hear the heartbeat of Christ just hours before the cross. Read Psalm 51 to grasp the bitterness of sin. Read Psalm 91 to grasp the scope of God's protection. Enjoy the Song of Songs to find the warm and intimate language of love. Be as personal with God as he is with you!

Joni Eareckson Tada

TAKE ACTION!

Read Psalm 91, Song of Songs 2, and Matthew 23:37. Choose an image of God's intimate love from one of these passages, or the verse of the day, and illustrate it in some way. Label your artwork with the verse.

RELY ON GOD

Read: Isaiah 50:4–10

Who among you fears the LORD and obeys the word of his servant? Let him who walks in the dark, who has no light, trust in the name of the LORD and rely on his God. —Isaiah 50:10

One summer, my family and I traveled to see a gigantic wonder called Carlsbad Caverns. I clasped my mother's hand as the tour guide led us down into the cavern. When we reached the bottom, our guide turned out the lamps so we could see, just for a moment, how thick the darkness really was.

I gasped as oppressive and utter blackness enveloped me. Panic seized me and I thrust my hand into the darkness to reach for my mother. In an instant, her hand was around mine, washing away my fear and anxiety. "Joni," she said, "you're safe. I would never lose you."

You probably have days that seem like cavernous holes. You can't find your way, and you search in vain for a single ray of light. Don't be alarmed! Remember that your walk is not by sight but by faith. And God, according to Isaiah 50:10, agrees with you: there are times when it's hard to see even a single ray of brightness in your circumstances. But even in the blackness, God promises you will find him, close by. He says, "You're safe. I would never lose you!"

Joni Eareckson Tada

FOR FURTHER REFLECTION

How dark would the world be without the Light of the World? Do a search of the Scriptures for the word "light" using a concordance or Bible software. What do you discover? You may want to include Exodus 13; 2 Samuel 22:29; Psalms 19:8; 27:1; Isaiah 60; and John 1:4–9; 3:19–21 and 8:12.

BEAUTIFUL FEET

Read Isaiah 52:6–10

How beautiful on the mountains are the feet of those who bring good news, who proclaim peace, who bring good tidings, who proclaim salvation, who say to Zion, "Your God reigns!" —Isaiah 52:7

*A*ll through his seventies and eighties, my father hobbled around on crutches due to arthritis. When I was in the hospital, I could always tell when my father was coming for a visit. "Click-click" his crutches would echo on the hallway tile. *Oh boy, Daddy's here!* I would think, grinning. I felt that he, more than anyone else in the family, understood my situation. This is why for me that clicking sound was so welcome.

How beautiful are those who bring encouragement and good news! Our heart lifts even as we hear the familiar footsteps. Are your footsteps pleasantly familiar to someone you know? When you walk through the front door of your office in the morning, what do people think when they hear you enter? When you climb the stairs to wake your husband after a nap, what do you believe comes to his mind when he hears you? Do your footsteps carry a smile or a happy hello? Try it, and feel the pleasure of having "beautiful feet."

Joni Eareckson Tada

PATH TO PRAYER

My Lord, may I see the real beauty behind sharing simple words and gifts of encouragement. Help me to understand that the smallest of graces lifts the spirit, strengthens the heart, and glorifies you.

NO EXPLANATION NECESSARY

Read: Isaiah 55

"For my thoughts are not your thoughts, neither are your ways my ways," declares the LORD. "As the heavens are higher than the earth, so are my ways higher than your ways and my thoughts than your thoughts," declares the LORD. —Isaiah 55:8

Warren Wiersbe once said, "Nothing is harder to heal than a broken heart shattered by experiences that seem so meaningless. But God's people don't live on explanations; God's people live on his promises."

A grocery list of Biblical reasons explaining the whys and wherefores behind suffering doesn't always help when you're hurting. What do help are the promises of God. Even though God's promises are usually devoid of standard explanations and don't always detail the blueprint behind his plan, they *do* point to the loving character of our good and kind Lord. And when he sets out to do something, it is as good as done, "So is my word that goes out from my mouth: It will not return to me empty, but will accomplish what I desire and achieve the purpose for which I sent it."

God wants us to understand that he alone is our source of help and hope. God owes us no explanations. He did enough explaining on the cross to show that his love is sufficient to meet every need.

Joni Eareckson Tada

PATH TO PRAYER

Using Isaiah 55 as an outline, pray through today's passage, noting the promises of God and claiming as your own those that speak to you most urgently.

REDEEMED

Read: Isaiah 56:1–8

"Maintain justice and do what is right, for my salvation is close at hand and my righteousness will soon be revealed."—Isaiah 56:1

God offered Adam and Eve a path that led straight from Eden to an eternal Paradise. But since our first parents opted for a detour, since suffering is now a part of what it means to be a *homo sapiens*, God is going to use it. Not half-heartedly, but in delight.

Do you feel as if you've been excluded from the Lord's presence? To you he says, "I will give within my temple and its walls a memorial and a name better than sons and daughters; I will give you an everlasting name that will not be cut off."

Do you feel joyless, rootless, drifting? To you he says, "I will bring you to my holy mountain and give you joy in my house of prayer."

As dark and pernicious as it is, God will squash suffering like a grapefruit in the face of the devil, turning it inside out into something sweet. If suffering can't be avoided, God's going to redeem it to usher us into the highest echelons of heaven.

Joni Eareckson Tada

WHAT OTHERS HAVE SAID

There is no human wreckage, lying in the ooze of the deepest sea of iniquity, that God's deep love cannot reach and redeem.
—John Henry Jowett

"IF . . . THEN"

Read: Isaiah 58:1–12

"If you spend yourselves in behalf of the hungry and satisfy the needs of the oppressed, then your light will rise in the darkness, and your night will become like the noonday."—Isaiah 58:10

God's heart intent is to alleviate suffering. He is bending over backward to make it happen. God is moving heaven and earth to dry the tear, lighten the load, ease the burden, take away the pain, stop the wars, halt the violence, cure the disease, heal the heartbroken, and mend the marriage.

God is straining to feed the homeless, clothe the naked, visit the prisoner, adopt the orphan, comfort the grieving, console the dying, defend the children, bandage the battered, give to the poor, care for the widow, uproot injustice, clean up pollution, prevent abortion, right the wrong, rectify racism, support the elderly, sustain the downcast, stamp out crime, stomp out pornography, help the disabled, prevent abuse, muffle the cursing, turn stone hearts to flesh and dead men into living ones.

He rallies us to his noble cause, but we fall behind. If God is weeping, it is because he has made his heart intent regarding suffering abundantly clear, but few—even of his own people—are moved into action. It's time to start listening.

Joni Eareckson Tada

TAKE ACTION!

How can you be the hands of God today? Look for a concrete way to join God in working to alleviate suffering and injustice. Tutor a child, write a letter to a political figure, or join a group fighting for human rights. Whatever God is calling you to do, respond now.

A SPECIAL DAY

Read: Isaiah 58:13–14

"If you keep your feet from breaking the Sabbath and from doing as you please on my holy day, if you call the Sabbath a delight and the LORD's holy day honorable . . . then you will find your joy in the LORD."—Isaiah 58:13,14

How are you at memorizing Scripture? I think the best time to invest in this practice is the time that already belongs to the Lord. The Lord's Day is a twenty-four hour period set aside for you to spend on spiritual objectives. How does God ask you to spend your time on his holy day? He simply asks that you do not do as you please, or go your own way, pursuing your own pleasures; he asks you to find delight in honoring him on his special day.

When is the best time to meditate on what you've memorized? Rehearsing God's Word is a great way to close out the evening. After all, God established that our day should begin in the evening anyway: "and the evening and the morning were the first day" (Genesis 1:5). This was how the Sabbath day was observed, and for good reason. The last important thoughts on our minds in the evening remain in our subconscious throughout the night and unconsciously set our mental attitudes for the day.

Joni Eareckson Tada

TAKE ACTION!

Begin a habit of memorizing Scripture on the next Lord's Day. Write out these verses and begin this week by memorizing and meditating on them.

ARISE, SHINE!

Read: Isaiah 60:1–5

"Arise, shine, for your light has come, and the glory of the LORD rises upon you."
—*Isaiah 60:1*

*I*t is the nature of light to expose and to show things for what they are. It is the nature of light to heal and nurture, to warm and soothe. It is the nature of light to push back the darkness. (Have you ever noticed how a room can be illumined by just one candle?) Darkness does not overtake light; light invades darkness. Light is always on the offensive. Light is a little like God. No, it is very much like God!

So Isaiah says of a future time when Jesus reigns, "Arise, shine, for your light has come, and the glory of the LORD rises upon you."

Heaven will shine by the Lamb who is the Lamp. Light will so much *be* in heaven that that sun will be ashamed (24:23). The Lord Almighty will reign gloriously. God's glory and his light go hand in hand. Heaven is a place full of glory and light—and it's where we're going one day!

Joni Eareckson Tada

PATH TO PRAYER

Light a candle and sit quietly in front of it in adoration of God, the source of Light. Express your praise for the Jesus, the Lamb who is the Lamp. Express your love for him and thank him for the hope of heaven, where there will be no darkness, but everlasting day.

THE LORD'S FAVOR

Read: Isaiah 61:1–6

The Spirit of the Sovereign LORD is on me, because the LORD has anointed me to preach good news to the poor. He has sent me to bind up the brokenhearted, to proclaim freedom for the captives and release from darkness for the prisoners, to proclaim the year of the LORD's favor and the day of vengeance of our God, to comfort all who mourn. —Isaiah 61:1–2

Would you like to have assurance that you are enjoying the Lord's favor? There is a way to know, and it's simpler than you might realize. The surest evidence that the Lord's hand of blessing is upon us comes when others are blessed through us. When we encourage friends and family in the midst of our trials, we know beyond a shadow of a doubt that God's hand of favor is on us. The best part is that those who are being blessed are at the same time being drawn closer to the Lord.

To be blessed by God means being drawn deeper, higher, and further into his heart. Being blessed means *feeling* his favor, his pleasure, and his delight. It means understanding him in his ways. What a gift to pass on to others!

Joni Eareckson Tada

POINTS TO PONDER

* How do you define blessing?
* In what ways are you being blessed?
* In what ways can you be a blessing?
* How can you help someone else be assured of God's favor?

You Are the Potter

Read: Isaiah 64:1–12

Yet, O Lord, you are our Father. We are the clay, you are the potter; we are all the work of your hand. —Isaiah 64:8

*I*saiah lived in a time when God's people were openly rebelling against him. The Lord called the prophet to peer into the future to give Israel a foretaste of what was coming—and the sight was awful. The prophet foresaw a day when the nation lay in ruins, the temple burned with fire and the people scattered, their cities abandoned and desolate.

But in Isaiah 64:8 we come to one of the Bible's big little words: "Yet." Although the whole rotten story is true, although Israel would be justly punished for her sins, *yet* God was the Potter who had taken some clay and shaped the nation. He was their Father, and though he was not in any way responsible for their sins, *yet* they belonged to him. Isaiah appealed for mercy on that basis.

It is not much different today. God is still using clay—only now the clay is you and me. Some of that molding and shaping we may not like. We may be tempted to ask indignantly, "What are you making?" or "Why did you make me like this?" We're especially prone to ask questions like that after we've been placed in the oven. Time spent in the oven is no fun.

But God knows all this. He is constantly at work forming us into a new creation. And even though some of his pottery seems to shatter into shards, in his hands even broken pottery can be made into something new and whole and beautiful. Our job is to work with him.

Dave Dravecky

Points to Ponder

* What are the forces in your life that you see as "time spent in the oven? How have those times shaped you? What wisdom have you gained from them?

A New Earth

Read: Isaiah 65:17–25

"Behold, I will create new heavens and a new earth . . . be glad and rejoice forever in what I will create, for I will create Jerusalem to be a delight and its people a joy."—Isaiah 65:17,18

I once was talking to a girl in a wheelchair about heaven. I asked her what she'd like to do when she got there. "Uh . . . I'd like to knit," she said. I replied, "Then let's make a date to meet in a cabin, pull up a couple of rocking chairs by the fireplace, and reach for our knitting needles, okay?" My friend scoffed, "You're just saying that. Heaven's not going to have cabins and rocking chairs. That stuff is only on earth."

Is that so? I believe heaven will have all that and more. Isaiah 65:17–25 says that God is planning new heavens and a new earth. Isaiah even foresees people dwelling in houses, planting vineyards, and eating fruit.

God does not switch dictionaries on us and suddenly redefine what earth is. If there are streets, rivers, trees, and mountains in the new earth, as the Bible says, then why wouldn't there be all the other good things? Why not cabins and rocking chairs?

Joni Eareckson Tada

For Further Reflection

Read also Isaiah 11:1–9; John 14:1–4; Revelation 21:1–4,9–27; 22:1–5 for more about God's plans for you and all of his people in heaven.

In God's Arms

Read: Isaiah 66:7–14

"As a mother comforts her child, so will I comfort you; and you will be comforted over Jerusalem."—Isaiah 66:13

*A*h, a child's life, wrapped in a warm blanket, sleeping peacefully in his mother's arms. Worries aren't his responsibility. A baby seems to know that mother will always be close by, tending to every need.

Do you ever wish your life were like that? If so, God has a reminder for you: "I will extend peace to her like a river . . . you will nurse and be carried on her arm and dandled on her knees. As a mother comforts her child, so will I comfort you; and you will be comforted over Jerusalem."

That seems an odd description for our heavenly Father, but God paints this tender picture to remind you that his breast is a place of comfort. In him, you can be satisfied. You, too, can rest peacefully knowing that Someone will always be close to you, tending to every need.

The Lord is your father, friend, husband, and brother. And according to Isaiah 66, He is also your mother. He is everything to you, just as a parent is to a child. And in his arms, you will find rest.

Joni Eareckson Tada

Path to Prayer

O God, you are father and mother to me; hold me close in your gentle arms. Comfort me as I long to be comforted. In you I will put all my trust in you, knowing that you will care for me as a parent does a child. I love you; help me to love and serve you more each day. Amen.

AN HONEST CRY

Read: Jeremiah 8:18—9:2

"O my Comforter in sorrow, my heart is faint within me." —Jeremiah 8:18

*A*s gloomy as Jeremiah can seem, you have to give the prophet one thing: he was totally honest about his feelings. Throughout his book he says thing like, "O my Comforter in sorrow, my heart is faint within me." I wish I had been so honest in my fight with cancer.

After my amputation removed the immediate threat of death, I genuinely praised God for my life and the opportunities he gave me, and I just kept going full speed ahead. Meanwhile, Jan had been falling apart emotionally. She begged me to let her get help. She was crying all the time and basically became bedridden. Yet I couldn't admit that she was depressed, much less that I was.

As an athlete, I had learned how to push past the pain. If I stopped pushing myself whenever I felt physical pain, I never would have made it to the big leagues. So naturally I applied the same jock mentality to emotional pain—and it didn't work.

But a neat thing happens when I'm honest and transparent with God. In some way, by being honest with him, I connect with his love for me as my heavenly Father. And that's a hard thing for me to do. It's probably one of the greatest struggles I have, outside of communication itself. I still wonder sometimes, *Does God really love me? How do I respond in love to him?* In ways I don't understand, being open and honest with him helps me to connect with the One who truly is "my Comforter in sorrow."

Dave Dravecky

TAKE ACTION!

Write a letter to God, being as honest and transparent as you can about the issues you are struggling with this very day—your pain and sorrow, your sins, your hopes and fears, and your questions.

WHY, LORD?

Read: Jeremiah 12:1–4

You are always righteous, O LORD, when I bring a case before you. Yet I would speak with you about your justice: Why does the way of the wicked prosper? Why do all the faithless live at ease?—Jeremiah 12:1

God's plan is specific. He doesn't say, "Into each life a little rain must fall," then aim a hose in earth's general direction and see who gets the wettest. He doesn't reach for a key, wind up nature with its sunny days and hurricanes, then sit back and watch the show. He doesn't let Satan prowl about totally unrestricted. He doesn't believe in a hands-off policy of governing. He's not our planet's absentee landlord. Rather, he screens the trials that come to each of us—allowing only those that accomplish his good plan because he takes no joy in human agony. These trials aren't evenly distributed from person to person. This can discourage us, for we are not privy to his reasons. But in God's wisdom and love, every trial in a Christian's life is ordained from eternity past, custom-made for that believer's eternal good, even when it doesn't seem like it. Nothing happens by accident . . . not even tragedy . . . not even sins committed against us.

Joni Eareckson Tada

WHAT OTHERS HAVE SAID

I am never afraid for my brethren who have many troubles, but I often tremble for those whose career is prosperous. —Charles Haddon Spurgeon

Consent

Read: Jeremiah 17:5–8

"Cursed is the one who trusts in man [human nature], who depends on flesh for his strength and whose heart turns away from the Lord. . . . But blessed is the man [or woman] who trusts in the Lord, whose confidence is in him."—Jeremiah 17:5–7

One day I was so angry with God. I paced the floor as my anger grew into rage. I spoke out loud, "You know what? I can't feel you, I can't see you, I can't sense you, I don't even know if you exist anymore. And if you *do* exist, why aren't you helping me?"

Still fuming with anger, I said, "You know what I need to do? I need to run. I'll just go back to the world. Just like in the beginning when I didn't understand you. I need to get busy; I need to fill my life up with things. I have enough money now. I could fill myself up with material things. I ought to just turn my back on you!"

But I couldn't. I knew I couldn't. Even with all its pleasures and promising distractions, I knew that the world could offer only a temporary solution. God offered the only eternal answer. I agreed to give my consent for God to do whatever he wanted in my life. I was surprised by the release and peace I found by surrendering my life to God and not relying on myself. I somehow knew God would walk me through this life. For me, this was a whole new way of looking at life, a perspective born of suffering and enduring many trials.

Dave's surgery was a one-time deal; the surgery God was doing on my sinful nature was ongoing. But we both came through our respective surgeries in the protective care of our heavenly Father.

Jan Dravecky

What Others Have Said

Trust God where you cannot trace him. Do not try to penetrate the cloud he brings over you; rather look to the bow that is on it. The mystery is God's; the promise is yours. —John R. MacDuff

HEAL ME

Read: Jeremiah 17:12–18

"Heal me, O LORD, and I will be healed; save me and I will be saved, for you are the one I praise." —Jeremiah 17:14

*I*n the early days of my injury my father would come to the hospital every day and whisper to me with wet eyes, "In every day and in every way, you're getting better and better and better." He'd say it every time he came.

But my body never did shake off the paralysis. The pragmatist would say, "See, your father's words were wishful thinking. You didn't get better, Joni; instead you got stuck with a wheelchair."

That's not the way I choose to look at it. Daddy was right. Every day I did get better. Maybe not on the outside but on the inside. My soul became settled. My hope became clear. This is the sort of healing described here: "Heal me, O LORD, and I will be healed; save me and I will be saved, for you are the one I praise." God is interested in healing the inside of a person. For me, a healed and happy heart is the best "better." By a long shot.

Joni Eareckson Tada

PATH TO PRAYER

Pray that the Great Physician will bring healing to you, whether in mind, body or spirit or all of these. Praise him for his goodness and kindness to you and for keeping you in his presence. Thank him very specifically for the blessings he has brought into your life.

"PLANS TO PROSPER YOU"

Read: Jeremiah 29:10–14

"For I know the plans I have for you," declares the LORD, "plans to prosper you and not to harm you, plans to give you hope and a future."—Jeremiah 29:11

*M*y sweetest memories are ones that inspire hope. Many of them are of life before my accident. I recall the grating sensation of a nail file against the tip of my fingers and the sound of my nails tapping cool, ivory piano keys. I can still "feel" my fingers plucking the tight nylons strings of my old guitar, digging under an orange skin and peeling it.

Why would memories like these inspire hope? They remind me that one day I'll have new hands. Fingers that work and feel, touch and pluck and pick and scrub and dig and caress. Hands that will embrace loved ones. The first thing I'm going to do is reach for Ken's new, glorified hand and give it a squeeze, just to see what it feels like. It'll happen! God promises me in Jeremiah 29:11, "For I know the plans I have for you . . . plans to prosper you and not to harm you, plans to give you hope and a future."

My best memories give shape to that hopeful future.

Joni Eareckson Tada

POINTS TO PONDER

* What are the losses you have suffered?
* What are the memories of the things you have lost?
* How might they inspire hope in you?
* How can you look forward to the restoration of your losses?
* Can you catch a glimpse of the plans God has for your future—plans that give you hope?

NO MORE

Read: Jeremiah 31:31–37

"For I will forgive their wickedness and will remember their sins no more."
— *Jeremiah 31:34*

God tells us that he will remember our sins no more. Why, then do we feel so bad about our past sins? Because we confuse sin with its impression. Let me show you how this can be so. Write the word "sin" on the page of a notepad. Press hard. Now tear off that sheet of paper, crumple it up, and throw it across the room. That's how God forgets your sin. Now take your pencil and rub it on the new page at an angle, back and forth, over the same location where you wrote. Guess what? The ghost of the word "sin" appears.

That's what our flawed memories do. We go back over the deep impression left by transgressions in our life, and we feel just as guilty. But be encouraged, the impression of sin is not the same thing as sin! God has forgotten our transgressions . . . and he can tenderly help us deal with the scars that remain.

Joni Eareckson Tada

PATH TO PRAYER

Lord Jesus, you know that I have sinned against you, and I confess it now as I have confessed my sin in the past. (*Confess your own sins and shortcomings.*) And yet, my Savior, I feel the impression of that sin yet. I have hurt you, and others, and myself in sinning against you, and that still troubles my soul. In your mercy forgive me. I pray that you will heal the wounds I have caused others, especially my loved ones, and that you will heal me, too.

AGAINST THE DARKNESS

Read: Lamentations 2:22—3:20

[The LORD] has besieged me and surrounded me with bitterness and hardship. He has made me dwell in darkness like those long dead. —Lamentations 3:5–6

Sometimes, the excellence of a jewel can best be seen when viewed against a dark background. Such is the case with Lamentations. Despite the horror and the suffering and the fear and the stench of death, Jeremiah reached out in the darkness and laid hold of the one gem of truth he could still see: God does not cast off his people forever (though it may seem that way). He will show compassion. Why? Because that is the greatness of his unfailing love (3:31–32).

I hope that is your own confidence! It may not seem to you that God cares. You look around and all you see is suffering and tears. You can't understand why God does not act. You may have laid bitter complaints at God's door.

Yet now is the time to reach out for the jewel that blazes even more brilliantly because of the dark backdrop of your circumstances. Though God may have allowed grief to invade your life for a little while, he *will* show compassion. That is the greatness of his unfailing love—not only for Jeremiah, but for you.

Dave Dravecky

FOR FURTHER REFLECTION

Look up Isaiah 54:10; Matthew 14:13–14; 2 Corinthians 1:3–4; and James 5:10–11 to discover more about God's compassionate love for you.

NEW EVERY MORNING

Read: Lamentations 3:22–38

Because of the LORD's great love we are not consumed, for his compassions never fail. They are new every morning; great is your faithfulness.
—Lamentations 3:22–23

*A*fter only a year of adjusting to life in a wheelchair, I began to tire of the self-pity. When I turned to the Bible, God's Spirit and a Christian friend named Steve Estes became my guides.

"Look," I said to Steve, "there's no way I can face a life of total paralysis with a happy attitude. It's just too much, too big."

He had a wise and ready reply: "I couldn't agree more. It is too much to ask. And God doesn't ask it of you, either. He only asks you to take one day at a time."

This wasn't simply a pious platitude plucked off a cross-stitched plaque; this was a powerful and fundamental signpost from Scripture pointing to the path away from pain. I began to "wheel" the path, beginning with verses 22–23: "Because of the LORD's great love we are not consumed, for his compassions never fail. They are new every morning; great is your faithfulness." I quickly learned this was the only way to live: one day at a time with God's enabling.

Joni Eareckson Tada

TAKE ACTION!

Print out the words of today's verse on a small piece of card. Tape it on your bathroom mirror and, each morning for the next week, reflect on it as you begin your day.

FACE TO FACE

Read: Ezekiel 1

This was the appearance of the likeness of the glory of the LORD. When I saw it, I fell facedown. —Ezekiel 1:28

When we sorely need encouragement, when tough challenges cause our hearts to sink, there can be no better place to look than into the loving eyes of our heavenly Father.

Even if the sight also drops us to our knees.

Ezekiel made that bracing discovery at the beginning of his ministry, when he came face-to-face with the God of the universe. The awesome sight so took away his breath that he groped for words, finally admitting that what he saw had "the appearance of the likeness of the glory of the LORD." The overwhelmed prophet immediately fell facedown—and God immediately gave him the strength to stand and to walk the difficult road ahead of him (2:1–8).

The prophet Daniel had a similar experience (Daniel 10:4–12), as did the apostle John (Revelation 1:10–19). All three men found great encouragement and the strength to move forward through a single glimpse of God's face—a joyous terror that first sent them crashing to the ground.

Do you need encouragement today? Then discover for yourself what vast strength is to be found in gazing into God's face—a joyous terror that brings us to our knees.

Dave and Jan Dravecky

WHAT OTHERS HAVE SAID

Holy, holy, holy, Lord God Almighty! / All Thy works shall praise Thy Name in earth and sky and sea; / Holy, holy, holy! Merciful and mighty, / God in Three Persons, blessed Trinity. —Reginald Heber

How Much Will It Cost?

Read: Daniel 3

"Praise be to the God of Shadrach, Meshach and Abednego, who has sent his angel and rescued his servants! They trusted in him and defied the king's command and were willing to give up their lives rather than serve or worship any god except their own God."— Daniel 3:28

What a remarkable testimony of faithfulness they left us! Even their persecutor, the pagan king Nebuchadnezzar, said of them and their awesome God, "Praise be to the God of Shadrach, Meshach and Abednego, who has sent his angel and rescued his servants! They trusted in him and defied the king's command and were willing to give up their lives rather than serve or worship any god except their own God."

Centuries later, Jesus, with eyes full of love and compassion, extends his hand and offers us life abundant and joyful, here and for eternity. "But how much will it cost?" you ask. The answer is short, simple, and painful. "It will cost you everything," the Lord replies (Matthew 10:37–39).

Is it worth taking up your cross, losing your life, and following the Lord? Jesus wraps his loving arms around us, reminding us, "Everyone who has left houses or brothers or sisters or father or mother or children or fields for my sake will receive a hundred times as much and will inherit eternal life" (Matthew 19:29). Yes, it's worth it. No matter the cost.

Joni Eareckson Tada

Points to Ponder

* What has it cost you to follow Jesus?
* What has it been worth to you to be called and saved by Jesus?
* Have you ever thought what it would be like to face death because of your confession of Jesus Christ?
* How would you respond?

DRAWING NEAR

Read: Daniel 6:1–10

[Daniel] went home to his upstairs room where the windows opened toward Jerusalem. Three times a day he got down on his knees and prayed, giving thanks to his God, just as he had done before. —Daniel 6:10

Daniel knew very well that, as the prophet Isaiah had said, God is our Great Shepherd who longs to gather the lambs in his arms and carry them close to his heart (Isaiah 40:11). How his divine heart must leap for joy when we ask for his help and protection! That is no doubt what Daniel was doing when he got down on his knees and three times a day prayed and gave thanks to God.

When we feel vulnerable and uncertain, we can always pray for God's help in:

- allowing him to instruct us
- trusting him to lead us
- resisting the temptation to "go it alone"
- rejecting the lure of self-pity
- resting in God's strength and care rather than our own

The Bible assures us that we can draw near to God in prayer, even as Daniel did. And he who heard that man of God will certainly hear us, as well.

Dave and Jan Dravecky

TAKE ACTION!

Do you ever get down on your knees to pray? Three times a day? If not, try it for three days, using the guidelines above as an outline for your prayers. What new things do you discover about praying this way?

DANIEL'S WITNESS

Read: Daniel 6:10–28

"My God sent his angel, and he shut the mouths of the lions. They have not hurt me, because I was found innocent in his sight. Nor have I ever done any wrong before you, O king."—Daniel 6:22

D runk drivers, irresponsible friends, and corrupt leaders—all of these can cause innocent people to suffer. The Bible provides numerous examples of righteous men and women who suffered at the hands of others. Daniel, for example, spent his life in captivity (and some scholars believe he was made into a eunuch by his Babylonian captors) and often was threatened with death—even though he is one of the most upright and pious men in the Scriptures.

There is great comfort in knowing that God will use anything—even the wickedness of humankind—to fulfill his purposes. Even though he suffered greatly, Daniel chose to honor God when he was a captive. His actions eventually led to a position of leadership in the nation of his captivity, a position that enabled him to display God's power and faithfulness to a watching world. Daniel realized that although others meant to harm him, God used his difficulties to work for good.

Dave and Jan Dravecky

POINTS TO PONDER

* Can you think of other Biblical characters who were harmed by others, and yet God used their suffering for good? (Hints: Genesis 37, 39–50; Matthew 27:11–26 and Mark 10:45; Acts 28:17–31)
* What is often the human response when someone hurts us?
* How did these others react? What qualities did they have in common?
* How should we pray when we are hurt by the sin of others?

HIGHLY ESTEEMED

Read: Daniel 10

"Do not be afraid, O man highly esteemed," he said. "Peace! Be strong now; be strong."—Daniel 10:19

How would you like to be called a man or woman "highly esteemed"—by God himself? Daniel was called exactly that, but not because of his job or his stature in the community. God called him "highly esteemed" because he first highly honored God by the way he lived.

While I have to say that my life as a baseball player was great, it did not give me the fulfillment I had expected. The day came when the baseball card with my picture on it became nothing more than a memento of past glories.

It took me awhile, but now I know I am worth as much today as I was the day I pitched a shutout during the National League playoffs. I have discovered that a person's true worth is found in who he or she is before God, not in what he or she does. And when we make that discovery, the world opens up like never before.

Dave Dravecky

PATH TO PRAYER

Tell God that there is no one else whose esteem you want more. Ask God if there is more you need to do to honor him by the way you live.

GETTING TO KNOW GOD

Read: Hosea 4:1–6

"My people are destroyed from lack of knowledge."—Hosea 4:6

S uffering can help us to get to know God better. Have you ever thought about that? It seems a quaint thought—then again, there's that high school buddy who never *did* take God seriously until trouble hit. Bagging a football scholarship to a Big Ten university consumed all his attention, but in his sophomore year at Michigan, he got slammed on the five-yard line. Two surgeries and three sidelined seasons later, he had done some serious thinking: Life was short; where were his priorities? Today, he is still into sports (he coaches the Tiny Tornadoes after work), but his priorities are straighter. Bible study and prayer get their chunk of time in his schedule.

Hosea wrote, "my people are destroyed from lack of knowledge"—and sometimes God uses suffering to add to our knowledge base. Specifically, he uses it to help us get to know *him* better.

Joni Eareckson Tada

POINTS TO PONDER

* What is your own experience? How has suffering helped you to know God better?

* How has suffering matured your view of God?

* How has suffering increased your desire to seek God and "worship him in spirit and in truth"?

July

July 1

RENOVATION PAIN

"I will be like the dew to Israel; he will blossom like a lily. Like a cedar of Lebanon he will send down his roots. . . . Men will dwell again in his shade."—Hosea 14:5,7

*E*ven in the Old Testament, in passages that drip with judgment, we are reminded continually that our God is a restoring God. Just moments after pronouncing divine judgment, God says, "I will be like the dew to Israel; he will blossom like a lily. Like a cedar of Lebanon he will send down his roots. . . . Men will dwell again in his shade."

When the Holy Spirit moves into our lives, he begins a massive renovation project on our souls. Day by day he builds into us the Christlike qualities of patience, endurance, kindness, gentleness, goodness, joy, and peace.

Perhaps this is why so much of life hurts—the third Person of the Trinity is busy tearing down old walls, pulling up warped floors, yanking out worn cupboards, and putting in new and wear-proof replacements, sent direct from the Manufacturer. He's so good at his work that every "home" he's ever renewed stays in perfect condition for eternity. And when he's finished, nobody ever misses the old place.

Dave and Jan Dravecky

WHAT OTHERS HAVE SAID

I should as soon attempt to raise flowers if there were no atmosphere, or produce fruits if there were neither light nor heat, as to regenerate men if I did not believe there was a Holy Ghost. —Henry Ward Beecher

A Worthy Lament

Read: Joel 2:12–19

"Even now," declares the LORD, "return to me with all your heart, with fasting and weeping and mourning." Rend your heart and not your garments. Return to the LORD your God, for he is gracious and compassionate, slow to anger and abounding in love. —Joel 2:12–13

My best companion during Lent is my old Book of Common Prayer. Just listen to the Collect for the beginning of Lent:

Almighty and everlasting God, who hatest nothing that thou hast made, and dost forgive the sins of all those who are penitent; Create and make in us new and contrite hearts, that we, worthily lamenting our sins, and acknowledging our wretchedness, may obtain of thee, the God of all mercy, perfect remission and forgiveness; through Jesus Christ our Lord. Amen.

If that prayer sounds a bit out of fashion, it may be we aren't reminded often enough that our sin is a stinking offense to God. Only an honest view of our sin will give us a full appreciation of God's mercy. Only when we understand how lost we really are, do we grasp how great is our salvation.

Christ did not die merely for the general sins of the world; he died specifically for *your* sin. If you have grown dull to the offense of your sin, ask God to help you to "worthily lament" in the spirit of Joel 2:12–13.

Joni Eareckson Tada

PATH TO PRAYER

My Lord and my God, I know that I so easily become dull and callous when it comes to my own failings and wrongdoing. Work in my heart so that I will come to know how much I have grieved and hurt you and so that I will truly grasp how great a treasure your love and forgiveness are to me. Create in me a clean, soft, heart, O God, and give me a right spirit. Amen.

July 3

WASTED YEARS

"I will repay you for the years the locusts have eaten. . . . You will have plenty to eat, until you are full, and you will praise the name of the LORD your God, who has worked wonders for you."—Joel 2:25–26

Recently I took inventory of my spiritual growth, beginning with that November afternoon in 1964 when I confessed Christ. As I marked off the milestones, I came across chunks of spiritual wastelands.

In my early teens I memorized the words of entire Beatles albums but felt bored with memorizing Scripture. I turned down a summer mission trip because I didn't want to be away from my boyfriend. Then came my accident in 1967 and more years of spiritual dryness as I sneered at nurses and took out my anger on my family.

Even after I got my spiritual act together, I wasted time. For almost a year I let die a habit of prayer. For ages I ignored Bible reading. Worthless years. Futile. Wasted.

At the close of my spiritual inventory, I grieved to think I would never recover or redeem what had been lost. But my grief lasted only a moment. God brought to mind the promise of Joel 2:25! The Lord promises that my losses shall be repaired. He will make good on the damage I've done. God vows that he will restore our loss.

Restore my wasted years, O Lord!

Joni Eareckson Tada

TAKE ACTION!

Conduct your own spiritual inventory. Make a timeline of your life, charting your spiritual growth and marking the spiritual milestones. Take note of the dry periods as well. Ask God to restore your lost and wasted years and redeem the time and opportunities you have wasted.

A TEMPORARY PARTNER

Read: Amos 9:11–15

"In that day I will restore David's fallen tent. I will repair its broken places, restore its ruins, and build it as it used to be. . . . New wine will drip from the mountains and flow from all the hills."—Amos 9:11,13

The book of Amos can seem a lot like life itself: page after dark page of pain, sorrow, tears and terror. You look in vain for much relief. It seems to offer nothing but uninterrupted misery.

And then comes the last page! Suddenly the clouds dissipate, the sun shines in full strength, and your skin warms in the brilliance of a bright summer day. Even Amos, who spends nine chapters proclaiming God's terrible judgment on sinful humankind, ends his book with a hopeful look ahead to that day when God will "restore David's fallen tent" when "new wine will drip from the mountains and flow from all the hills."

That is always the divine pattern. God wants us to know that pain and sorrow will never have a place on the victor's stand. Pain may be our companion for the moment, but he is nothing but a temporary partner. We must wait in hope for God's restoration, for it will surely come.

Dave Dravecky

WHAT OTHERS HAVE SAID

Every painful event contains in itself a sea of growth and liberation.
—Anthony de Mello

DON'T RUN AWAY

Read: Jonah 1:1—2:6

"In my distress I called to the LORD, and he answered me. From the depths of the grave I called for help, and you listened to my cry."—Jonah 2:2

There have been many times I haven't felt like praying. But that doesn't mean I lack a desire to communicate with God. I have a burning desire to communicate with him, and that desire has grown deeper over the years. I have a longing to talk to God about what's going on in my life. I've gotten beyond the point of bogging myself down in wondering whether he's hearing me and whether he's going to respond to me.

I often feel like Jonah, the prophet who admitted he was "running away from the LORD." After he was tossed into the sea and swallowed by a great fish, he prayed like this: "In my distress I called to the LORD, and he answered me. From the depths of the grave I called for help, and you listened to my cry."

God *does* hear, he *does* listen, and he *will* act. We just need to reach out to him in prayer.

Dave Dravecky

WHAT OTHERS HAVE SAID

It is not that prayer changes God, or awakens in him purposes of love and compassion that he has not already felt. No, it changes us, and therein lies its glory and its purpose. —Hannah Hurnard

STINGING WORDS

Read: Jonah 3—4

"I will have mercy on whom I will have mercy, and I will have compassion on whom I will have compassion."—Exodus 33:19

God has this thing about showing compassion to whomever he wants. Sometimes we don't like that. The *nerve* of God to save that child abuser, to reach out to that rapist on death row, to show compassion to that drug pusher!

Jonah felt exactly that way about those drug-pushing, idol-worshiping, fornicating Ninevites. Never had Jonah had such joy in preaching fire and brimstone! But what happens? The Ninevites repent—and God forgives them. That really makes Jonah mad. He says to the Lord, "Isn't that just like you?" God responds, "Have you any right to be angry, Jonah?" Those words stung.

And they sting today when we hear of serial killers who come to Christ or deathbed conversions of tyrants. But God will have compassion on whomever he wishes. God wants to make a difference in someone's life, including yours. Don't let your resentment stand in the way.

Joni Eareckson Tada

POINTS TO PONDER

* Have you ever felt resentment like Jonah's?
* What attitude is at the root of that kind of resentment?
* How does it stand in the way of your relationship to God?
* How might it stand in the way of the other person's relationship with God?

THOUGH . . .

Read: Habakkuk 3:2–19

"Though the fig tree does not bud and there are no grapes on the vines, though the olive crop fails and the fields produce no food, though there are no sheep in the pen and no cattle in the stalls, yet I will rejoice in the LORD, I will be joyful in God my Savior." —Habakkuk 3:17–18

*I*n our wilderness Jan and I learned to trust God, even though at times every visible trace of him had vanished. But we finally came to the point that Habakkuk did. Those verses brought us such comfort. We took encouragement in knowing that the wilderness was part of the spiritual landscape trudged by many people whom God has greatly used. This knowledge didn't take away our pain, but it did give us hope that we were not banished to the desert forever. We found comfort in realizing that Moses spent forty years in the desert and that God used that time to teach him lessons that would later equip him for mighty exploits. We put our trust and hope in God, that he would do something like that for us.

Dave and Jan Dravecky

PATH TO PRAYER

O God my Savior, sometimes it seems that I have gone so long without sensing your presence or seeing the fruit of my hard work and my faith. Yet I can see with the eyes of faith that you are not gone from the desert that seems to be my life right now. I will rejoice in you anyway, knowing that in your wisdom you have many things to teach me. You are still, and always will be, my hope and my joy.

QUIETED WITH LOVE

Read: Zephaniah 3:9–20

"The LORD your God is with you, he is mighty to save. He will take great delight in you, he will quiet you with his love, he will rejoice over you with singing."
—Zephaniah 3:17

When my heart is restless and my soul is downcast, I often surround myself with the calming strains of a favorite hymn. I sing to myself. I sing to God. But I'm astonished to think that God sings to me.

God sings! Do you think he sings all four parts at once? Maybe his music, so celestial and heavenly, resounds like a great choir. No doubt he has invented chords and major and minor keys that our ears have never heard. And I'm touched that he rejoices over you and me with an actual melody. What's more, he quiets us with his loving song.

I have often thought of this when a beautiful hymn rolls over and over in my mind. Always, its tune lifts my spirit and carries me through the day. No, I'm not playing a broken record in my head; the song, I'm convinced, is God's melody to me, direct from his heart. He is rejoicing over me with singing—hallelujah!—and all I need to do is listen and be inspired.

Joni Eareckson Tada

PATH TO PRAYER

Today, spend some time just listening to God and enjoying his presence. Empty your mind and quiet your spirit to prepare to hear God's voice.

BY MY SPIRIT

Read: Zechariah 3:3–4:10

"Not by might nor by power, but by my Spirit," says the LORD Almighty.
—Zechariah 4:6

G od specializes in irony. I was reminded of that when I was invited to speak at Billy Graham's Mission in Moscow.

My interpreter, a young blind student named Oleg, listened intently as I described the incredible scene before us. People were crammed shoulder-to-shoulder in the aisles and on the stairs. Just before I moved to the microphone, Oleg said to me, "I can hardly believe that God has picked you, a paralyzed woman, and me, a blind young man, to give his gospel to my countrymen in this stadium. It's amazing!"

Oh, the irony of God that he would choose to voice his message to a nation, not through the powerful or the mighty but through a most unlikely twosome. A paralyzed woman. A blind young man.

Zechariah 4:6 teaches us that God delights in showing the power of his Spirit through weak and unlikely people. He specializes in irony, always choosing a combination of circumstances opposite to what one might expect. There are plenty of ironies in your life, and each one is a reason to give God praise. His power always is best displayed through weakness.

Joni Eareckson Tada

TAKE ACTION!

Make a bookmark with the words of today's verse on it. Decorate it with markers or other art materials. Keep it in your Bible as a reminder to depend on the power of the Spirit of God to meet the challenges that face you.

A Fountain of Joy

Read: Zechariah 12:7–13:1

"On that day a fountain will be opened to the house of David and the inhabitants of Jerusalem."— *Zechariah 13:1*

One hot summer day when I was a little girl, my mother took me to the park. I remember a big fountain just over the hill from the zoo and arboretum. As we strolled by the fountain, I looked longingly as neighborhood children waded and splashed in the pool. I begged to join them, and my mother did the most amazing thing: she let me.

We took off my shoes and socks and I splashed into the fountain with the other children. My shorts and shirt got soaked, but there we were, a bunch of giggling boys and girls with arms widespread and faces uplifted, squealing as the water showered on us from the fountain above. Our hearts were free. Exuberant. Uninhibited. Full of life and in high spirits.

A fountain is a place of joy. That's what I think of when I read this verse. God has opened up a fountain to you through the Lord Jesus. He invites you to come on in and enjoy his love. Don't stand on the edges of his joy. He has washed away your sin and you, like a child, can be free and full of life.

Joni Eareckson Tada

PATH TO PRAYER

Reflect today on Jesus as the fountain at the very center of your being. Imagine how it would feel to splash in a pool of sparkling water on a hot day and have the cool water misting over you. Open your mouth and let it run down your dry throat. Open your spirit like you did when you were a child and let the joy of Jesus sink in.

SHINE

Read: Malachi 3

A scroll of remembrance was written in his presence concerning those who feared the LORD and honored his name. "They will be mine," says the LORD Almighty, "in the day when I make up my treasured possession."—Malachi 3:16–17

I love my wedding ring to shine. About once a week, I ask a friend to use my toothpaste and toothbrush to scrub it. Real gold and diamonds can take a good scrubbing; they're not as delicate as we think. And when they're polished, my, they look lovely!

Today's passage describes the Lord's "Book of Remembrance" in which the names of all those who meditate on his name are written down. He calls these people his "treasured possession." And how do we become a treasure that gleams and shines in his sight? He refines us and tests us.

Maybe you feel as if someone has taken a gigantic toothbrush and is scrubbing your soul raw. It hurts. You wince at the pain, the disappointment. But take heart—there's a purpose. And let me remind you: you're not as delicate as you think. You are a jewel, someone very precious to God. He promises that he's going to shine you up. He will polish you bright so that everyone will see what a treasure you are.

Joni Eareckson Tada

PATH TO PRAYER

Ask Jesus to help you understand the ways in which you are precious to him. Ask him to help you visualize yourself as his precious jewel, his treasured possession. Thank him for polishing you in every facet so that you can reflect his light to others.

This Is My Son

Read: Matthew 3:13–17

"This is my Son, whom I love; with him I am well pleased."—Matthew 3:17

*I*n the Bible, the Son commands center stage. He is God, absolute divinity, on a par with the Father and the Spirit in every way. The Father never tires of bragging about him: "This is my Son, whom I love; with him I am well pleased."

The two are so close that the Son is "in the bosom of the Father"—that is, resting his head on his chest, as close friends did while reclining on carpets around a low dinner table in the Middle East. Furthermore, God has taken the universe and turned the shop over to the Son: "All things have been committed to me by the Father" (Luke 10:22).

Why does the Father treasure him so? Because he sees himself in his Son. His own perfections are flawlessly reflected there. The Son is God standing in a mirror. In him God sees the fountain of all the intelligence, grandeur, and goodness that ever was.

And that fountain works ceaselessly on *your* behalf!

Joni Eareckson Tada

FOR FURTHER REFLECTION

Read John 14:6–21 and John 16 and 17 and meditate on the relationship between God the Father and God the Son.

BLESSED ARE YOU

Read: Matthew 5

"Blessed are those who mourn, for they will be comforted. . . . Blessed are you when people insult you, persecute you and falsely say all kinds of evil against you because of me. Rejoice and be glad, because great is your reward in heaven."
—Matthew 5:11–12

*A*ll suffering is within God's sovereign will. Not a sparrow falls without his knowledge nor is a soul lost for eternity without his tearful purpose being accomplished. In the words of Amos, "When disaster comes to a city, has not the LORD caused it?" (Joel 3:6).

There are many ways to suffer in this world. My wheelchair is a suffering that came from the sovereign purpose of God. And since that time more than three decades ago, I've also suffered things that have come upon me as a result of being in the kingdom. I have chosen to flee temptation, to drag my body from church to hospital, to endure the scorn of those who don't know God. And I have suffered as a result. Such is the will of God for my life.

The result? The common suffering he comforts. The godly suffering he rewards. And I wouldn't want to exchange either for anything.

Joni Eareckson Tada

POINTS TO PONDER

* What does being blessed mean to you?
* In what ways have you been insulted and scorned because of your belief in Jesus Christ?
* How did you respond to those who treat you that way?

THE FOCUS OF PRAYER

Read: Matthew 6:5–15

"But when you pray, go into your room, close the door and pray to your Father, who is unseen. Then your Father, who sees what is done in secret, will reward you."—Matthew 6:5–8

O ur Lord commanded us to pray in secret so that we would not be tempted to try to impress others with our vocalized piety. He is to be the focus of our prayers. If today you feel up against a wall, if your sin is heavy on your heart, let Christ come into the corner with you. Feel free to borrow the following words and make them your personal prayer.

Joni Eareckson Tada

PATH TO PRAYER

Lord Jesus, I have not allowed my suffering to draw me to you. But instead I have resisted you. I see now how my sin has separated me from you. Forgive me, I pray, and sit on the throne of my life as I lay before you my old way of doing things. Help me to live a life that pleases you, and as you do, I will wait patiently to see how you work through my trials. Amen.

WHERE IS YOUR TREASURE?

Read: Matthew 6:19–21

"For where your treasure is, there your heart will be also."—Matthew 6:21

S o far as we know, Jesus never asked to see anyone's bank statement. He didn't have to because he could see everyone's heart, and that told him everything he needed to know.

Someone might claim his heavenly deposits made him a millionaire, but if Jesus looked into his soul and saw a heart crusted over with greed, materialism and a preoccupation with "success," he knew he had found a liar. On the other hand, if Jesus encountered a man whose heart beat to the rhythms of heaven, he knew he had located a very wealthy man.

"Do not store up for yourselves treasures on earth, where moth and rust destroy, and where thieves break in and steal," the Master said. "But store up for yourselves treasures in heaven, where moth and rust do not destroy, and where thieves do not break in and steal. For where your treasure is, there your heart will be also."

Dave and Jan Dravecky

WHAT OTHERS HAVE SAID

Lives based on having are less free than lives based either on doing or being. —William James

ASK, KNOCK, SEEK

Read: Matthew 6:25—Matthew 7:8

"Ask and it will be given to you; seek and you will find; knock and the door will be opened to you. For everyone who asks receives; he who seeks finds; and to him who knocks, the door will be opened."—Matthew 7:7–8

There is no such thing as a bad question. The issue is not with the questions we ask, or even how we ask them. The issue is where we go with our questions. Any question that brings us to God for an answer is a good question. Anytime we come to God, it is an act of faith. When we knock on heaven's door, regardless of how hard we knock, how long we knock, or how stubbornly or angrily we knock, we state by our presence at that door that we believe God is there, that he is in charge of the world and therefore in some way responsible for what goes on here.

Dave Dravecky

POINTS TO PONDER

Read Genesis 18:22–33 for a story about Abraham, a man who questioned God about his intentions. Think about these questions: What did Abraham's motive seem to be? What were his attitudes? What phrase did Abraham keep repeating?

OUR LOVING FATHER

Read: Matthew 7:9–11

"If you, then, though you are evil, know how to give good gifts to your children, how much more will your Father in heaven give good gifts to those who ask him!"—Matthew 7:11

God knows that when we are in greatest distress we are in greatest danger of doubting his goodness. Jesus understood this completely. You can almost hear the pleading tone of his voice when he asked, "Which of you, if his son asks for bread, will give him a stone? Or if he asks for a fish, will give him a snake?"

A great preacher from a bygone era once asked his audience, "Did any of you parents ever hear your child wake from sleep with some panic-fear and shriek the mother's name through the darkness? Was not that a more powerful appeal than all words? And, depend upon it, that the soul which cries aloud on God, 'The God and Father of our Lord Jesus Christ,' though it have 'no language but a cry,' will never call in vain."

Dave and Jan Dravecky

PATH TO PRAYER

Write down all the attributes of a good parent that you can think of. After each attribute, try to think of some way in which God has shown that to you. Pray in gratitude for all the ways in which God has nurtured you, provided for you, comforted you, etc.

NOT YET COMPLETE

Read: Matthew 8:5–17

"He took up our infirmities and carried our diseases."—Matthew 8:17

We'd all like to think that Jesus came to take up our diseases—therefore we don't need to put up with them anymore. But that's akin to saying: "There's an oak in every acorn—so take this acorn and start sawing planks for picnic tables," or "Congress just passed a Clean Water Act—so Manhattan residents can start drinking from the East River tomorrow."

Forty years will pass before that white oak is ready for lumbering. Purging industrial ooze will take time, even if Congress can guarantee the outcome. So it is with the Rescue. What Jesus began doing to sin and its results won't be complete until the Second Coming. "It is finished," he uttered from the cross; the *purchase* of salvation was complete, the outcome settled with certainty. But the *application* of salvation to God's people was anything but finished.

Joni Eareckson Tada

POINTS TO PONDER

* Consider the verse for today. What does it mean to you?

* In what way does Jesus "take up" your infirmities? How might he "carry" your diseases?

* Can you imagine what it will be like when this verse comes to full fruition? (See Isaiah 65:17–25.)

WHO NEEDS A DOCTOR?

Read: Matthew 9:9–12

Jesus said, "It is not the healthy who need a doctor, but the sick."—Matthew 9:12

*A*lthough Jesus himself declared the sick need a doctor, some believers continue to insist that seeking medical help demonstrates a lack of faith—especially when the help that's needed is psychological.

But the human brain is a physical organ. Why can't we accept that the brain can get sick, just as a heart or a liver can? Our mental state is partially a result of what is happening in the part of our bodies called the brain. Depression, for example, involves a lack of seratonin necessary to transport the responses between the neurons in the brain.

So don't just sit there and let someone tell you to pull yourself together; you may be physically incapable of pulling yourself together. Even if you're afraid of what you might find out, face that fear and get professional help to find out what is causing your problems and what can be done to help you.

Jan Dravecky

WHAT OTHERS HAVE SAID

To have a curable illness and to leave it untreated except for prayer is like sticking your hand in a fire and asking God to remove the flame.
—Sandra L. Douglas

HIS EYE IS ON THE SPARROW

Read: Matthew 10:26–33

"Are not two sparrows sold for a penny? Yet not one of them will fall to the ground apart from the will of your Father."—Matthew 10:29

E nglish sparrows. They're worth barely a penny (Jesus said so). Yet of the world's nine thousand bird species, the Master singled out the least-noticed and most insignificant of birds to make a point.

If God takes time to keep tabs on every sparrow—who it is, where it's going, whether its needs are being met—then surely he keeps special tabs on you. Intimately. Personally. And with every detail in mind.

The Bible may point to eagles to underscore courage and power, and it may talk about doves as symbols of peace and contentment. But God's Word reserves sparrows to teach a lesson about trust. Just as God tenderly cares for a tiny bird, even making note of when it is harmed, or when it falls to the ground, he gently reminds you that he is worthy of your greatest trust, your deepest confidence.

Joni Eareckson Tada

TAKE ACTION!

Take a few crusts of bread or some birdseed and go to a natural area or a park. See if you can spot some sparrows and throw breadcrumbs out for them. Watch them for a while and meditate on how your Father cares for you. Say a prayer of thanks.

GOD WORKS WONDERS

Read: Matthew 11:1–20

"The blind receive sight, the lame walk, those who have leprosy are cured, the deaf hear, the dead are raised."—Matthew 11:5

I believe in a God of miracles. Not only because of the message Jesus sent to John the Baptist as recorded in Matthew 11:5, but also because I've seen him work wonders in my own life.

Before the surgeon operated on my left arm for the first time (and long before I made my comeback to the major leagues), I told him, "If I never play again, Doc, I'll know that God has someplace else he wants me. But I'll tell you something else. I believe in a God who can do miracles. If you remove half my deltoid muscle, that doesn't mean I'll never pitch again. If God wants me to pitch, it doesn't matter whether you remove *all* of the deltoid muscle. If God wants me to pitch again, I'll be out there."

And on August 10, 1989, I pitched against the Cincinnati Reds—winning 4-3. Chalk up another miracle!

Dave Dravecky

POINTS TO PONDER

* How do you define a miracle?

* Have you witnessed miracles?

* What do you think about this statement by St. Augustine: "Miracles are not contrary to nature but only contrary to what we know about nature"?

His Burden is Light

Read: Matthew 11:25–30

"Come to me, all you who are weary and burdened, and I will give you rest. Take my yoke upon you and learn from me, for I am gentle and humble in heart, and you will find rest for your souls."—Matthew 11:28–29

Have you ever wondered why Jesus called his yoke easy and light? A yoke appears to be a weighty burden, but it makes the workload light for the animal. A plow would be intolerable to the animal if it were attached any other way. A yoke, then, is not a contrivance to make work hard. It's a gentle device to make hard labor light.

Work is a fact of life. Burdens are inevitable. But you have a choice: either drag your workload under your own strength or put on the yoke of Christ. Jesus says, "Come." If you're weary and burdened, let him give you rest. You'll find a deep, sweet, peaceable rest even in the midst of your labors when you put on Christ's yoke.

Joni Eareckson Tada

Path to Prayer

Jesus, Lover of my soul, let me to thy bosom fly, /while the nearer waters roll, /while the tempest still is high; /hide me, O my Savior, hide, till the storm of life has passed;/safe into the haven guide. O receive my soul at last. —Charles Wesley, 1738

HAVE NO FEAR

Read: Matthew 12:15–21

"A bruised reed he will not break, and a smoldering wick he will not snuff out, till he leads justice to victory."—Matthew 12:20

Y ou never have to fear coming to Jesus. Yes, he is called "the Lord of glory" (1 Corinthians 2:8). Yes, into his hands all judgment has been placed (John 5:22). And yes, his almighty hands can quiver with wrath (Revelation 6:16).

But never forget that he is forever the infinitely gentle Savior, the One whom God promised will never break a bruised reed nor snuff out a smoldering wick.

You may feel like a bruised reed—stooped, battered, about to snap off in a puff of wind. Jesus sees your frailty, and far from despising it, he longs to lift you up. Or maybe you feel like a smoldering wick—depleted, gasping for air, nearly spent. Jesus wants to rekindle your flame and help you to burn brightly once more.

So have no fear. Approach the Savior with confidence. And be astonished at how expertly his gentle hands can remake your life.

Dave and Jan Dravecky

PATH TO PRAYER

Lord Jesus, I admit that I often let my fears keep me from coming to you with my problems. Sometimes I feel broken beyond repair, and I know that my reluctance to open my heart to you is because I have not always sought you when I should. I come to you now, bringing nothing but a desire to rest in your presence once again and to let you heal me. Rekindle in me the flame of your love and help me to burn brightly so that others may see you.

FIELD OF POSSIBILITIES

Read: Matthew 13:44–45

"The kingdom of heaven is like treasure hidden in a field. When a man found it, he hid it again, and then in his joy went and sold all he had and bought that field."
—Matthew 13:44

I wouldn't trade it for the world. I'm talking about God's will for my life—including this wheelchair. When we embrace God's will, everything changes.

It's very much like the parable of the hidden treasure. The key word in Matthew 13:44 is *bought.* We must buy the field. When we think of the field God wants us to buy, we assume it's attractive, something we would love to purchase anyway, a sun-drenched meadow dappled with wildflowers. It rarely is. The field—the thing God wants us to embrace—is often bleak (like a sandlot with broken bottles and old tires scattered here and there).

Of course, once we know the scrubby field contains a treasure, the whole picture changes. The empty scrap of land suddenly brims with possibilities. Now we're ready to sell everything to buy it. It's beautiful because underneath the surface lies the treasure, the priceless fortune of knowing Jesus better. I agree with Matthew 13:44: it's the kingdom of heaven.

Joni Eareckson Tada

POINTS TO PONDER

* In what "scrubby field" of trial or hardship has God hidden your treasure?

* How hard is it for you to envision that treasure buried there?

* What would you be willing to "sell" to "buy" it? Or what did you "sell" to "buy" it?

A DROWNING MAN

Read: Matthew 14:22–33

When [Peter] saw the wind, he was afraid and, beginning to sink, cried out, "Lord, save me!"—Matthew 14:30

So much of my professional life was concerned with pleasing others—my manager, my teammates, the fans. When I became a Christian, God seemed to be just one more person to please.

I had a hard time believing that God could love me regardless of my mistakes, despite my faults, even though I had not and never could perform perfectly. Could he really love me the way a father loves his toddling child, as the Bible claimed?

I mean, how could he? My prayer life stank. I had so little time to pray, and when I did, I felt guilty. I prayed out of desperation, not devotion. I felt as if I were drowning—and I don't mean dangling my feet in the deep end of the pool. I mean, I could feel myself going under.

So I called out to the Lord the way Peter did when he walked on the water and started to sink: "Lord, save me!" And do you know what? Jesus heard me, just as surely as he heard the burly old fisherman. That's how we could both rise up out of the deep!

Dave Dravecky

PATH TO PRAYER

Ask God the Father to rescue you today if you feel yourself sinking physically, spiritually, and/or emotionally. Ask your "*Abba* (Daddy)" to help you realize how much he loves you despite your imperfect devotion to him. Ask God to help you feel as safe and secure in him as a child is when he or she is being carried in daddy's arms.

THE GREATEST MIRACLE

Read: Matthew 15:21–39

Jesus called his disciples to him and said, "I have compassion for these people."
—Matthew 15:32

*M*atthew 15 records two supernatural incidents of divine compassion, both of which truly deserve the designation "miracle." But who's to say which is the greatest?

In the first (vv. 21–28), Jesus cast out a demon from the daughter of a Canaanite woman. Some readers are troubled by Jesus' initial unwillingness to hear out the woman. But they forget that the Old Testament commanded the exclusion of all Canaanites from Israel's worship (Zechariah 14:21) and even their annihilation (Deuteronomy 20:17). For Jesus to grant this woman's request was nothing short of a miracle.

In the second (vv. 29–38), Jesus looked at a crowd of lame, blind, and disabled people and told his disciples, "I have compassion for these people; they have already been with me three days and have nothing to eat." Then, to their astonishment, he took seven loaves of bread and a few fish, gave thanks, and multiplied these meager rations into a meal that fed four thousand men plus women and children (with plenty left over).

Which miracle was the greater? Perhaps we don't have to decide. For God's compassion itself is the greatest miracle of all.

Dave and Jan Dravecky

TAKE ACTION!

Be a mirror of Jesus' compassion today. Make a loaf of bread, a batch of cookies, or a meal and take it to someone who is ill or discouraged. Take time to visit with them for a short time. Tell them you will be thinking of them and that you will pray for them.

July 27

WONDERS GREAT AND SMALL

Read: Matthew 17:24–27

"Go to the lake and throw out your line. Take the first fish you catch; open its mouth and you will find a four-drachma coin."—Matthew 17:27

*I*f you made a list of all the big creation miracles Jesus did before he came to earth, what would be on it? My list contains galaxies, black holes, solar systems, the law of gravity, the law of thermodynamics, the atmosphere, the asteroid belt, constellations and photosynthesis. All of them are God-sized wonders.

When this same Lord lived in Palestine, he performed smaller-scale miracles, like the one recorded in Matthew 17:27, where he found a coin in a fish's mouth. While on earth, Jesus performed powerful miracles, but at a different speed and on a smaller scale than when he created the cosmos.

Make a point of looking up into the heavens tonight. Even if it's overcast, there's magnificence to it all. Contemplate how marvelous God's creation is, including you.

Joni Eareckson Tada

TAKE ACTION!

Go outside tonight and look at the sky. Sing a hymn of praise to God, or recite Psalm 19.

COURAGE TO CONFRONT

Read: Matthew 18:15–20

"If your brother sins against you, go and show him his fault, just between the two of you."—Matthew 18:15

There was a time when I just stuffed my complaints against a person and pretended to be fine, while I seethed inside. Now if I catch myself seething whenever I am around a person, I stop to examine why I'm seething. If I've been wronged or sinned against, I go to the person as Scripture instructs us in this passage. I still have to swallow hard before confronting those who might get mad at me or retreat from me. Courage is required to confront others when it is necessary, but at least I realize confrontation is necessary at times to keep relationships balanced and honest.

Jan Dravecky

TAKE ACTION!

Who are you angry with? Who is angry with you? Ask God for the courage to go and speak to that person. With a humble and gentle spirit, try to make peace with that person.

KINGDOM PLAY

Read: Matthew 19:13–15

Jesus said, "Let the little children come to me, and do not hinder them, for the kingdom of heaven belongs to such as these."—Matthew 19:14

When was the last time you experienced an "Aha!" moment of delight in God? These moments burst beyond happiness and call for rejoicing out of sheer exuberance. Like a child, you just *have* to go outside, beyond the four walls of normal human experience, and have some fun! I call this "kingdom play," based on Jesus' words about the children who were brought to him.

When was the last time you did something childlike out of sheer joy? Said something childlike? Express your delight in God today in the way a child would: finger-paint a wild and colorful poster; sing at the top of your lungs a song you learned in Sunday school; buy a Tootsie-Pop and lick it for fun. Most of all, do a little kingdom play, telling God in song, word, or deed how delighted you are in him.

Joni Eareckson Tada

TAKE ACTION!

Act on one of the suggestions from above or think up some "kingdom play" on your own. What did you enjoy doing as a child? Go back into your memories and revive your unique playfulness in some way.

GOD'S WILL FOR OUR CHILD

Read: Matthew 20:20–23

"What is it you want?" [Jesus] asked. —Matthew 20:21

The mother of James and John asked the Lord to bestow honor on her sons but was told instead they would drink from the same cup as the Lord's. No one knows if she realized that Jesus was describing his cruel death. We don't know if she understood that this meant martyrdom for her sons.

This dear mother is not all that unusual. Every parent wants to see his child promoted and honored. But God may have a different plan for that child, perhaps one not as glamorous or as full of accolades. Always, a parent's desire for a child's advancement must be held in check as the mother and father pray that God's will be done in his life.

Like the mother of James and John, parents need to consider carefully what they ask God to do for their children.

Joni Eareckson Tada

POINTS TO PONDER

* Take time to ponder what you truly want for your children.
* What will be the cost to them if they get it?
* What do you think God wants for them?
* How can you pray for them?

PRAISE JESUS REGARDLESS

Read: Matthew 21:1–11

When Jesus entered Jerusalem, the whole city was stirred and asked, "Who is this?"—Matthew 21:10

No wonder those people waving palm branches were so excited. They had great expectations of Jesus. This was the one who would throw the Roman oppressors out of the Holy City. He would feed and protect them, giving them back their national dignity. But by mid-week, the mood of the people soured. And the rest is history.

I wonder . . . are we all that different from those people? When we think we've got God's plan neatly figured, when we've convinced ourselves that the Lord's job is to make our lives easier, do our praises turn to curses? Do we sing our hosannas to the Most High when Palm Sunday turns into Blue Monday?

Let's not run away when God doesn't follow through on our expectations. Let's give Jesus praise for who he is, not for who we think he ought to be.

Joni Eareckson Tada

WHAT OTHERS HAVE SAID

I believe there is no one lovelier, deeper, more sympathetic and more perfect than Jesus—not only is there no one else like him, but there could never be anyone like him. —Fyodor Dostoevsky

August

A REJECTED STONE

Read: Matthew 21:33–46

Jesus said to them, "Have you never read in the Scriptures: 'The stone the builders rejected has become the capstone; the Lord has done this, and it is marvelous in our eyes'?"—Matthew 21:42

We may not like it much, but in a real sense Christianity is a faith of rejects—starting with its Founder.

In verse 42 Jesus quoted Psalm 118:22 to describe himself: "The stone the builders rejected." He saw himself as an unwanted stone—a reject. On many occasions those who heard him speak recoiled at his message—also a reject. And our Lord warned us that just as he was rejected, so would we be (John 15:20)—a family of rejects.

Of course, the story doesn't end there! Some might reject Jesus, but God would make him into "the capstone." His word might be rejected, but nevertheless it would last for eternity (Matthew 24:35). And we might be rejected by the world, but we will reign with him forever in heaven (Revelation 3:21).

Sometimes it's good to be a reject!

Dave Dravecky

WHAT OTHERS HAVE SAID

If you were not strangers here the dogs of the world would not bark at you. —Samuel Rutherford

LOVE THE LORD

Read: Matthew 22:34–40

"'Love the Lord your God with all your heart and with all your soul and with all your mind.' This is the first and greatest commandment." —Matthew 22:37–38

The more you center in prayer on God's attributes, the more those attributes become a part of your life. Focus on God's mercies, and you will become merciful. Plead with him for his wisdom, and wisdom will be yours. Center your thoughts on his holiness, and you will grow in holiness.

Grab onto an attribute of God with all your heart, and ask him to deal with you accordingly. Humbly hold him to his promises. God is delighted when you seek his will, his character, his glory—and yes, his heart—in your prayers.

Joni Eareckson Tada

PATH TO PRAYER

Make a prayer card and write on it an attribute of God, e.g. wisdom, holiness, mercy, kindness, compassion, loving, or forgiving. On the back, write a prayer humbly asking God to show himself to you with respect to that attribute. Ask God to deal with you accordingly and to make you a reflection of him.

HEART OF COMPASSION

Read: Matthew 23:37–39

"O Jerusalem, Jerusalem, you who kill the prophets and stone those sent to you, how often I have longed to gather your children together, as a hen gathers her chicks under her wings, but you were not willing."—Matthew 23:37

One of the most plaintive cries in the entire Bible has to be this verse where Jesus laments over the people of God's holy city.

Here we gain an immense window into the very soul of God himself. And what we see in the divine heart is this: unfathomable compassion wracked with grief. Jesus looks down the corridor of time and sees the awful destruction hovering over the city due to its stubborn rejection of the Savior's love. And his heart breaks.

When you wonder whether the Savior cares for you, when you worry that he has turned his back on you because of some real or imagined offense, remember this wail before the ancient walls of Jerusalem. And know that even now Jesus longs to gather you close, as a hen gathers her chicks under her wing.

Dave and Jan Dravecky

POINTS TO PONDER

Find a book or encyclopedia that discusses how birds care for their young. What do you learn about God from the birds? Imagine yourself a baby bird nestled under God's wing. What's it like there?

GOD REMEMBERS

Read: Matthew 26:6–13

"I tell you the truth, wherever this gospel is preached throughout the world, what she has done will also be told, in memory of her."—Matthew 26:13

*I*f we're honest, we have to admit that sometimes we're afraid that the Lord might forget us. He's so busy, after all. He has a universe to take care of. And even on this little world, full of billions of people and trillions of daily incidents, why should God take note of little old us? Why should he remember our puny attempts at service and devotion?

For all those troubled by that question, God answers with this story. An unnamed woman approaches Jesus just before his arrest and anoints him with a jar of expensive perfume. When the disciples react with indignation, Jesus insists she has done "a beautiful thing" for him and declares that her story will continue to be told wherever the gospel is preached.

The woman didn't do much. She poured a little perfume over the Master's head. That's all. But she did it in faith and devotion—and we're still talking about it 2,000 years later. Why? Because God doesn't forget. And neither will he forget you, no matter how small you feel.

Dave and Jan Dravecky

FOR FURTHER REFLECTION

Read more about God's perfect memory in Deuteronomy 4:29–31; Isaiah 49:13–16; and Hebrews 6:10.

WHEN GOD SAYS "NO"

Read: Matthew 26:36–46

"My Father, if it is possible, may this cup be taken from me. Yet not as I will, but as you will."—Matthew 26:39

For years I pleaded with God to give me hands and feet that would work. I never got what I wanted. Looking back, I can see God's wisdom in not granting my wish. My faith is stronger. My love for Jesus is brighter. It wouldn't be the same had my wish been granted.

Great things happen when God does not give us what we want. Even the Father did not abide by the pleadings of his Son. In the Garden of Gethsemane, Jesus longed to bypass the cross. He hoped it might be possible for his Father to take him in another direction. But at the close of his prayer, Jesus knew that his pleading was over. He was heading for Calvary.

But oh, the glorious things that happened as a result of the Father's "no"! Thank heaven that the Cross happened.

If God does not grant you your wish, please know that he wants to strengthen you as you accept what comes from his hand. Ultimately, that may be the very thing your heart desires most.

Joni Eareckson Tada

PATH TO PRAYER

Lord, teach me to trust you regardless of how you answer my prayers. Teach me to accept your *no*'s as well as your *yes*'s and to look for your blessings in all things, even in my hardest trials and biggest disappointments. Thank you for watching over me in all these circumstances.

HE KEPT SILENT

Read: Matthew 26:57–67

But Jesus remained silent. —Matthew 26:63

One after the other they slapped his bleeding face with rough, callused hands. Their arrogant sneers and cruel mockery seemed to consume their hard faces as they chanted in sing-song voices, "Prophesy to us, Christ. Who hit you?"

Of course, he could have—easily. The God-man who prophesied the manner and time of his own death and resurrection, who predicted how and when his best friend would betray him, would have no trouble naming those who struck him. And what would they have done, I wonder, had he slowly begun to announce their identities: "Saul . . . Judah . . . Levi"? But he didn't do that. He kept silent. Why? We could only guess.

You know, the same is true when we come to him with many of our own questions. Certainly he knows the answers. But still he remains silent. Why? We can only guess. One day, perhaps, we'll know. But until then, let's wait patiently. Better to follow his example of silence than to strike out like Levi.

Dave Dravecky

POINTS TO PONDER

* Why do *you* think Jesus remained silent?
* What would you have said to the mockers?
* What questions have you asked Jesus, and he remains silent?
* How might you pray in the face of Jesus' silence?

TAKE THE NEXT STEP

Read: Matthew 26:69–75

And [Peter] went outside and wept bitterly. —Matthew 26:75

I so identify with Peter after he denied the Lord three times! Jesus had told him he would disavow all personal connections "before the rooster crows," and that's exactly what happened, despite the fisherman's bold statement to the contrary (Matthew 26:34).

But then the rooster crowed. And Matthew says Peter "went outside and wept bitterly."

Many have been the times I have "denied" the Lord, despite my confident assertions to the contrary! And many have been the times I have felt absolutely worthless, to the point of bitter tears. C. S. Lewis wrote a great sentence that encourages me in these times: "If we only have the will to walk, God is pleased with our stumbles."

Ask anybody who knows me, and you'll discover that I stumble plenty. But God knows I have the will to walk. God knows I want to please him, and so I keep taking the next step. If I stumble, I get back up. I am trying to walk in a manner worthy of my Lord and Savior, even though I often hit the pavement.

Dave Dravecky

WHAT OTHERS HAVE SAID

Loyalty that will do anything, that will endure anything, that will make the whole being consecrate to Him, is what Christ wants. Anything else is not worthy of Him. —Burdett Hart

THE WOMEN WERE THERE

Read: Matthew 28:1–10

The angel said to the women, "Do not be afraid, for I know that you are looking for Jesus, who was crucified."—Matthew 28:5

*A*s awful as the days surrounding Jesus' crucifixion were, they show us that we women are vitally important to his plans and infinitely dear to his heart. Matthew goes out of his way in his Gospel to show the crucial place women played in the passion story—despite cultural pressures to downplay or hide such involvement. First, he tells us who was observing as Jesus took his last breath on the cross: "Many women were there, watching from a distance. They had followed Jesus from Galilee to care for his needs" (27:55). Next, he tells us who was taking note when the body of Jesus was placed in a tomb: "Mary Magdalene and the other Mary were sitting there opposite the tomb" (27:61). Third, he tells us this same pair of women showed up at dawn Sunday just after Jesus rose from the grave (28:1). Last, when the angel rolled away the stone from the tomb, he didn't speak to the guards who surrounded the site, but to the women. (The men were too busy being afraid, shaking, and becoming "like dead men.")

Yes, God has a special place for women in his eternal plans. Each of us.

Jan Dravecky

WHAT OTHERS HAVE SAID

Perhaps it is no wonder that the women were first at the Cradle and last at the Cross. They had never known a man like this Man—there never has been such another. A prophet and teacher who never nagged at them, never flattered or coaxed or patronized; who rebuked without querulousness and praised without condescension; who took their questions and arguments seriously; who never mapped out their sphere for them.
—Dorothy Leigh Sayers

"I Am With You Always"

Read: Matthew 28:16–20

"And surely I am with you always, to the very end of the age."—Matthew 28:20

*I*n the early days of my paralysis, pressures seemed greatest at night. Perhaps therapy had gone badly that day. Or no one came to visit. Or maybe Mrs. Barber was being mean to me again. Whatever the problem, I'd want to cry. I felt even more frustrated because I couldn't cry, for there was no one to wipe my eyes and help me blow my nose. Yet the Scriptures were encouraging, and I'd apply the reality and truth of them to my own special needs.

During these difficult midnight hours, I'd visualize Jesus standing beside my bed. I imagined him as a strong, comforting person with a deep, reassuring voice, saying specifically to me, "Surely I am with you always. If I loved you enough to die for you, don't you think I ought to know best how to run your life—even if it means your being paralyzed?" The reality of this Scripture was that he *was* with me, now. Beside me in my own room! That was the comfort I needed.

Joni Eareckson Tada

Path to Prayer

Tonight when you go to bed, lie quietly, visualizing Jesus standing beside your bed. If you have something you would like to tell him, do so. Otherwise enjoy his presence there with you as you drift into sleep.

ALONE WITH GOD

Read: Mark 1:29–37

Very early in the morning, while it was still dark, Jesus got up, left the house and went off to a solitary place, where he prayed. —Mark 1:35

Wonderful things happen when you're alone with the Lord. Look at the record:

Moses was alone when the Lord revealed himself through the burning bush. Paul was alone in the Arabian desert when the Lord gave him personal instructions about preaching the Word. Mary was alone when the angel brought her the message that she would give birth to the Savior. Isaiah was alone when he received his commission from the Lord. Elisha was alone when the mantle of prophet fell on his shoulders. And who can forget John alone on the island of Patmos when he received his startling revelation? Joshua, Jacob, and Daniel all received a special word from God when they followed the wisdom of this verse.

Guidance and real fellowship come only in those times of solitude, in an hour when you say to the Lord, "I need you."

Joni Eareckson Tada

PATH TO PRAYER

If you need a word from the Lord—direction, help, and hope—set aside time to be alone with him. Expect him to speak to you.

JESUS' REAL MESSAGE

Read: Mark 1:36–38

"That is why I have come."—Mark 1:38

Word spread through the night that Jesus had healed all the sick and the demon-possessed in Capernaum, and the next morning everyone was searching for the Great Physician. Only after searching high and low did Simon and his friends find Jesus away from the crowds, almost hiding, and praying alone.

Sick people and their families were frantic for his healing touch, but Jesus left them to go on. It's not that he didn't care about the cancer-ridden and arthritic. It's just that their illnesses weren't his focus; the gospel was. Jesus' miracles were merely a backdrop to his urgent message: sin will kill you; hell is real; God is merciful; his kingdom will change you; and I, Jesus, am your passport.

What are you seeking from God? The healing of a hurt? The meeting of a need? These things are good, but don't miss Jesus' deeper message. The core of his plan is to rescue you from sin. God cares most not about making us comfortable but about teaching us to hate our sins, to grow up spiritually, and to love him.

Joni Eareckson Tada

FOR FURTHER REFLECTION

Read more about Jesus' mission in John 1:7; 10:10; 12:46; and Ephesians 2:17.

SHAKING UP THE STATUS QUO

Read: Mark 3:1–5

[Jesus] looked around at them in anger and, deeply distressed at their stubborn hearts, said to the man, "Stretch out your hand." He stretched it out, and his hand was completely restored. —Mark 3:5

Often it's not *what* Jesus did, but *why* he did it. Healing people was, for Jesus, a daily part of his public ministry. But the point behind this story has to do with *why* Jesus performed the miracle.

The Lord was deeply disturbed by the indifference the congregation showed toward the handicapped person. He was upset that the people were more concerned about the letter of the law and the proper way to do things than meeting the need of a hurting person in their midst. It was their cold, stubborn apathy that prompted Jesus to act.

There are many reasons for reaching out to meet the needs of those around you. One reason may simply be to lend a helping hand. Another may be to put your gifts and talents to use. But a valid reason could be that you must take action against the nonchalance and indifference others display toward the needs at hand. Many a church has been sorely convicted when a believer steps out and shakes up the status quo!

Joni Eareckson Tada

POINTS TO PONDER

* What needs are people indifferent to in your church or community?
* What convictions has God called you to stand for?
* What can you do to "shake things up" with a caring spirit?

TIME TO DO THE FATHER'S WILL

Read: Mark 5:21–43

A large crowd followed and pressed around him. —Mark 5:24

If you struggle with battling "the tyranny of the urgent," as I do, then we both need to take another look at Jesus. At the end of his life, the Master could say, "It is finished!" even though many of the needs of those around him were left untended. Jesus' life "showed a wonderful balance, a sense of timing" because he "prayerfully waited for his Father's instructions and for the strength to follow them," says author Charles Hummel. "Jesus had no divinely drawn blueprint; he discerned the Father's will day by day in a life of prayer. By this means, he warded off the urgent and accomplished the important."

In this passage, Jesus had been urgently summoned to the bed of a dying little girl. On the way he encountered a woman with a long-term (but not imminently fatal) health problem. Probably to the distress of some of his disciples, he paused to minister to this woman's important need—and in so doing once again showed us how to ward off the urgent to accomplish the important.

Jan Dravecky

PATH TO PRAYER

Ask Jesus to give you the ears to hear his voice as he directs you in your daily struggle to balance your time and energy. Ask him to show you the difference between the urgent and the important and to show you his timing and his will.

A Quiet Place

Read: Mark 6:31–32

"Come with me by yourselves to a quiet place and get some rest."—Mark 6:31

Self-care is not self-absorption. Even Jesus took time to go away by himself to be with his Father. After he and his disciples had been out ministering, he pulled them away for a time of rest: "Then, because so many people were coming and going that they did not even have a chance to eat, he said to them, 'Come with me by yourselves to a quiet place and get some rest.' So they went away by themselves in a boat to a solitary place."

This really grabbed my attention because I was saying "yes" to my kids and "yes" to my husband and "yes" to friends, but I rarely said "yes" to myself. My set of rules dictated that if a need existed, I needed to fill it; but physically, I couldn't do it all. I felt relieved to read that even Jesus, God in the flesh, needed to take time for his own restoration.

Jan Dravecky

Take Action!

Resolve to take care of yourself so that you can continue to serve without burning out. Make an appointment with yourself for a period of rest, and keep it. If you are a caregiver, ask a friend or relative to take over for you, even if only for a couple of hours. Or look for respite resources in your community. You and your loved one will be better for it.

NOTHING IS WASTED

Read: Mark 6:30–44

They all ate and were satisfied, and the disciples picked up twelve basketfuls of broken pieces of bread and fish. —Mark 6:42–43

*I*n Mark 6 we read the heart-warming story of how Jesus took the loaves, broke them, multiplied the fish, and gave everybody lots to eat with lots left over. They gathered baskets full of leftover bread so nothing would be thrown away.

I think about that story when I watch a Christian go through tough times yet hang on to God's grace. Maybe you're such a person. Day-to-day heartache is your routine, and problems seem to have a permanent place in God's plan for you. What God is doing with you is like what he did with the barley loaves and fish. Jesus broke the bread. And out of the broken loaves of bread, he multiplied the blessing so thousands would be nourished. Yes, it hurts to be broken. But sometimes that's part of God's plan, especially if he wants you to feed others. Out of your brokenness, the blessing can be bestowed on more people than you ever dreamed possible—and you can be certain nothing will be wasted. God will gather up and use all the hurt; not a bit of it will be discarded or cast aside.

Joni Eareckson Tada

PATH TO PRAYER

Bread of Life, Lord of all, I pray that you take the hurt and the brokenness of my life and multiply it as you multiplied the loaves and fish. My suffering will be easier for me to bear if I know that you have used me to feed others and heal them. Thank you for blessing me and blessing others through me.

An Invitation to Suffer

Read: Mark 8:31–38

"If anyone would come after me, he must deny himself and take up his cross and follow me. For whoever wants to save his life will lose it, but whoever loses life for me and for the gospel will save it."—Mark 8:34–35

*P*rograms, systems and methods sit well in the ivory towers of monasteries or in the wooden arms of icons. Head knowledge comes from the pages of a theology text. But the invitation to know God—really know him—is always an invitation to suffer. Not to suffer alone, but to suffer with him.

Thankfully, Jesus was not imprisoned by death. He burst back to life. What power! If I'm to be held steady in the midst of my suffering, I want to be held, not by a doctrine or a cause, but by the most powerful Person in the universe.

Joni Eareckson Tada

What Others Have Said

Sacrifice releases power. The greater the sacrifice, the greater the power released. —John Wimber

THE LIFELINE OF THE SOUL

Read: Mark 9:14–29

"I do believe; help me overcome my unbelief!"—Mark 9:24

On this side of heaven, we are often like the man in Mark 9 who asked Jesus *if* he could do anything to help his demon-possessed son. Jesus replied, "If you can? Everything is possible for him who believes." To which the man wisely and immediately exclaimed, "I do believe; help me overcome my unbelief!"

Even though it is often difficult for us to pray when we find ourselves in the middle of great trials, that is exactly the time when we most need to pray. Every time we pray, whether it feels like it or not, we are brought into the very throne room of heaven. Jesus himself ushers our prayers into the presence of the Father, and that alone assures us that they will be heard and answered. Prayer is a matter of obedience, but it is also a matter of survival. Prayer is the lifeline of the soul, and we cannot afford to do without it.

Dave and Jan Dravecky

WHAT OTHERS HAVE SAID

Pray inwardly even if you do not enjoy it. It does good though you feel nothing, even though you think you are doing nothing.
—Julian of Norwich

No Longer Cast Aside

Read: Mark 10:46–52

Jesus stopped and said, "Call him." So they called to the blind man, "Cheer up! On your feet! He's calling you."—Mark 10:49

When it comes to being obnoxious, Bartimaeus would take the prize. He must have carried on and made quite a scene, because verse 48 says *many* rebuked him. But instead of putting a lid on it, Bartimaeus yelled all the more.

The blind man's tenacity and insistence caused the Lord to stop. But before he addressed Bartimaeus, Jesus had a thing or two to say to the people who were trying to shove the blind man aside. Jesus told them to call to Bartimaeus and then bring him forward. Boy, did those people change their tune fast! Suddenly the guy was given the VIP treatment. Once these people understood that Jesus thought this poor handicapped person was important—once they realized the Lord's priorities—their whole attitude toward the obnoxious social outcast switched from negative to positive.

What a lesson for us! O, that we, too, would bring the Lord's healing touch to those the world casts aside!

Joni Eareckson Tada

Points to Ponder

* What is your attitude when you encounter a person who is disabled, or one the world counts as a cast-off? How do you act?

* Why do so many of us avoid social outcasts? What are we afraid of?

* How can you revise your attitude toward the people, like Bartimaeus, that Jesus would have sought out?

KEY TO PRAYER

Read: Mark 11:20–25

"And when you stand praying, if you hold anything against anyone, forgive him, so that your Father in heaven may forgive you your sins."—Mark 11:25

When we walk through suffering, most of us have a multitude of opportunities to seek and offer forgiveness. We need the healing of heart and soul that forgiveness brings. We not only need it personally, we need it in our relationship with God.

When instructing his followers about prayer, Jesus said, "And when you stand praying, if you hold anything against anyone, forgive him, so that your Father in heaven may forgive you your sins." A lack of forgiveness can hinder our prayers. Just as we choose to praise God, we must choose to forgive so that we might have a whole and debt free relationship with God and with others.

It isn't easy to reach out in forgiveness to those who hurt us—especially when we're hurting too. But what's the alternative? Self pity . . . isolation . . . loneliness . . . despair. God commands us to reach beyond our comfort zones and give mercy and compassion to those who have hurt us, just as he has shown mercy and compassion to us. He commands this because he loves us. Forgiveness and reconciliation allow his purposes to prevail in our lives.

Dave and Jan Dravecky

FOR FURTHER REFLECTION

Read Luke 17:3; Colossians 3:13; and James 3:17–18 to understand more about forgiveness and reconciliation.

BE FAITHFUL

Read: Mark 13:32–37

"Be on guard! Be alert! You do not know when that time will come."—Mark 13:33

S omeone once said to me, "Joni, I wish I could be like you, because you'll get a great reward in heaven." I appreciate the accolade but I see it differently. I already have the reward of seeing the gospel go forth and of watching believers become encouraged because of this wheelchair. The glorious purposes for my suffering are clear to all.

But some saints have suffered for no apparent reason. When Jesus returns, I'm convinced, the highest accolades will go to those godly people who labored loyally yet received no recognition.

So when is our Lord coming back? We don't know. He said "It's like a man going away: He leaves his house and puts his servants in charge, each with his assigned task, and tells the one at the door to keep watch." But whenever he returns, what reward there will be for those who remain faithful to their "assigned task"!

Remember, success isn't the key. Faithfulness is. May you be faithful to God until he returns!

Joni Eareckson Tada

PATH TO PRAYER

Pray that God will give you the strength to remain faithful to the task he has given you, whether or not you see the reason for your suffering or the results of your labor and whether or not you receive recognition. Ask him to help you to be steadfast until he returns or until you join him in heaven.

FALLING OFF THE MOUNTAIN

Read: Mark 14:32–42

"Watch and pray so that you will not fall into temptation. The spirit is willing, but the body is weak."—Mark 14:38

*D*oes it mystify you that on one day you can be on top of the world, in love with the Lord, and the next day you fall off the mountain with a "splat"? It happens to you and it happens to me. And it happened to the Lord's three best friends.

On the Mount of Transfiguration, Peter, James, and John got a blinding look at the glory of the Lord. They dropped to their knees, jaws agape, dumbstruck with wonder (9:2–13). What ecstasy! Yet a short time later in the Garden of Gethsemane—when Jesus revealed another part of himself, showing them how deeply distressed and troubled he was—the tired trio yawned, then hit rock bottom.

How like all of us! We rise to some new level of spirituality, then are bewildered at the depths to which we fall almost the next day. Friends, our spiritual life must not hinge on our commitment to Christ; that only sets us up for defeat. Rather, let's glory in his commitment to us. He is the one whose arms are underneath us as we rise to the mountaintop and he is the one who preserves us as we descend on the other side.

Joni Eareckson Tada

WHAT OTHERS HAVE SAID

To realize God's presence is the one sovereign remedy against temptation.
—François de la Mothe Fénelon

THE VIGIL

Read: Mark 14:32–42

"My soul is overwhelmed with sorrow to the point of death," he said to them. "Stay here and keep watch."—Mark 14:32

*F*or the first time in his life the Shepherd was asking for something from his disciples. *He wanted human comfort that night.* But somebody's yawn tipped the first domino, and in no time everyone's prayers had degenerated into dreams.

Now, the Son of God dropped to the dirt in an olive grove and vomited in his soul at the prospect before him. Eleven men who would later change world history—some accustomed to working all night on their fishing boats—could not keep awake for the scene. Yet sixty feet away their eternal destinies were being fought over.

Except for the heaving of those shoulders that bore the weight of the world, nothing could be seen in that shadowy spot where the Son of God groaned. But the bleachers of heaven filled to capacity that night—and hell strained its neck to see how the spectacle in that lonely acre would end. The Father gazed down and gave his sober nod. The Son stared back, and bowed his acceptance.

The torches arrived. The sheep fled. The shepherd stood. The hurricane struck.

Joni Eareckson Tada

PATH TO PRAYER

Read this devotion again. Sit quietly and imagine the scene in the Garden of Gethsemane—see the deep darkness, hear the rustle of the grass in the night breeze, witness the figure of Jesus bent over in prayer, sweating blood. What is your prayerful response?

THE RESCUE

Read: Mark 15:33–39

And at the ninth hour Jesus cried out in a loud voice, "Eloi, Eloi, lama sabachthani?"—which means, "My God, my God, why have you forsaken me?"
—Mark 15:34

The Son is innocent, blamelessness itself. The Father knows this. But the divine pair has an agreement, and the unthinkable must now take place. Jesus will be treated as if personally responsible for every sin ever committed.

The Father watches as his heart's treasure, the mirror-image of himself, sinks, drowning into raw, liquid sin. Jehovah's stored rage against humankind from every century explodes in a single direction.

"Father! Father! Why have you forsaken me?!"

But heaven stops its ears. The Son stares up at the One who cannot, who will not, reach down or reply.

The Trinity had planned it. The Son endured it. The Spirit enabled him. The Father rejected the Son whom he loved. Jesus, the God-man from Nazareth, perished. The Father accepted his sacrifice for sin and was satisfied. The Rescue was accomplished.

God set down his saw.

This is who asks us to trust him when he calls on us to suffer.

Joni Eareckson Tada

PATH TO PRAYER

Nothing in my hand I bring, / Simply to Thy cross I cling. Naked, come to Thee for dress; / Helpless, look to Thee for grace; / Foul, I to the fountain fly; /Wash me, Savior or I die. —Augustus Montague Toplady

THE SOVEREIGN TIMETABLE

Read: Luke 2:1–7

While they were there, the time came for the baby to be born, and she gave birth to her firstborn, a son. —Luke 2:6–7

*U*npleasant circumstances often have a way of being the best part of God's most magnificent design. Consider Mary and Joseph's trip from Nazareth to Bethlehem where the Savior was to be born. This was no short hike but a trek over sixty miles of rugged terrain. Despite Joseph's attempts to make the trip comfortable, it must have been extremely difficult for Mary, into her ninth month of pregnancy, to make the three-day journey. But God decreed to have his Son born in the City of David, and he used an external circumstance—a Roman census—to get the Holy Family from point A to point B.

Sometimes we mistakenly think that only the *right* things, the *comfortable* things, are a part of God's design. And when inconvenience or hardship hits, we wonder what went wrong.

Maybe nothing has gone wrong. Maybe we just need to realize that our most unpleasant circumstances, much like Mary and Joseph's, often have a way of being the best part of God's most magnificent design. God's sovereign timetable is working in the life of your family, too.

Joni Eareckson Tada

PATH TO PRAYER

Ask God to teach you how to accept the difficult terrain that you and your family are journeying through. Pray for the faith to wait for God's timing and for the strength to keep on going.

JESUS COMES TO *YOU*

Read: Luke 4:38–41

The people brought to Jesus all who had various kinds of sickness, and laying his hands on each one, he healed them. —Luke 4:40

*E*verybody from the surrounding countryside brought sick people to see Jesus. He could have simply waved his hand over the whole crowd with one grand flourish and said, "Be healed!" But he didn't. Instead, he laid his hands on *each one* who came to him. His gentle touch healed the deaf, and he gave nothing but kind words for the blind people who reached out to him. He ministered to each one . . . individually. In so doing, he performed divine feats in a loving and highly personal way.

That's the kind of miracle God wants to perform in your life. Today he encounters you with the same tenderness and humanity he showed two thousand years ago. You are not a face in a sea of nameless people whom he divides into groups like the deaf, the blind, the cancer-stricken, and the paralyzed. He wants to give you his highly personal touch.

Joni Eareckson Tada

PATH TO PRAYER

Do you feel God's touch on you? Do you have faith that he sees you individually and knows you personally? Sit quietly, imagining God's hand on your head, or his arm around your shoulders. Imagine him looking deep into your eyes. What do you want to say to him, if anything?

NARROW ESCAPE?

Read: Luke 8:22–25

[Jesus] got up and rebuked the wind and the raging waters; the storm subsided, and all was calm. —Luke 8:24

R eading in Luke 8, I began noticing phrases like "the boat was being swamped" and "they were being swamped" and "they were in great danger." There's no soft-pedaling it. The disciples' narrow escape was just that: narrow. They were inches from death. But those inches were really miles. Why? They had God in the boat with them!

It may feel as if God is asleep when danger strikes, but he's not. No matter if it's by the skin of their teeth or with miles to spare, God helps his people. If it's not your appointed time, he will always, always deliver you . . . sometimes in the nick of time.

Joni Eareckson Tada

PATH TO PRAYER

Lord, thank you for the many times you've rescued me. Whether it was too close for comfort or not, I was—I am—always safe and secure when being held by you.

ETERNAL RECOGNITION

"Master, it is good for us to be here. Let us put up three shelters—one for you, one for Moses and one for Elijah."—Luke 9:33

Some folks are afraid that when they get to heaven, they won't recognize anyone. They're fearful that they won't know a husband or wife of thirty-five years without a nametag pinned to the robe. Luke's account of the transfiguration seems to settle that troubling question. Not only will you know your loved ones; it's likely you'll know everyone else, too—even without an introduction.

When two men, Moses and Elijah, appeared in glorious splendor talking with Jesus, Peter immediately recognized them. He blurted out, "Master, it is good for us to be here. Let us put up three shelters—one for you, one for Moses and one for Elijah." Yet how did Peter know those two men? They lived hundreds of years before Peter's time, so he had never met them. There were no photographs or artist's sketches. How did he recognize them? He just knew them—that's all.

The Transfiguration was a preview of heaven . . . a place where there will be no need for introductions.

Dave and Jan Dravecky

WHAT OTHERS HAVE SAID

In that sweet by and by we shall meet on that beautiful shore.
—Ira David Sankey

CERTIFIED LOSERS ONLY

Read: Luke 14:15–24

"Go out quickly into the streets and alleys of the town and bring in the poor, the crippled, the blind and the lame."—Luke 14:21

The Gospel is only "good news" to those who consider themselves losers—to those who recognize the helplessness of their spiritual condition. Whether it's crane operators or bag ladies, schoolteachers or drug addicts, the tennis pro on world tour or the homeless drunk living in an alley. Each must consider himself a loser if he wants a seat at the King's banquet. And the price of a seat? That each dies to himself or herself (John 12:24–25).

The price of salvation is high and, yes, you should sit down and count the cost. But when you've finished counting, you have the absolute certainty that *everything you've got* turns out to be exactly the right price for a seat at the banquet. All you have to be is a certified loser and God will send his servant, Jesus, to positively drag you into his house.

Joni Eareckson Tada

POINTS TO PONDER

* In what way did you see yourself as a loser when you recognized the gospel as "good news"?

* What does the phrase "dying to self" mean to you?

* At what point did you, (or will you) count the cost of your seat at the banquet of God?

ONGOING LOVE

Read: Luke 16:19–31

"But Abraham replied, 'Son, remember that in your lifetime you received your good things, while Lazarus received bad things, but now he is comforted here and you are in agony.' " —Luke 16:25

T he story of Lazarus is not a parable, but an amazing real-life occurrence. The rich man was very conscious of his hellish surroundings. He saw and recognized his family, remembered them, was concerned for them, and pleaded on their behalf. Here is the lesson: *If lost souls can feel and care, how much more can those who have died in the faith!*

Our Christian loved ones who have graduated into glory presently reside with the great I AM, the Lord of love. How deeply they must feel, pray and see. How fervent and ongoing must be their love. When we die, we are not in some soul-sleep of a stupor, not in purgatory, and we're certainly not unconscious; we are "away from the body and at home with the Lord" (2 Corinthians 5:8). The departed are full of the joy of having come home!

Joni Eareckson Tada

PATH TO PRAYER

Pray with praise and thanksgiving that your loved ones who are with God are full of joy and deep pleasure in God's presence. Ask God to help you grasp this wonderful reality.

THE KINGDOM IS WITHIN YOU

Read Luke 17:20–21

"The kingdom of God does not come with your careful observation, nor will people say, 'Here it is,' or 'there it is,' because the kingdom of God is within you."
— *Luke 17:21*

God wants us to have a present-tense excitement, a right-around-the-corner anticipation of heaven. He wants us to believe that we have already come to the heavenly Jerusalem (Hebrews 12:22–23). He wants us to realize that we are already seated with Christ in heavenly places (Ephesians 2:6). As far as God is concerned, the coming of the Lord is at hand, ready to explode on the world's stage at any moment.

The resurrection throbs with present-tense excitement when we learn to invest our days in eternity. When we make certain we are building for eternal glory, then heaven will seem as close as a heartbeat. The future, the distant, and the vague will appear as the present, the near, and the real. The kingdom of God is within you, Jesus said, and it whets our appetite for kingdom fulfillment at any day, any moment.

Joni Eareckson Tada

WHAT OTHERS HAVE SAID

Heaven is not a space overhead to which we lift our eyes; it is the background of our existence, the all-encompassing lordship of God within which we stand. —Helmut Thielicke

PERSISTENT PRAYER

Read: Luke 18:1–8

Jesus told his disciples a parable to show them that they should always pray and not give up. —Luke 18:1

*A*uthor Don Baker has suggested at least six reasons why our prayers seem to go unanswered: 1) We don't deserve the answer yet. 2) We need to learn something first. 3) It isn't the right time yet. 4) It's not what we really want. 5) It's not what we really need. 6) God wants to give us something better.

I have learned through my own struggles that after I have brought a matter to God in prayer, I can release it and know that he is in charge of it. I don't have to worry about it any more. Oh, I will continue to pray for that concern—Jesus also taught us that we "should always pray and not give up"—but the answer, whatever it may be, is in his hands.

Dave Dravecky

POINTS TO PONDER

* What is your response to Don Baker's list above? Can you place any of your prayers in one of his categories?

* When you have brought a matter to God, how good are you at releasing it?

* How persistent are you in prayer? Are you ever tempted to give up? Why?

September

HE KNOCKS BOLDLY

Read: Luke 19:1–10

"The Son of Man came to seek and to save what was lost."—Luke 19:10

Why it is that Jesus singled out the little man in the sycamore tree, no one knows. But what is clear is this: the Lord stepped boldly into Zacchaeus's life. Jesus not only invited himself to the tax collector's home, he hardly gave the little man time to think twice about it.

Some would say Jesus was a bit presumptuous—*telling* a host to open his home for him. Bold, yes. Presumptuous, no. It was the boldness of love. Jesus ensured that his command would be well received, for he inclined the ear of Zacchaeus to welcome him.

The love of God *is* daring and courageous. But wait. When you consider that it's the Lord of the universe who steps up to the door of your heart and knocks for entrance, only a fool would refuse him entry. Jesus invites himself into your life, bringing his own joy and welcome. And just as he did with Zacchaeus, he tells you not to hesitate.

Joni Eareckson Tada

PATH TO PRAYER

The words of Revelation 3:20 are Jesus' invitation to you: "Here I am! I stand at the door and knock. If anyone hears my voice and opens the door, I will come in and eat with him, and he with me." Open the door and respond to Jesus. Invite him into your heart.

JUST DO IT

Read: Luke 19:28–44

Those who were sent ahead went and found it just as he had told them.
—*Luke 19:32*

*I*t's always wisest to do what the Lord directs, even if it doesn't seem to make much sense. That's the lesson two of Christ's disciples learned on the day of their Master's Triumphal Entry into Jerusalem.

Jesus had instructed them to go into a particular village where they would find a never-before-ridden colt. They were to untie the animal and bring it back to him. And if anyone questioned their actions, they were to say, "The Lord needs it." Pretty skimpy instructions, aren't they? You can just see the questions rising in the disciples' minds: *But what if. . .? Supposing they . . . ? Can't you at least give us the owner's name?*

Nevertheless, Luke says, "Those who were sent ahead *went and found it just as he had told them.*" Of course they did! He always knows what lies ahead—and that's why it's always wisest to do exactly what he instructs. When we obey—even if the instructions seem a bit skimpy—we'll always find things "just as he had told" us.

Dave and Jan Dravecky

WHAT OTHERS HAVE SAID

I can say from experience that 95% of knowing the will of God consists in being prepared to do it before you know what it is.
—Donald Grey Barnhouse

No Effort Too Small

Read: Luke 20:45—21:4

"All these people gave their gifts out of their wealth; but she out of her poverty put in all she had to live on."—Luke 21:4

S ome time ago our ministry delivered three wheelchairs to the Ghana Society for Crippled boys. Most of these young men are disabled from polio. Without wheelchairs they have to drag themselves through the dirt, using their hands. They spend their weekends begging on the streets, then during the week come to the Society and learn how to use sewing machines so they can develop a job skill.

You should have seen the boys' smiles when we presented the three wheelchairs—not much, but all we had to give. They stopped in the middle of their work to sing and clap for us with that wonderful African harmony.

But I couldn't help wondering about our small gift. It barely scratched the surface of need. Were we really making a difference? Was the gift meaningful? Answer: *Yes*! Nothing is unworthy of the Lord when it is given in his name—especially when it's all we have to give, such as the two copper coins given by the widow. No action is unimportant, no effort too tiny. And the Lord takes notice of them all!

Joni Eareckson Tada

For Further Reflection

Read 1 Kings 17:12–17 and John 6:5–13 to discover how two people gave a little to God—and God multiplied their gifts.

SON OF MAN

Read: Luke 21:25–31

"At that time they will see the Son of Man coming in a cloud with power and great glory."—Luke 21:27

One of Jesus' favorite titles for himself in the Gospels is "the Son of Man" (used 78 times). He probably chose this name for at least two reasons: 1) To identify completely with us in our humanity. 2) To identify himself with the divine figure described in Daniel 7:13–14.

In Luke 21:27 Jesus clearly is making a connection with the text in Daniel. Compare the two passages:

Luke: "At that time they will see the Son of Man coming in a cloud with power and great glory."

Daniel: "There before me was one like a son of man, coming with the clouds of heaven. He . . . was given authority, glory, and sovereign power . . ."

Jesus wants us to know both that he understands us and sympathizes with us, for he is one of us; and that he has the power to ultimately triumph over whatever threatens us, for he is God. It's a one-two punch that can't be beat.

Dave Dravecky

FOR FURTHER REFLECTION

Look up each of these verses from the book of Luke that contains the title for Jesus, "son of man." Decide if each verse shows Jesus as human—one of us—or divine: 5:24; 7:34; 9:22; 9:44; 12:8; 21:27. What is your response?

ONLY WITH PERMISSION

Read: Luke 22:31–38

"Simon, Simon, Satan has asked to sift you as wheat. But I have prayed for you, Simon, that your faith may not fail."—Luke 22:32–32

"Satan has asked . . . ," observed Jesus. We can be certain that the old snake didn't check in with God out of politeness or protocol. He *had* to get permission, and this means the devil operates under constraints. He can't do what he wants whenever he wishes. He has to clear it with God.

God *must* control evil. And he does so because he is good. Imagine a God who didn't deliberately permit the smallest details of your particular sorrows. What if he didn't screen your trials? The devil would be without constraints—free to do whatever he pleased. This means the world would be much worse than its present state of war, violence, greed and misery.

Evil can raise its ugly head only when God deliberately backs away for a specific and intentional reason—always for a reason that is wise and good, even if hidden from this present life. God permits what he hates in order to achieve what he loves—it's just that most of us won't see it until the other side of eternity.

Joni Eareckson Tada

TAKE ACTION!

When you're reading the newspaper tonight, look for stories that show Satan's action in the world. Could the situation be worse? Is there evidence that he is restrained? Look also for a story that shows that God is working in the world.

BRUTALLY HONEST

Read: Luke 22:39–46

And being in anguish, [Jesus] prayed more earnestly. —Luke 22:44

There's no right way to suffer. When I am talking with a mother whose child is dying of cancer, it does no good to say, "Don't feel sad," or "Don't be angry at God." There is no point in saying, "You shouldn't feel that way." If she feels that way, she feels that way. Feelings are not right or wrong; but it is wrong to lie about how you feel. And you're no less of a Christian if you express those human emotions that come to the surface when you suffer. To me, you're more of a Christian because you are being honest.

Jesus was brutally honest in the Garden of Gethsemane. Luke says he was "in anguish" and "his sweat was like drops of blood falling to the ground," a rare condition known as hematidrosis in which hemorrhage into the sweat glands, caused by a highly emotional state, makes the skin fragile and tender. Now, if Jesus could feel so deeply (and he never sinned), why do we think we must hide or deny our emotions?

Jan Dravecky

POINTS TO PONDER

❋ Why should Christians allow others to experience and express their emotions honestly?

❋ What happens when people are not allowed to express honest emotion?

❋ How do you feel when you are allowed to express emotion without fear of judgment?

IN PARADISE—TODAY

Read: Luke 23:26–43

"Today you will be with me in paradise."—Luke 23:43

When my friend Debbie, a polio quadriplegic, died and went to be with the Lord, I said to a woman in church, "Just think, she's free of her paralysis and pain!" The woman shook her head "no" and insisted that Debbie is "asleep" and won't join the Lord until the dead are resurrected.

That woman's frame of reference is limited. We operate within the confines of time and space in this world, but God exists outside of time. It's mind-boggling to think that he lives as the great "I AM," always in the present tense, always observing the past and present now. Probably that's why the Lord Jesus could say to the thief on his dying day, "Today you will be with me in paradise."

It takes faith to have this heavenly perspective. Faith that is the substance of things hoped for. Exercise this kind of faith the next time a believing friend dies and goes to be with the Lord.

Joni Eareckson Tada

WHAT OTHERS HAVE SAID

Faith tells us of things we have never seen, and cannot come to know by our natural senses. —St. John of the Cross

GRACE

Read: John 1:14–18

We have seen his glory, the glory of the One and Only, who came from the Father, full of grace and truth. —John 1:14

Grace is what beauty looks like when it moves. God's grace is what he looks like when he moves, acting out his will through us.

Those on whom God's grace rests are truly . . . gracious. They are truly beautiful: the cerebral-palsied young man who smiles despite a dreary existence in a nursing home; the elderly woman who always seems to think of others rather than her aches and pains; the mother of two toddlers who is happy to baby-sit the neighbor's little boy; the pastor and his wife who take in a homeless couple for a week while they look for lodging. These people shine with a hint of glory. They shine because of God's grace.

Grace is God's energy, all bright, beautiful, and full of power. And grace is most beautiful when God is moving through us to touch the lives of others who hurt.

Joni Eareckson Tada

FOR FURTHER REFLECTION

Look up the following Scriptures and ponder what they say about grace: Luke 2:40; Proverbs 4:7–9; James 4:6. What attributes accompany grace?

ON THE TEAM

Read: John 1:35–50

"Follow me."—John 1:43

*T*he first thing Jesus did when he began his ministry was to start building a team. Have you ever thought about that? When the Creator of the worlds, the Lord of the universe, wanted to set about changing this planet forever, he started by first putting together a team.

What's so great about being part of a team? You are chosen. You are important because others depend on you to play your position; they need you. Something powerful happens to your sense of worth when you look at a group whose members you respect and honestly think, *I'm one of them.* You are an accepted part of something bigger than yourself.

To make it in this world, you need to be part of a team. Who's on yours?

Dave Dravecky

POINTS TO PONDER

❋ How did Jesus go about choosing his team?

❋ Think about what you know of the disciples. What kind of people were they?

❋ What team(s) are you a part of? Is your church or assembly your "team"? Do you have a sense of being "an accepted part of something bigger than yourself"? Why or why not?

❋ How can you pull together a team that will show God's love to others?

SQUARED OFF AGAINST SIN

Read: John 2:13–22

His disciples remembered that it is written: "Zeal for your house will consume me."—John 2:17

*I*t's easy to picture a kindly, loving Jesus. But it's challenging to visualize an angry—violently angry—Jesus Christ. You can almost see him overturning cash registers, grabbing the moneychangers by the scruff of their necks and heaving them out of the temple door on their self-righteous backsides.

Jesus, full of fury, took a stand. No one, he asserted, was going to make his Father's house into a haven for con men and rip-off artists. Jesus tore the mask off hypocrisy. He exposed dark recesses of the hearts of greedy, materialistic men. Jesus squared off against sin.

We need to fully meditate on portions of Scripture such as John 2:13–22 in order to get a more complete picture of the way the Lord dealt with sin. And we need to remember that he didn't always confront sin gently.

Joni Eareckson Tada

FOR FURTHER REFLECTION

Read Matthew 23:23–36 and Luke 11:42–52 to discover another occasion when Jesus was angry. With whom was he angry? Why?

DRINKING WATER

Read: John 4:1–26

"Whoever drinks the water I give him will never thirst. Indeed, the water I give him will become in him a spring of water welling up to eternal life." —John 4:14

*J*esus told the woman at the well that he would give her living water, but he also said she needed to drink it!

We can't go for long intervals without prayer and Bible reading and then, in a clinch, grab for grace and find—voilà—strength is there. We all need to drink in God's Word at regular intervals. That's the only way you and I are going to be prepared when we are faced with those tough uphill climbs.

Jesus is offering you a drink today. Take a long, refreshing drink of the Living Water.

Joni Eareckson Tada

TAKE ACTION!

You've already begun to drink the Living Water by working through this book and the Bible. Continue to challenge yourself to go deeper into the Word and prayer. Consider seeking out and reading a classic Christian book such as Richard Foster's book, *Celebration of Discipline* to find out more about building your life around the fountain of living water.

A LIMITLESS GOD

Read: John 6:1–15

When Jesus looked up and saw a great crowd coming toward him, he said to Philip, "Where shall we buy bread for these people to eat?" He asked this only to test him.
—John 6:6

God laughs in the face of limited resources. In fact, he often uses limitations on our resources to strengthen and test our faith as we step out and believe he will supply the need.

That's something to remember if you are faced with a need, a project or a problem with which you feel bound and gagged because of your lack of resources. Remember: when you roll up your sleeves and dig into the task God has put before you, your resources will expand. Out of nowhere you will find you have the strength, you will see you have the time, and, if money is the problem, watch to see how God will supply what's needed. Our God is a God of limitlessness!

Joni Eareckson Tada

PATH TO PRAYER

What need, project, or problem has you stymied because you don't have the resources? Ask God to supply what you need. Ask him to show you how to proceed and what you need to do to begin.

RESURRECTION DAY

Read: John 6:35–40

"For my Father's will is that everyone who looks to the Son and believes in him shall have eternal life, and I will raise him up at the last day."—John 6:40

*M*y mother-in-law recently purchased a family grave plot at a cemetery called Forest Lawn, but she would not sign the papers until Ken and I looked at the lot and gave our approval. So one afternoon we trekked to the gravesite located in a section called "Murmuring Pines," and listened to the realtor (that's what she was actually called) remind me that what with my head "here," I would have a grand view of the valley and distant mountains. That's important, I told her. I also told her I did not have plans to stay there very long.

While the realtor and my mother-in-law conferred over the papers, I looked around at the hundreds of tombstones. It suddenly struck me that I was sitting on the exact spot where my body will rise, should I die before Christ comes. Sitting on that grassy hillside did more to ignite the reality of the Resurrection than hearing sermons or reading essays on the subject.

The Resurrection is not something to be spiritualized away. One day actual spirits will return to actual graves and reunite to rise. Dead people, one day, shall live. Hallelujah!

Joni Eareckson Tada

WHAT OTHERS HAVE SAID

The edges of God are tragedy; the depths of God are joy, beauty, resurrection, life. Resurrection answers crucifixion; life answers death.
—Marjorie Hewitt Suchocki

THE BREAD OF LIFE

Read: John 6:25–69

"I am the bread of life."—John 6:48

The Lord Jesus wants us to know him in an intimate way, to realize a deep, personal union with him. To press home the point about intimacy, Jesus gave this emphatic analogy to his disciples, after which many deserted him.

The disciples were right about one thing: This is a hard teaching. Taken literally, these words were repulsive to them and Jesus knew it, but he told them that he, the "bread that came down from heaven," was their only option for spiritual life: "The Spirit gives life; the flesh counts for nothing. The words I have spoken to you are spirit and they are life."

Symbolically, Jesus' words teach us the beautiful truth that the Christian depends on the indwelling presence of God for everything. Jesus asks us to feed on him as in Psalm 34:8: "taste and see that the Lord is good." And as the Song of Songs tells us, "your love is more delightful than wine." In other words, we must abide in him and let his Word abide in us if we are to know Christ in a deep and intimate way.

Joni Eareckson Tada

POINTS TO PONDER

* For what is your spirit hungry today?
* What does the phrase "letting God's word abide in you" mean to you?
* What do you need to do to "feed" on the "bread of life"?
* What do you need to ask for from Jesus, the Bread of Life, today?

CHOOSING TO DO GOD'S WILL

Read: John 7:14–24

"If anyone chooses to do God's will, he will find out whether my teaching comes from God or whether I speak on my own."—John 7:17

*I*f you really want to know the truth, what should you do? Study harder? Enroll in seminary? Hire a private tutor? Not at all, according to Jesus. He tells us that if we really want to know the truth, we must choose to do God's will. When we decide to rely on him, the truth will become clear.

Of course, it's difficult to rely on God. I won't deny it. It's scary to put things in his hands when you're used to doing everything yourself. Yet I think if Jan and I hadn't been brought to the point of total weakness, we would never have known how much we could trust God and how faithful he is. It doesn't depend on me after all. What joy there is in that discovery! And what truth!

Dave Dravecky

POINTS TO PONDER

* How do you determine what God's will for you is?
* What is God's will for every Christian?
* What do you learn about God's will from Romans 12:2–21?

STREAMS OF LIVING WATER

Read: John 7:37–39

"Whoever believes in me, as the Scripture has said, streams of living water will flow from within him."—John 7:38

The encroachments of my limitations often feel like the cutting edge of a spade, digging up twisted vines of self-centeredness and the dirt of sin and rebellion. Uprooting rights. Clearing out the debris of habitual sins. Shoveling away pride. To believe in God in the midst of suffering is to empty myself; and to empty myself is to increase the capacity—the pond area—for God. *The greatest good suffering can do for me is to increase my capacity for God.* Then he, like a spring, is free to flow through me.

Not a rivulet, but a powerful river of peace!

Joni Eareckson Tada

PATH TO PRAYER

Ask God to make you a conduit of living water to those around you. Ask him to clean out the debris and sludge from your heart and spirit that block the flow of his life through you. Ask him to fill you with his clean, refreshing water—water that is so needed in your own life and in the lives of your family members and friends.

SPEAKING THE TRUTH

Read: John 8:31–41

"Then you will know the truth, and the truth will set you free."—John 8:32

One by one the women at the conference took turns pouring out their hearts. I had been speaking about being honest with our struggles, about admitting our weaknesses and refusing to put up a front any longer, and my audience responded. After each woman shared her story, we would stop and pray for her. These women were being set free because they were able to share the truth.

Truth always frees. We need to speak the truth to each other. But just sharing our pain is not the end of the story. Love is the conclusion. When we reach out to each other in the midst of our pain, we learn to give and receive love. I didn't stay stuck in my pain. I came through it—and so can you.

Jan Dravecky

POINTS TO PONDER

* Why do you think that telling the truth about ourselves is so difficult?

* Why might speaking the truth about ourselves to God be liberating?

* Why might speaking the truth about ourselves to another human being be liberating?

* What truth about yourself do you need to speak to God about today? To a safe and godly person?

TO DISPLAY THE WORK OF GOD

Read: John 9:1–7

"This happened so that the work of God might be displayed in his life."—John 9:3

*P*ain forces us to live in reality, to deal with issues we would rather ignore, to shift our focus off the concerns of life on earth and onto things eternal. Pain forces us to ask the question, "Is this all there is?"

It can be difficult to accept God in this role unless we remember that he is a loving Father who is determined to bring us to maturity. He will use suffering in his children's lives in the same way that a sculptor uses a chisel. As the craftsman of the human soul, God knows best which edges need to be smoothed and where fine lines must be etched to bring out the true beauty of his creation. He loves us too much to allow us to remain trapped in our rough, stony state.

God not only uses suffering to train us, he uses it to accomplish his perfect purpose, to draw us into relationship with him, and to display his glory to others.

Dave and Jan Dravecky

WHAT OTHERS HAVE SAID

God whispers to us in our pleasures, speaks in our conscience, but shouts in our pains; it is his megaphone to rouse a deaf world.
— C.S. (Clive Staples) Lewis

THE GOOD SHEPHERD

Read: John 10:1–18

"I am the good shepherd."—John 10:11

Ever get the feeling you're somewhere out in front of God as you move through your week? You bump up against a trial, and you know from Scripture that God is going to work all things together for good, but somehow you have the idea he's *behind* you, armed with a dustpan and broom, ready to do a cleanup job on you and your problem.

If you feel as though God's principal activity in your life is to follow behind you and throw a rope after you've fallen headlong into a trial, then you need to read John 10:2–4 over and over A shepherd never follows his flock, he leads them. Jesus himself says that he goes on ahead. He blazes a straight path and charts the way.

Never is God surprised by your trials. Never does he push you out ahead and back you up with a dustpan and broom. God is out in front.

Joni Eareckson Tada

POINTS TO PONDER

* When did Jesus call your name?
* How have you been led by the Good Shepherd?
* How do you know that Jesus is leading you?

ALWAYS IN GOD'S CARE

Read: John 10:22–41

"My sheep listen to my voice; I know them, and they follow me. I give them eternal life, and they shall never perish; no one can snatch them out of my hand. My Father, who has given them to me, is greater than all; no one can snatch them out of my Father's hand." —John 10:27–29

*D*uring the long watches of the night, when sleep would not come, I comforted myself with stories of great saints like Elijah, who also experienced depression immediately following great spiritual victories. He even asked God to take his life. *Well*, I thought with a small measure of relief, *at least I'm not that far gone*. I was not suicidal, but whenever I heard about someone who had committed suicide, I went bonkers. It scared me, not because I wanted to die, but because I feared that I was losing my mind and might do something dangerous.

Even when I was suffering such emotional trauma, I found great comfort in John 10:27–29. And when I paired this with Romans 8:38–39—"For I am convinced that neither death nor life, neither angels nor demons, neither the present nor the future, nor any powers, neither height nor depth, nor anything else in all creation, will be able to separate us from the love of God that is in Christ Jesus our Lord"—the effect was incalculably powerful. These verses reassured me that no one—not me, nor Satan—could take me out of God's care. I had seen that God was faithful to his many other promises; I would trust him again with this one.

Jan Dravecky

PATH TO PRAYER

Jesus, teach me to recognize your voice whenever you call me so that I can follow you wherever you lead me. Thank you for the assurance that you watch over my soul and deliver me safe into the hollow of the your Father's hand.

WE HAVE ETERNAL LIFE

Read: John 11:1–31

"I am the resurrection and the life. He who believes in me will live, even though he dies; and whoever lives and believes in me will never die. Do you believe this?"
—John 11:25–26

D o we believe that if we have placed our faith in Jesus, we already have eternal life? Do we believe that even if our bodies should stop breathing, we will never die? Do we believe this?

Martha did believe it. Her sister Mary also believed it. And you know the rest of the story—Jesus raises Lazarus from the grave after four days of entombment so that everyone else would have reason to believe it as well.

But where is Lazarus today? Have you seen him lately? I haven't. And I know you haven't, either, because his body died a second time a little later on. He might even have been murdered because John 12:10–11 tells us, "the chief priests made plans to kill Lazarus as well [as Jesus], for on account of him many of the Jews were going over to Jesus and putting their faith in him."

And yet Lazarus *never* died, even though his vital signs flat lined twice (the second time, for good). How can we say this and still be completely accurate? *Because eternity begins here and now for a child of God.*

Dave and Jan Dravecky

PATH TO PRAYER

Jesus, I believe that you are the resurrection and the life. I believe that when my body dies, my soul, my essence, my spirit, will never die, but be with you. I believe that, because I am your child, eternity begins now. Lord, I do believe; help my unbelief. Amen.

FULLY HUMAN

Read: John 11:32–44

Jesus wept. —John 11:35

The Son of Man was completely and utterly human, which means that he experienced the entire range of human emotions (yet untainted by sin). We can easily imagine Jesus crying over the graveside of Lazarus. Smiling over children at play. Scowling at moneychangers in the temple. We can even picture him laughing, perhaps over a joke Peter may have played on John.

So why is Scripture devoid of any reference to Jesus laughing? I think it's because the Gospel writers held a sober and circumspect view of the world that deeply possessed an eternal perspective on all things. While a wellspring of joy filled their hearts, yet these authors were serious. Reflective. Compassionate. Merciful. They reflected the wisdom of God in not conveying moments of laughter from our Lord.

When grieving mothers and brokenhearted widows open their Bibles in search of comfort, they don't have to worry about being assaulted by passages depicting Jesus breaking out in a belly laugh. Instead they open God's Word and find a man of sorrows with whom they can deeply identify. It is in *this* picture the suffering find comfort.

Joni Eareckson Tada

FOR FURTHER REFLECTION

Read Isaiah 53:3–4. What does that passage tell you about Jesus? How does that enlighten you about today's verse? In what way is it comforting to you?

BROKEN BUT BRILLIANT

Read: John 12:20–26

"I tell you the truth, unless a kernel of wheat falls to the ground and dies, it remains only a single seed. But if it dies, it produces many seeds."—John 12:24

*M*y art studio is a mess of half-chewed pastel pencils, old tubes of paint, and piles of illustrations overflowing my file drawers. Recently while cleaning up, I discovered some broken glass on the counter by the window. I also discovered that when sunlight struck the shattered glass, brilliant, colorful rays scattered everywhere.

What's true of shattered glass is true of a broken life. Shattered dreams. A heart full of fissures. Splintered hopes. A life in pieces. But given time and prayer, such a person's life can shine more brightly than if it had never been broken.

Only our great God can reach down into what otherwise would be brokenness and produce something beautiful. Your life may be shattered by sorrow, pain, or sin, but God has in mind a kaleidoscope through which his light can shine more brilliantly. When the light of the Lord Jesus falls upon a shattered life, hope bursts forth in a thousand brilliant hues.

Joni Eareckson Tada

POINTS TO PONDER

* What kind of dying is Jesus referring to?
* In what ways have you already died?
* What in you needs to die so that you can be more productive? (See Romans 6:11)

GOING TO HEAVEN

Read: John 13:31–38

"Where I am going, you cannot come." —John 13:33

*P*oetic they are; metaphorical they are not. Comforting they are; figurative they are not. Veiled they are; abstract they are not.

The "they" in this case are the words of Jesus, uttered to his disciples on the eve of his crucifixion. The Master did not talk about "going" merely to announce his death. He did not speak this sentence only to calm the troubled spirits of his followers. He did not make this statement just to paint over a harsh reality. No, he spoke these words—exactly these words—because they are *true*.

Jesus was about to leave this world and return home, to heaven—the ultimately real place. He told Peter, "You cannot follow now, but you will follow later" (13:37). Again, not a metaphor, not a figure, not an abstraction, but a solid promise. Peter may not have understood, but the truth nevertheless had been spoken—and one day we, too, will experience the fullness of this glorious truth.

Not as metaphor. Not as sentiment. Not as abstraction. But as warm, vital reality. We're going to heaven, where Jesus walks this very moment!

Dave and Jan Dravecky

WHAT OTHERS HAVE SAID

When I get to heaven, I shall see three wonders there—the first wonder will be to see any people there whom I did not expect to see; the second wonder will be to miss many people whom I did expect to see; and the third and greatest wonder of all will be to find myself there. —John Newton

A Place for Us

Read: John 14:1–14

"I am going there to prepare a place for you."—John 14:2

There's nothing escapist about pondering heaven. Jesus told us about it, not so that we could escape from our troubles, but so that we could better endure them. He wants us to think about heaven, especially when anxious thoughts seize our hearts. Although we won't enjoy its full benefits until we arrive, even now we can allow its atmosphere to fill our lungs with hope.

Jesus wanted us to know that, when the time is right, there won't be any problem in getting us to heaven. He won't entrust this task to some third-level angel or to some celestial scoop that would mechanically pluck us out of earth and dump us in paradise. He wanted us to know that he will come for us himself: "And if I go and prepare a place for you, I will come back and take you to be with me that you also may be where I am."

Dave and Jan Dravecky

Points to Ponder

* What kind of place do you think Jesus is preparing for you?
* What kind of place would you like it to be?
* How does knowing about that place affect you today?

September 26

REMAIN IN ME

Read: John 15:1–17

"If you remain in me and my words remain in you, ask whatever you wish, and it will be given you. This is to my Father's glory, that you bear much fruit, showing yourselves to be my disciples."—John 15:7–8

The way I live affects God's hearing. Not even an offering-plate full of sincerity can replace a careful life of obedience when it comes to getting prayers answered. I can have enough faith to move mountains—enough faith to make the annual congregational meeting interesting—and still my prayers will flop if Christ's words don't remain in me and I ignore his teaching. Have we really grasped this link between getting our prayers answered and steeping our minds in Christ's words? The longer the tea bag sits in the cup, the stronger the tea. The more God's Word saturates our minds, the clearer our grasp on what's important to him and the stronger our prayers.

Joni Eareckson Tada

PATH TO PRAYER

Jesus, my Savior, I do want to remain in you, and I want your words to remain in me, but I confess that my commitment to obedience wavers too often. Root your word in me and change my heart, I pray, so that obeying you will become more and more joyful and ever more a part of my nature, a nature patterned after yours. Teach me to pray so that my will becomes entwined with yours and so be done.

NO ONE WILL TAKE AWAY YOUR JOY

Read: John 16:19–24

"Your grief will turn to joy . . . I will see you again and you will rejoice, and no one will take away your joy." —John 16:20–22

*J*esus knew well the awesome power of hope, and that is why he poured an ocean of it on his disciples shortly before the soldiers took him away to be crucified. And yet how honestly he poured! Who among us would begin a warm bath of hope with a bracing shower of reality? Yet that is just what the Master did. Before he lavished on his men this gift of hope, he declared to them why they would need it so badly: "I tell you the truth," he said, "you will weep and mourn . . . you will grieve."

Jesus is always candid with his followers, both then and now. He knows the end from the beginning and is aware that the middle is often filled with pain, tears, and grief. But he also knew that no grave of granite could long entomb his glory, so he also told his men, "Your grief will turn to joy."

That is the glorious hope promised us. And that is the hope that is able to see us through all of our tears, all of our groans, and all of our grief. It's as certain as the promise of Jesus.

Dave and Jan Dravecky

FOR FURTHER REFLECTION

Find out what Isaiah 61:1–3; Matthew 5:4; and 1 Thessalonians 4:13 have to say about grief, hope, and the promises of God.

THE SIN OF THE WORLD

Read: John 19:28–37

"It is finished." With that, he bowed his head and gave up his spirit. —John 19:30

*I*t encourages me to keep going in my trials when I consider how infinitely greater were the sufferings of Jesus. No one ever knew suffering as Jesus knew it. His physical suffering was horrible enough; read a medical description of what happens during crucifixion, if you can stand it. But many others in history have been put to death in exactly the same way.

What made Jesus' death so incomparably worse than any other was that God placed on him—a man who had never known even a moment of sin's contamination—the entire vile volume of the sin of the whole world. "God made him who had no sin to be sin for us, so that in him we might become the righteousness of God," Paul wrote in 2 Corinthians 5:21.

Dave Dravecky

PATH TO PRAYER

Meditate on Jesus' words, "It is finished," considering what it was that he finished and what it cost him. Stay with those thoughts until you know how to respond to God in prayer.

YOU MUST FOLLOW ME!

Read: John 21:18–22

"You must follow me."—John 21:22

*I*n this passage, Jesus revealed that Peter would be led to a martyr's death, but he spoke not a word about John. To Peter, John appeared to be getting a better deal. So he blurted out, "Lord, what about him?"

Jesus' shocking answer allowed no room for deserved indulgence, no luxury of self-pity. In effect, Jesus said, "What I have planned for John is none of your business. Get your eyes off him and follow me." Rather harsh words for a man facing martyrdom! But the Lord knew the greater devastation of competing and comparing.

We need to learn that God's will for each one of us is good and acceptable and perfect. I have no need to compare myself with others: I have his best for me!

Joni Eareckson Tada

POINTS TO PONDER

* Why do you think Jesus insisted that Peter not worry about John's fate?

* In what ways are you tempted to compare your own relationship with God with that of other people?

* Read Galatians 6:4–5. What does it tell you about comparing your lot in life with someone else's?

HE IS COMING BACK

Read: Acts 1:1–11

"Men of Galilee," they said, "why do you stand here looking into the sky? This same Jesus, who has been taken from you into heaven, will come back in the same way you have seen him go into heaven."—Acts 1:11

"*I*t's one of the rules of the church nursery," my friend with three little girls told me. "When you drop off your child, always tell them you'll come back. And then by all means, come back! It's the only way they'll accept being in the nursery."

What would it be like for us if the angels on the Mount of Olives had said, "Jesus has gone," and nothing more? I'd be like a child in the nursery, standing alone in the middle of toys and books, staring at the door. And I'd cry. There are few things in life more frightening to a child than being left alone without hope that Mom or Dad will return.

But Jesus *is* coming back! I need not spend my days in tears or pain. I can enjoy the fellowship of others who are also expecting his return. And I can tell others about Jesus, friends who wonder why they came into this world in the first place.

Joni Eareckson Tada

PATH TO PRAYER

Father God, thank you for this promise: that Jesus will come again to this earth. More than ever, I am looking for him to come and restore the kingdom in all its wonder and awesome beauty. May your promise keep me ever hopeful and ready to share the kingdom with others who need your hope and your salvation.

October

THROUGH ANOTHER'S EYES

Read: Acts 2:42–47

They devoted themselves to . . . the fellowship . . . Every day they continued to meet together in the temple courts. They broke bread in their homes and ate together with glad and sincere hearts. —Acts 2:42,46

W hy did the early church grow so explosively? Without a doubt, one major reason is the close relationships it fostered.

If we want to get close to God and know his love, we must realize that he has chosen to deliver that love, primarily, through people. That means that if I cut myself off from relationships, I have cut myself off from receiving God's love. And who wants that?

Sometimes the only way I can see God is through the eyes of another human being who is willing to stay with me despite the pain. Sometimes we ask, "How does God show his faithfulness to us?" Often all we need to do is look in the eyes of the people around us.

Dave Dravecky

TAKE ACTION!

Do you need to renew a friendship that you have let fade? Call or write an old friend today and renew your fellowship with that person. You might both need to see God's love in each other's eyes.

TAKE HEART

Read: Acts 5:19–20

"Go, stand in the temple courts," he said, "and tell the people the full message of this new life."—Acts 5:20

God doesn't command us to stay encouraged without giving us a reason to do so. He knows there is plenty in life to cause even the stoutest soul to lose heart. Calamities and mishaps and disease and accidents and foul play and a thousand other devastations can pulverize our lives at any moment. Life in this fallen world has countless nasty ways of causing us to lose heart.

But God is greater than any calamity, mightier than any disaster. When the angel of Acts 5 told Peter to "stand in the temple courts and tell the people the full message of this new life," he was commanding him to speak not only of crucifixion, but also of resurrection.

Death does not have the final say—Jesus does! And so long as we are connected to Jesus by faith, death has no more say over us than it did over him. Truly, this is the most powerful reason in the universe for taking heart, no matter what happens. God wins! And we win with him.

Dave and Jan Dravecky

TAKE ACTION!

How would you define this message of life? Sit down and summarize the message of the gospel. First make a list of the points you want to make, then fill in connecting words until you have a couple of paragraphs. Review your message several times until you can say it by heart. Be ready to share it with someone when the Spirit prompts you.

Rejoicing in Suffering?

Read: Acts 5:17–42

The apostles left the Sanhedrin, rejoicing because they had been counted worthy of suffering disgrace for the Name. —Acts 5:41

Is it really possible to rejoice in suffering? After the apostles were flogged for preaching the good news of Jesus, they "left the Sanhedrin, rejoicing because they had been counted worthy of suffering disgrace for the Name."

Probably we are not suffering for our faith, as did the apostles. Our suffering is more likely due to a body gone awry. Yet the principle is exactly the same in both cases.

We can rejoice, even exult, in our sufferings *because they bring us another step higher and closer to our Hope, Jesus Christ.* As Nicholas Wolterstorff has written in his poignant *Lament for a Son*, "In the valley of suffering, despair and bitterness are brewed. But there also character is made. The valley of suffering is the vale of soul-making."

And in such a vale, we really can rejoice . . . without the slightest contradiction.

Dave and Jan Dravecky

PATH TO PRAYER

Look up 1 Peter 1:3–9 and copy it into your journal or on a piece of paper. Substitute the pronouns "us" and "you" with the pronouns "I" and "me" to make it your personal prayer. Keep it handy and refer to it when your suffering is threatening to overwhelm you or you feel despair coming on.

Motive Is Everything

Read: Acts 6:8–15

All who were sitting in the Sanhedrin looked intently at Stephen, and they saw that his face was like the face of an angel. —Acts 6:15

W as the seizure and eventual martyrdom of Stephen a bad thing, in and of itself? Surely. Did evil men, spurred on by Satan, bring it about? Unquestionably. So was it a demonic disaster, a regrettable tragedy?

Hardly.

Suppose God the Father had taken the view many modern Christians take—the view that says anything Satan wants must be bad for God's people. Such a view implies that if Satan wants one thing, God must want the opposite. The result? God would have canceled the crucifixion. And none of us would be saved!

The truth is, Satan and God may want the exact same event to take place—but for different reasons. Satan's motive in Stephen's stoning and Jesus' crucifixion was rebellion; God's motive was love and mercy. And love really does conquer all.

Joni Eareckson Tada

What Others Have Said

Love makes the whole difference between an execution and martyrdom.
—Evelyn Underhill

"I Have Heard"

Read: Acts 7:23–38

"I have indeed seen the oppression of my people in Egypt. I have heard their groaning and have come down to set them free."—Acts 7:34

*T*here have been times when I don't feel anything for God. Do you know what I mean? Sometimes I feel God's presence, but other times I do not. That's scary for me, because it can prompt me to start doubting my salvation. So what can I do?

When I lack an emotional connection with God, I have to rely on my faith and God's faithfulness regardless of my feelings. Probably the ancient Israelites didn't "feel" God when they suffered under the lash of Egyptian slavery. And yet God was at work on their behalf, as he said: "I have indeed seen the oppression of my people in Egypt. I have heard their groaning and have come down to set them free."

I like the saying I heard somewhere, "Your relationship with God doesn't depend on the puny pebble of your fluctuating faith, but on the massive boulder of his unchanging character."

Dave Dravecky

Points to Ponder

* How much does your faith depend on an emotional connection with God?

* What reassurance does the verse of the day provide you with?

* What is your response to the saying at the end of the devotional?

WHAT STEPHEN SAW

Read: Acts 7:54–60

Stephen, full of the Holy Spirit, looked up to heaven and saw the glory of God, and Jesus standing at the right hand of God. —Acts 7:55

*A*t the moment of his death, Stephen fixed his eyes not on what was seen, but on what was unseen (invisible to the angry members of the crowd, anyway). He could have filled his vision with the jagged rocks and stones that were hurtling toward his head, but he didn't. In the midst of his deadly troubles, he chose to lock his eyes on something no one else either saw or could see—his Savior.

Curiously, the Savior he saw was not *sitting* at the right hand of God (his rightful position on the divine throne), but *standing* there. Why standing? To welcome home the church's first martyr? To applaud a job well done? To be ready for an imminent embrace? I'm not sure. But I do know the sight filled Stephen with the courage to die well. As the rocks kept coming, this man cried out, "Lord Jesus, receive my spirit." Then a pause, then another request: "Lord, do not hold this sin against them." And then he was safe in the arms of Jesus.

Dave Dravecky

WHAT OTHERS HAVE SAID

Be Thou my vision, O Lord of my heart, naught be all else to me save that Thou art. Thou my best thought, by day or by night, waking or sleeping, Thy vision my light. —Celtic hymn attributed to Dallan Forgaill, 8th Century

MOURN WITH THOSE WHO MOURN

Read: Acts 8:1–3

Godly men buried Stephen and mourned deeply for him. —Acts 8:2

I used to be one of those who never wanted people to cry. I'd change the subject or try to cheer them up. It makes me sad to realize that I didn't help them by doing so. Now, I don't change the subject; I listen to their stories. I stand beside them and cry with them, holding their hands. I have learned that those who mourn will be comforted, so I let them mourn. I even encourage it. I understand that mourning is a necessary part of dealing with loss. It is not a weakness in faith.

Certainly it was no weakness of the men who buried Stephen and mourned for him! In fact, God *commands* us to show our grief: "mourn with those who mourn" (Romans 12:15).

I know I can't relieve the pain, but I also know there's no way to get on the other side of the pain except to go through it.

Jan Dravecky

TAKE ACTION!

Resolve to encourage people to go ahead and mourn in your presence if they need to. Decide that you won't run from the grief of others, but rather that you will listen and hold the hand of the next person who needs you.

GOD'S CHOSEN INSTRUMENT

Read: Act 9:1–19

"This man is my chosen instrument to carry my name before the Gentiles and their kings and before the people of Israel. I will show him how much he must suffer for my name."—Acts 9:15–16

There is great comfort in knowing that we are God's chosen ones. Jesus has chosen us to serve and worship him, to receive every spiritual blessing and a heavenly inheritance.

But to some of his loved ones God whispers, "I have chosen you for the furnace of affliction." Consider the apostle Paul. God said of him, "This man is my chosen instrument . . . I will show him how much he must suffer for my name."

Chosen to serve God, yes; to praise him, of course; but to suffer for him? After being paralyzed for more than three decades, I am able to say yes. God gives special promises to those who have been specially chosen. If you have severe aches and pains, a husband gone astray, a wife with bi-polar syndrome, or some other painful circumstance, he has a word that is spoken particularly for you: you are a chosen vessel, chosen to suffer.

Joni Eareckson Tada

PATH TO PRAYER

If you can do so honestly, thank God for choosing you to be his chosen instrument. Ask him to make you a communicator of his grace to others through your suffering. Ask him to help you bear your suffering with a sense of purpose and with courage and patience.

WHY PRAY?

Read: Acts 10:1–33

[Cornelius] gave generously to those in need and prayed to God regularly.
—*Acts 10:2*

Why pray when God doesn't answer? Why pray when, apparently, he doesn't hear? Why pray when our prayers seem to rise no higher than a couple of feet above our heads?

The answer Dave and I now give can be boiled down to one thing: we pray because God tells us to pray and he promises that he both hears and answers our prayers. It comes down to choosing to believe what God tells us in his Word.

Cornelius, the Roman centurion described in Acts 10, made this discovery. Who knows for how long he had prayed before he received an answer to his requests? Verse 2 says he "prayed regularly." But not until one special day did he learn (from an angel!) that "God has heard your prayer and remembered your gifts to the poor." Do you think Cornelius was glad he continued to pray, even when he seemed to get no answer? Is there any doubt?

Jan Dravecky

TAKE ACTION!

A "rule of prayer" is a plan that gives one a framework for regular prayer so that the days don't slip by without one having prayed at all. Do you have one? If not, sit down and decide the best times for you to pray and write down a rule of prayer. (Note that a rule of prayer doesn't mean you can't pray at other times as well.) If you wish, you can research rules of prayer others have established.

PLEASE SPEAK!

Read: Acts 13:13–15

"Brothers, if you have a message of encouragement for the people, please speak."—Acts 13:15

*E*veryone needs frequent words of encouragement. But it's just as true that God has given each of us a word of encouragement to give someone else, as an incident in the synagogue of Pisidian Antioch demonstrates. When congregational leaders spotted Paul and his companions attending their service, they said to them, "Brothers, if you have a message of encouragement for the people, please speak." And the apostle obliged.

What word of encouragement might you have to give? When I was making my comeback, we received scores of letters from fans encouraging us and thanking us for sharing our faith. It was an incredible feeling to sense we were being lifted up and above our own workaday concerns, that our lives were being used to encourage and help and challenge others whom we did not even know. Clearly, it wasn't our doing. All we'd thought about was making a comeback in baseball, doing it the best way we could, always trying to keep our focus on God's will, not our own. But God took that and made much more of it than we could have imagined. He can do that in your life, too.

Dave Dravecky

WHAT OTHERS HAVE SAID

Correction does much, but encouragement does more. Encouragement after censure is as the sun after a shower. —Johann Wolfgang von Goethe

LET IT SHINE

Read: Acts 13:44–48

"I have made you a light for the Gentiles, that you may bring salvation to the ends of the earth."—Acts 13:47

There is a church in England that has no lights. Many visitors are shocked that the architect left out something as important as overhead lighting. But the architect had a plan. The various families who regularly attend the church are given their own pew, as well as a lamp and a book. When the family comes to church, their lamp is lit. If they are not in church, the pew remains dark.

What difference can one darkened pew make? Not much. But what if several pews lack lamps? Then the whole church is affected.

What a beautiful picture of the body of Christ! Through us, the light of Jesus shines to bring salvation to others. As we use our gifts, the whole body will be full of light. This is how intimately we are linked one with another. The Lord has made us a light in order to shine for the sake of others.

Joni Eareckson Tada

PATH TO PRAYER

Jesus, Light of the world, you are our light and our salvation. I praise you that you have given your light to your people. Thank you for providing me with people who give me encouragement and hope. Help me to let my light shine for others, too, as they have shone for me. Amen.

A DIVINE HELP

Read: Acts 26:9–29

"I have had God's help to this very day." —Acts 26:22

*I*t's quite a claim Paul makes. But it's a claim I'm convinced all believers in Christ can make still today.

What a comfort this is when we run into troubles and hardships! Remember, Paul made this claim in the middle of a tremendously stressful period of life. His enemies had tried to kill him. The Romans had thrown him in jail. He'd been beaten by one group and chained by another. And yet he can declare confidently to the authorities, *"I have had God's help to this very day."*

But how had he received God's help? What did that help look like?

Well, it didn't get him out of custody. It didn't free him from death threats. But it did give him great peace in the midst of his storm. It did give him words that brought others to Christ. It did give him the assurance that he would accomplish all God had planned for him.

And *that*, friends, is help! A divine help that we, too, enjoy "to this very day."

Dave Dravecky

POINTS TO PONDER

* In what ways have you received God's help?
* What did that help look like?
* How do you look for and recognize God's help?
* Why is gratitude important in recognizing God's help?

HURRICANE HOPE

Read: Acts 27:13–26

"I have faith in God that it will happen just as he told me."—Acts 27:25

How could Paul maintain an even keel even when his ship capsized? And what can we learn from him that will help us when our own "northeasters" strike with hurricane force?

First, we need to realize that Paul felt the blows of life like any of us. "When neither sun or stars appeared for many days and the storm continued raging," Luke tells us, "we [including Paul!] finally gave up all hope of being saved." But, of course, God intervened. The Lord told Paul that he would appear before Caesar—and that God would spare the lives of everyone on board.

Paul maintained an even keel because he placed his confidence in the God of the storms. Paul might have been like a strong oak tree, but he knew that if a two-ton meteorite hit him, the meteorite would win. On the other hand, he also knew that if God sustained that tree and gave it his own strength, no meteorite was going to budge it, even if the rock was as big as Jupiter. It is *that* kind of hope that can keep anyone's keel even.

Dave and Jan Dravecky

WHAT OTHERS HAVE SAID

Fear imprisons, faith liberates; fear paralyzes, faith empowers, fear disheartens, faith encourages; fear sickens, faith heals; fear makes useless, faith makes serviceable—and most of all, fear puts hopelessness at the heart of life, while faith rejoices in its God. —Harry Emerson Fosdick

UNUSUAL KINDNESS

Read: Acts 28:2–10

The islanders showed us unusual kindness. —Acts 28:2

*I*magine the scene. Two hundred and seventy-six people—prisoners, soldiers and crew—all standing helpless on the Malta shore. Each one drenched, frozen to the bone, with nothing to their names but the clothes on their back. No trunks with goods to trade. No potential for spending lots of money to boost the island's economy. Just themselves.

Yet the islanders welcomed them with "unusual kindness"—unusual because they responded to the need of the moment and not to the reputation of the castaways. What hospitality! And later when the party left, the islanders gave them all they needed.

We learn from history that the entire island of Malta was converted to Christianity. Somehow we're not surprised. They welcomed the good news of God as readily as they welcomed the dying strangers.

What is the nature of our hospitality? Is it based on what we perceive the stature of the person to be? May God help us to show the hospitality of the Maltese! Today. To everyone.

Joni Eareckson Tada

TAKE ACTION!

What kindnesses can you show others? Be on the lookout for a way to show God's grace to someone at the earliest opportunity. Do it without an agenda or ulterior motive. Do it because God has been kind to you.

An Essential Grain of Sand

Read: Acts 28:17–31

"God's salvation has been sent to the Gentiles, and they will listen!"—Acts 28:28

*P*aul was preeminently a preacher of hope. Even when under house arrest, he couldn't stop preaching the good news of Jesus Christ. When some in the Jewish community refused to receive his message, he turned to others. "I want you to know," he declared, "that God's salvation has been sent to the Gentiles, and they will listen!"

Yes, they did. Countless millions of them not only listened, but also received the news with joy and so were added to the multitude of the redeemed. C. H. Spurgeon, an nineteenth-century pastor, suggested that the reason redeemed people will number more than the grains of sand on the beach or the stars in the sky is that an endless number of saints will be required to fully reflect the infinite facets of God's love. Everyone is necessary in heaven—including you. For without you, some wonderful nuance of God's love (dare I say?) might not get reflected. And that can never be.

Joni Eareckson Tada

Path to Prayer

Pray that God will show you what facet of his love you can show to someone else. Pray that he will reveal the special and unique role you have in bringing his kingdom to the world. Thank him for sending salvation to you through the ministry of all the people that have given his message to you.

GRATITUDE

Read: Romans 1:21–25

For although they knew God, they neither glorified him as God nor gave thanks to him, but their thinking became futile and their foolish hearts were darkened.
—Romans 1:21

Ingratitude carries serious penalties. Probably the oldest story is found in here in Romans 1:20–21. It is an ageless problem, says Paul. The wonder of God's divinity and power is all around people, plainly shown in the beauty of the world he created and in the provision he has made for their food and shelter and enjoyment. Yet they refuse to see. And God punished them for their thankless hearts.

That should say something to you and me; because if a thankless spirit was the undoing of a generation long ago and far away, is it any different today? In fact, you know God far better than those to whom he revealed himself through creation—that means that you have even more to be thankful for!

Look around you. The blessings abound: The smiles of children, the beauty of a glorious sunset, the comfort of a warm bed at night. Small and great, there are plenty of reasons to say to God, "Thank you."

Joni Eareckson Tada

WHAT OTHERS HAVE SAID

Life without thankfulness is devoid of love and passion. Hope without thankfulness is lacking in fine perception. Faith without thankfulness lacks strength and fortitude. Every virtue divorced from thankfulness is maimed and limps along the spiritual road. —John Henry Jowett

SATISFIED!

Read: Romans 3:21–31

All have sinned and fall short of the glory of God, and are justified freely by his grace through the redemption that came by Christ Jesus. —Romans 3:23–24

Propitiation is a word rarely found in newer translations of the Bible. It's out of fashion, even in Christian circles. Propitiation carries the idea of appeasement or satisfaction; in this case Christ's violent death satisfied the offended holiness and wrath of God against those for whom Christ died. In pagan religions it is the worshiper, not the god, who is responsible to appease the wrath of the offended deity. But in reality man is incapable of satisfying God's justice apart from Christ, except by spending eternity in hell. In Christianity it is God, not the worshiper, who took the responsibility of satisfying his own wrath.

Herein lies the amazing love of God—the Father's wrath was appeased through the willing sacrifice of the Son. This is what makes the good news so *great*. God has no more anger left for us, only mercy, pardon, forgiveness, compassion and grace upon grace.

Joni Eareckson Tada

PATH TO PRAYER

"And can it be that I should gain / an interest in the Savior's blood? / Died he for me, who caused his pain—/ for me, who caused his bitter death? / Amazing love! How can it be / that you, my Lord, should die for me?"
—Charles Wesley, 1738

PRESENT SUFFERING, FUTURE GLORY

Read: Romans 5:1–5

And we rejoice in the hope of the glory of God. Not only so, but we also rejoice in our sufferings, because we know that suffering produces perseverance; perseverance, character; and character, hope. —Romans 5:2–4

There is a direct relationship between earth's suffering and heaven's glory. I'm not glorifying suffering here. There's no inherent goodness in injury, illness, or loss. There's nothing to applaud about the agony. Problems are real, and I'm not denying that suffering hurts. I'm just denying that it matters in the grander scheme of things. It is light and momentary compared with what our response is producing for us in heaven—yes, suffering is pivotal to future glory.

The Lord inferred that if his followers were to share in his glory, they would also have to share in his sufferings. And the deeper the suffering, the higher the glory.

Does this mean that those who suffer greatly, yet nobly, will have a bigger halo? A shinier face? No, but it does mean they may enjoy a greater capacity to serve God in heaven. Those who suffer beyond comparison will, if they honor Christ with an uncomplaining spirit, be glorified beyond all comparison.

Joni Eareckson Tada

WHAT OTHERS HAVE SAID

God often digs wells of joy with the spade of sorrow. —Anonymous

GOD'S BRIGHTEST STARS

Read: Romans 5:1–11

But God demonstrates his own love for us in this: While we were still sinners, Christ died for us. —Romans 5:8

The overwhelming data we now have about the immensity of outer space often sparks conversations about who created the universe and why. During a college astronomy lecture, a student asked his professor, "Why would God go to all the trouble to create all that?" The professor, who happened to be a Christian, replied, "Trouble? What trouble? Creating the suns and stars was no trouble for God. He accomplished it with simply his Word. You and I are the ones who have caused him trouble."

Never does God's glory shine brighter than when we stand in the shadow of the cross. It's one thing for God to make a star; it's another thing to redeem sinful man to "shine like the stars forever and ever" (Daniel 12:3). Today contemplate the humility and love of God in that "while we were still sinners, Christ died for us" (Romans 5:8).

Joni Eareckson Tada

FOR FURTHER REFLECTION

Read and meditate on John 15:13; Ephesian 3:14–19; and Hebrews 2:14–15.

October 20

LOOK UP!

Read: Romans 8:18–27

I consider that our present sufferings are not worth comparing with the glory that will be revealed in us. —Romans 8:18

When terrible pain comes into our lives, we are often tempted to give in to the idea that Romans 8:18 is little more than wishful thinking. Never fall for this devilish trap! Remember that the writer of this verse was no dreamy-eyed idealist. No, Paul was the consummate realist. Yet his reality was not confined to the fishbowl of earthly existence but encompassed the vast, unsearchable riches of heaven. Paul never downplayed the jagged pain of life here below; he simply emphasized the infinitely greater rewards of life above. Paul would never think of telling someone, "Oh, please grow up. Your pain is not so bad." He would be more likely to say, "Oh, please, *look* up! The glory that awaits you is worth it all!"

Dave and Jan Dravecky

PATH TO PRAYER

Jesus, my strength and my hope, help me to be like your servant, Paul, who though he faced the evil that the world often offered him, could keep the best that heaven offered in his sights. Draw my eyes toward you— toward heaven—and keep me looking at the vast riches you are holding for me and toward the glory that will be revealed in me and in all your people. Help me look up, I pray. Amen.

NEITHER . . . NOR

Read: Romans 8:28–39

For I am convinced that neither death nor life, neither angels nor demons, neither the present nor the future, nor any powers, neither height nor depth, nor anything else in all creation, will be able to separate us from the love of God that is in Christ Jesus our Lord. —Romans 8:39

I grieve to think how I treated my friends when I was in the hospital. They would sit by my bedside while I lay there in stubborn silence. They would bring magazines, and I would say I wasn't interested. I'm sure that I provoked my friends to exasperation. A few stopped coming around, and who could blame them?

We sometimes feel that way about God. Deep down we know we probably provoke him with our sloppy prayers and ho-hum approach to Bible study. We're certain that he's irritated with our sins and annoyed with our constant ups and downs. We assume he must be exasperated to the point that he will "stop coming around."

Yet if we are truly God's children, we can be sure that he will love us right through the tough times. Children can be exasperating—even children of God—but the Lord will never give up on us. *Nothing* will be able to separate us from God's constant and abiding love.

Joni Eareckson Tada

TAKE ACTION!

Memorize today's verse and recite it when pain or trouble seems about to overwhelm you.

THE MASTER POTTER

Read: Romans 9:16–24

Shall what is formed say to him who formed it, "Why did you make me like this?"
—Romans 9:20

From the moment you and I become children of God, he is constantly molding and shaping us according to his own plans. Some of that molding we may not like. We may ask, "What are you making?" or "Why did you make me like this?" We might gaze upon the work of his hands, dislike what we see, and ask, "How could any true artist create something like this?"

We're especially prone to ask those questions after we've been placed in the oven. Clay isn't pottery until it's fired in a kiln, but time spent in the oven is no fun! And even though pottery is far more useful than mere clay, it's also far more brittle. It breaks. So do we.

But God knows all this. As both our Father and our Potter, he is constantly forming us into a new creation. And even though some of his pottery seems to shatter into shards, in his hands even broken pottery can be made into something new and whole and beautiful. Our job is to work with him, to yield to the touch of the Master Potter.

Dave and Jan Dravecky

FOR FURTHER REFLECTION

Look up Isaiah 45:4–12; 2 Corinthians 4:7–10; and 2 Corinthians 5:17. What do these verses tell you about God, the great Potter, and what he is doing in your life?

THE PUZZLE

Read: Romans 11:33–36

Oh, the depth of the riches of the wisdom and knowledge of God! How unsearchable his judgments, and his paths beyond tracing out!— Romans 11:33

*L*ife is a puzzle where many of the pieces don't fit. Especially at first, when the puzzle is dumped in our lap. It takes a while to sort through the pieces, to turn them all right side up, to see the overall pattern, to spot the connections. I don't think God holds it against us when we can't understand everything that happens in this jigsaw world of ours, especially at first. And especially because some of the key pieces to that puzzle are missing.

Maybe what God wants us to do is to put together as much of life's puzzle that we can, and then to trust him with the missing pieces—however many those pieces may be, however large, however gaping the holes that are left in our theology as a result.

The question changes from, "Why, God?" to "Can I trust him with my unanswered questions?"

Dave and Jan Dravecky

WHAT OTHERS HAVE SAID

Trust God where you cannot trace him. Do not try to penetrate the cloud he brings over you; rather look to the bow that is on it. The mystery is God's; the promise is yours. —John R. McDuff

BE JOYFUL

Read: Romans 12:9–13

Be joyful in hope, patient in affliction, faithful in prayer. —Romans 12:12

Why does God ask us to be "joyful in hope"? I can understand why he reminds us to be faithful in prayer or patient in affliction, but why the words about hope? After all, the focus of our hope is yet to be fulfilled; we don't yet possess that for which we hope. It's hard to be joyful about something we don't yet have!

Recently, it hit home that God wants me to be joyful about future things. How can God command joy? It's easy once we realize what's over the heavenly horizon.

Does the idea of heavenly glories above put a smile on your face? Do you get a charge when you talk about the return of the Lord? Words like "pleasure," "happiness," and "delight" should come to mind when you hope in the Lord. Heaven will seem more near and real to you as you stir up your joy over that for which you hope. It's a command for your own good!

Joni Eareckson Tada

FOR FURTHER REFLECTION

Look up Titus 3:4–7; Hebrews 3:6; 6:11; 10:23; and 11:1. How do these passages define this hope? What do we have to do to cultivate it? How might that hope make *you* joyful?

DAY OF THE LORD

Read: Romans 12:17–21

Do not take revenge, my friends, but leave room for God's wrath, for it is written:
"It is mine to avenge; I will repay," says the Lord. —Romans 12:19

God has given us many good gifts: gifts of health, food, work, friends and especially the gift of himself. His gifts to us overflow in abundance, meeting our needs far more than we realize. There is at least one thing, however, that God has not given us. God tells us that vengeance is his and his alone. He reminds us to keep hands off when it comes to backbiting or evening the score. You may say that vengeance is sweet, but God says, "It is mine to avenge."

God has good reasons for warning you against getting even or retaliating against friend or foe. He knows that revenge can too easily infect you with anger, resentment, or a spirit of bitterness. He also wants you to know that it is not your place to judge and condemn another person. Leave judgment to God. That's what "the Day of the Lord" is all about.

One day on the other side of eternity, we who are saints will judge the world with the Lord Jesus (1 Corinthians 6:2). Until that time, however, leave in God's hands what is rightfully his.

Joni Eareckson Tada

PATH TO PRAYER

Father God, I confess I become angry with others when they hurt my loved ones or me. But I know that you hold the scales of ultimate justice in your hands. So I give to you now any desire for revenge or retailiation that lingers in the dark corners of my heart. Create in me a heart of peace, O God, and renew in me your spirit of love and mercy. Amen.

FIRST THINGS FIRST

Read: 1 Corinthians 3:10–15

[His work] will be revealed with fire, and the fire will test the quality of each man's work. —1 Corinthians 3:13

W hen Jan and I began to see life from the perspective of "first things first," we stopped trying to meet everybody's needs and demands. As we began to understand where all the demands of life fit into our lives in light of our commitment to God, we realized there was a whole lot of "stuff" that was just that: stuff, excess baggage. It was junk that didn't need to be there. So instead of pouring our energies into those things, we began focusing on the things that were most important in life. We began to put our efforts into those areas where God had gifted us. Only then did we begin to put things in perspective and realize that even if some of those extraneous things fell away or disappeared, we still had incredible worth in our relationship with God.

Dave Dravecky

WHAT OTHERS HAVE SAID

Let us give up our work, our plans, our health, our lives, our loved ones, our influence, our all, into God's right hand. Then, when we have given over all to him, there will be nothing left for us to be troubled about, or to make trouble about. —J. Hudson Taylor

No Proper Suffering

Read: 1 Corinthians 4:1–5

Therefore judge nothing before the appointed time; wait till the Lord comes.
—1 Corinthians 4:5

We are not to judge how people suffer; we are to love them. We teach people at our ministry that there is no proper way to suffer. Suffering is not tidy because suffering is a purifying process, a process of cleaning out impurities. When suffering causes impurities to rise to the surface, naturally we are going to see the worst of people. Their selfishness is going to come out; their wrong priorities are going to become apparent, and they are not going to be able to mask their sinfulness anymore. Suffering breaks down the walls that people put up to hide what's really inside. When you suffer, you can't keep up the nice facade.

The last thing that people need at those times is to be judged. Instead they need a safe place to go through the process, someone to listen, someone to accept them right where they are, someone to offer them God's own kindness and forgiveness.

Jan Dravecky

Points to Ponder

❋ Why might judging people while they are suffering be devastating to them?

❋ How do you want to be treated when you are suffering?

❋ Look at each of the acts of grace listed in the last paragraph. Is there anyone to whom you can offer one or more of them?

HOW LONG?

Read: 1 Corinthians 7:29–31

For this world in its present form is passing away. —1 Corinthians 7:31

*I*t's good to remember this verse. God doesn't tell us when everything will be wrapped up, but he does assure us that, even now, the old order of pain is being phased out.

God may never answer our question "How long?" He may never tell us how much farther we must trudge through the desert. But if our wilderness journey leads us to him, then the road we travel is as surely a highway to heaven as is any more rapid thoroughfare.

Who knows when the trip will be over? Maybe tomorrow, maybe next week, maybe next year. God does not give us an ETA, an Estimated Time of Arrival. But if we belong to him, he does give us a GTA—a Guaranteed Territory of Arrival. And from what we can glimpse in the official travel brochure of his Word, the place is spectacular.

Dave and Jan Dravecky

FOR FURTHER REFLECTION

Read Revelation 21:1–22:5. What are the new heavens and the new earth going to look like? How can you depict that new earth in a poem, a short essay, a picture or other artwork?

HAND-TAILORED TRIALS

Read: 1 Corinthians 10:11–13

And God is faithful; he will not let you be tempted beyond what you can bear. But when you are tempted, he will also provide a way out so that you can stand up under it. —1 Corinthians 10:13

Have you ever looked at someone going through a tough time and thought, *Boy, I'm glad that's not me. I could never handle that situation.* Sure you have. I have, too. And I'll tell you someone else who thinks that: my friend Charlene. She was recently in the hospital, having temporarily lost control of her muscles. She had to be fed and had to wear an indwelling catheter. That meant no trips to the bathroom (she carried her bathroom with her) and lots of discomfort.

Charlene later told me, "Joni, I don't know how you do it. I'm glad you're the quadriplegic rather than me. I love my independence."

I couldn't believe my ears. Charlene is blind and deaf. She was saying, "Hey, I can do the deaf-blind thing. But that's it; no quadriplegic stuff for me."

Which just goes to show that God will never push you past your limit. He hand-tailors your trials just as he limits your temptations. God knows— and he is the only one who knows—what you can bear.

Joni Eareckson Tada

WHAT OTHERS HAVE SAID

The perseverance of the saints is only possible because of the perseverance of God. —J. Oswald Sanders

MUTUAL BLESSINGS

Read: 1 Corinthians 12:12–26

But in fact God has arranged the parts in the body, every one of them, just as he wanted them to be. . . . The eye cannot say to the hand, "I don't need you!" And the head cannot say to the feet, "I don't need you!"—1 Corinthians 12:18,21

Through our experiences and the suffering we have witnessed in the lives of others, we have learned that we *need* one another. Most of us, though, are uncomfortable with asking for help, with exposing our needs. A wise friend of mine who nursed her husband through nearly two decades of total incapacitation shared a powerful insight with me about our need for each other.

Like most of us, at first my friend resisted asking for help. She didn't like feeling needy and weak. But God showed her early on in her husband's illness, that he wanted to teach her family to trust him to meet their needs, *and* he wanted to teach the local body of Christ the true meaning of serving him. Her family was blessed by the people who brought meals, repaired appliances, and cut firewood. God's people were blessed because they were learning to give, to sacrifice and to put their faith in action. God showed my friend that not asking for help, not sharing her family's needs, was actually robbing the local body of Christ of a blessing.

Dave Dravecky

POINTS TO PONDER

* Are you shy about asking for help? Why or why not?
* In what areas of your life are you most reluctant to ask for help?
* In what ways might you be blessing others if you ask for their help?

IMPERISHABLE

Read: 1 Corinthians 15:35–58

When the perishable has been clothed with the imperishable, and the mortal with immortality, then the saying that is written will come true: "Death has been swallowed up in victory."—1 Corinthians 15:54

*P*aul tells us that our resurrection bodies will be "imperishable." That means they won't wear out, burn out, or rot out. After you've used your glorified body for a trillion billion years, it will still be as good as new. These bodies won't come with 50,000-mile warranties because they won't need any warranties at all. Fifty thousand miles or 50,000 light years, the tread on your tires will still be the same.

Our bodies will also be strong. Paul says they will be "raised in power." That means there won't be any wheelchairs in heaven. No pneumatic lifts. No crutches, no hospital beds, no braces, no personal trainers. No need to take vitamins A, B, or even C, and you won't ever have to eat spinach if you don't want to.

Dave Dravecky

PATH TO PRAYER

Offer thanksgiving to God for this wonderful promise that your body will be imperishable in the resurrection—that your pain and discomfort will be a thing of distant memory and that your body will be strong and "raised in power."

November

A Ministry of Comfort

Read: 2 Corinthians 1:3–5

Praise be to the God and Father of our Lord Jesus Christ, the Father of compassion and the God of all comfort, who comforts us in all our troubles, so that we can comfort those in any trouble with the comfort we ourselves have received from God. —2 Corinthians 1:3–4

God really does comfort his children—and most often he chooses to do so through the arms and legs and voices and ears and faces and tears of men and women who have been to the front lines and returned with battle scars. Someone who has "been there" has the understanding to know what it is that the person in pain is going through—the questions, doubts, and fears. They can speak both compassionately and authoritatively because of their own experience.

I am amazed at what God had to take me through to change me from one who avoided suffering people to someone who is able to comfort those who are in pain and distress. He had to take me through a tremendous amount of pain to prepare me for this ministry of comfort. He had to change my heart.

I wonder . . . have you considered how God might want to use you to comfort someone in pain? "But I'm in pain myself," you reply. Yes, but who better to reach out with understanding, empathy and genuine concern? If you have suffered, and God has stepped in with his comfort, then you qualify to join his army of comforters.

Jan Dravecky

Path to Prayer

I praise you, God and Father of our Lord Jesus Christ, that you are the Father of compassion and the God of all comfort. You comfort us in all our troubles, so that we can comfort those in any trouble with the comfort we ourselves have received from you. Amen.

UNFAILING PROMISES

Read: 2 Corinthians 1:12–22

For no matter how many promises God has made, they are "Yes" in Christ.
—*2 Corinthians 1:20*

He stood out in a crowd—a tall, handsome, black man from Jamaica with a big smile. I saw him shaking people's hands and heard each person tell him how encouraging his testimony was. I wheeled up to him, leaned forward, and lifted my arm. He smiled and leaned forward to extend his hand. Then a surprising thing happened: I realized he had no hands! This joyful Christian wore black fiberglass hands. We commented that even though we couldn't feel it, our "handshake" sure looked good!

He smiled broadly and said, "Sister, aren't you glad we have Jesus? We have his promises!" Jesus and his promises. They are virtually one and the same. To believe in Christ is to believe in God's promises.

Joni Eareckson Tada

PATH TO PRAYER

Father, help me to sink my anchor deep in your promises. As life's waves broadside my boat, enable me to remember that every promise has its beginning and ending in Jesus.

THE AROMA OF CHRIST

Read: 2 Corinthians 2:14–16

For we are to God the aroma of Christ among those who are being saved and those who are perishing. —2 Corinthians 2:15

*I*t's amazing how a scent—even a fragrance—evokes powerful feelings. These verses speak of the power of fragrance. It's another way of saying, "I want to live in a way that will perpetually remind God of the obedience, sacrifice, and devotion of the Lord Jesus. I want my words and deeds to bring to God's mind fragrant memories of the earthly life of his Son."

What's more, our godly words and deeds not only remind God of his Son but remind others of him, too—whether they believe in Jesus or not. To be obedient among the fellowship of believers is to carry with you the fragrance of Christ. To be obedient in a wicked world is to remind others of the stench of death. But that's not bad! Sometimes the wicked need to face their own mortality to be awakened out of their spiritual slumber. No matter how others interpret it, just be certain to waft Jesus their way.

Joni Eareckson Tada

TAKE ACTION!

Find or buy a scented candle that reminds you of holiness. Light it during your times of prayer to remind you that you are the aroma of Christ to those around you.

November 4

LIGHT TROUBLES?

Read: 2 Corinthians 4:8–18

Therefore we do not lose heart. Though outwardly we are wasting away, yet inwardly we are being renewed day by day. For our light and momentary troubles are achieving for us an eternal glory that far outweighs them all.
—2 Corinthians 4:16–17

*L*ight troubles? It's not easy putting paralysis into that category. And I hesitate to call over three decades in a wheelchair "momentary." Yet it truly is when you realize that "you are a mist that appears for a little while and then vanishes" (James 4:14). Scripture is constantly trying to help us view life in this way. Our life is but a blip on the eternal screen. Pain will be erased by a greater understanding, it will be eclipsed by a glorious result. Something so superb, so grand is going to happen at the world's finale, that it will suffice for every hurt and atone for every heartache.

Joni Eareckson Tada

PATH TO PRAYER

Have you lost heart? In what way? Do you feel that you are "wasting away"? Ask God to give you a sense of renewal "day by day." Pray for a greater understanding of the suffering you are undergoing. Pray for the eyes to see your situation with eternal perspective.

EXCITED BY HEAVEN

Read: 2 Corinthians 5:6–10

We are confident, I say, and would prefer to be away from the body and at home with the Lord. —Corinthians 5:8

Why did the apostle Paul get so excited whenever thoughts of heaven crowded into his mind? For him, it wasn't so much the golden streets or the gleaming mansions or even rushing water of life at the heavenly city's center that got him excited. No, he was going home, and that meant only one thing: he'd soon be seeing his Savior.

No doubt Paul appreciated knowing something about the layout of heaven, and something of its appearance, radiance, and exquisite beauty. Apparently he had seen part of it himself, for in 2 Corinthians 12:2–4 he describes being "caught up to the third heaven . . . caught up to paradise" where he "heard inexpressible things, things that man is not permitted to tell." And yet when it came right down to it, all he ever wanted to write about was Christ. He was going home, and that meant going to see Jesus, the One who appeared to him on the Damascus road. In his mind, heaven is heaven because Jesus is there.

Dave and Jan Dravecky

WHAT OTHERS HAVE SAID

Our Father refreshes us on the journey with some pleasant inns but will not encourage us to mistake them for home. — C.S. (Clive Staples) Lewis

WE CAN ADMIT IT

Read: 2 Corinthians 7:2–13

For when we came into Macedonia, this body of ours had no rest, but we were harassed at every turn—conflicts on the outside, fears within. But God, who comforts the downcast, comforted us. —2 Corinthians 7:5–6

While I had cancer, we attended a church that taught it was impossible for a Christian to be depressed if he or she were truly walking with the Lord. I bought into that teaching and denied all my symptoms (as well as Jan's) of depression. In that setting, admitting that I was depressed and seeking professional help would have been like confessing sin. I really believed that if I kept a positive attitude and kept trying to help others, I could and should get around my own grief without going through it.

I was wrong. I needed to realize if someone with the stature of the apostle Paul could say he had "conflicts on the outside, fears within," and that he was "downcast," then who was I to deny my own struggles?

Dave Dravecky

POINTS TO PONDER

* Why do you think Christians tend not to admit their struggles? What might they be afraid of?

* Why might confessing problems such as depression seem like confessing sin?

* Why should Christians seek to be more open about their struggles? What good might come of it?

WHAT IS HAPPINESS?

Read: 2 Corinthians 8:1–5

Out of the most severe trial, their overflowing joy and their extreme poverty welled up in rich generosity. —2 Corinthians 8:2

*L*et's face it, some people are never going to be happy. Maybe they're in a dead-end marriage—or constantly tangle with their supervisor at work—or despair of ever losing that extra 25 pounds. Life, to them, seems a never-ending drudgery of the same, sad routine.

Are you this way? Do you feel as though true happiness has somehow passed you by? The fact is, life is hard—for some more than others. If happiness relates only to "present circumstances," it may always dance ahead of us—just out of reach. But it doesn't have to be this way. The answer is not to get rid of unhappiness but to find a new *definition* for it.

My friend Elisabeth Elliot has suggested we redefine happiness as duty and honor, sacrifice and faithfulness, commitment, and service. Circumstantial happiness may certainly seem fleeting and elusive, but joy is an overflow of the perseverance and hope growing out of faithful sacrifice and committed service to our loving Lord.

Joni Eareckson Tada

POINTS TO PONDER

* How do you define happiness?
* What are your thoughts about Elizabeth Elliot's definition of happiness?
* What kind of service, commitment, or duty can you joyfully perform that will help you find happiness?

CAPTIVE THOUGHTS

Read: 2 Corinthians 10:1–6

We take captive every thought to make it obedient to Christ. —2 Corinthians 10:5

When I catch myself, I'm aghast at how many lazy, anxious or lustful imaginations wheedle their way into my head. When they do, the "thought patrol" goes on alert and I ask myself, "What are you doing in my mind, you silly thought? You have no business thinking those things in my head, so in Jesus' name, *scram!*"

Can you identify? Perhaps for you, it's a problem with daydreaming. Keeping track of another's wrongs. Stewing over worries. Whatever, God expects you to take responsibility for the ponderings that creep into your brain. You are accountable.

Let the Holy Spirit set up watch, keep guard, and prevent harmful thoughts from roosting in your head. How is this possible? Because "the weapons we fight with are not the weapons of the world. On the contrary, they have divine power to demolish strongholds." Remember, Satan's strongholds are nothing but human dungeons—and it's time to break out of prison.

Joni Eareckson Tada

PATH TO PRAYER

Ask the Holy Spirit to stand guard over your mind and to help you banish harmful, unhelpful and unholy thoughts from creeping in. Ask the Holy Spirit to give you a spirit of power and love and self-discipline so that your thoughts will be pleasing to God (2 Timothy 1:7).

SUFFICIENT

Read: 2 Corinthians 12:7–10

"My grace is sufficient for you, for my power is made perfect in weakness."
—*2 Corinthians 12:9*

*T*he apostle Paul went to God for help with his physical weakness (whatever it was—the Bible doesn't say). He writes, "But [God] said to me, 'My grace is sufficient for you, for my power is made perfect in weakness.' " Every committed Christian longs to experience God's power flowing through his or her life. However, God's power at its best is only manifested through a believer who acknowledges his weaknesses.

God is not the sort of father who wants his children to grow up, leave the nest, and "get out there on your own!" Rather, he desires that we always stay "close to home" so that he can shelter, protect, and provide. So go ahead and boast of your weakness! The more you boast of your need in God, the more you avail yourself of his power.

Joni Eareckson Tada

WHAT OTHERS HAVE SAID

I have been driven many times to my knees by the overwhelming conviction that I had nowhere else to go. My own wisdom, and that of all about me, seemed insufficient for the day. —Abraham Lincoln

But He Is Strong

Read: 2 Corinthians 12:7–10

For Christ's sake, I delight in weaknesses, in insults, in hardships, in persecutions, in difficulties. For when I am weak, then I am strong. —2 Corinthians 12:10

On a hot and windy evening, as we prepared to board our jet to leave Ghana, I talked on the tarmac with an African airport employee. When I told her about the hurting yet happy people we met in the slums, she replied, "We have to trust God. Our people have no other hope." She flattened her whipping hair with her hand and gave me a knowing look, her eyes unblinking, her broad smile, unflinching. She meant every word. I asked how she kept smiling. She shrugged her shoulders. "I too have God."

Hardships press us up against God. It's a universal truth we all learned in the old Sunday school song, "We are weak, but he is strong."

This is what I saw that night in Africa. A pastor-friend spread wide his arms and beamed, "Welcome to our country where our God is bigger than your God." It was a happy-faced fact: God always seems bigger to those who need him most. And suffering is the tool he uses to help us need him more.

Joni Eareckson Tada

Path to Prayer

Make a list of your weaknesses and offer them to God in prayer. Ask him to take them and use them as he will for his kingdom.

THE GIFT

Read: 2 Corinthians 13:11–14

May the grace of the Lord Jesus Christ, and the love of God, and the fellowship of the Holy Spirit be with you all. —2 Corinthians 13:14

*P*aul ends his second Corinthian letter with a prayer that "the grace of the Lord Jesus Christ . . . be with you all." *Grace*. It's one of the most beautiful words in the whole world.

Grace is a gift. The smell of hot roasted peanuts at the ballpark is grace. The passing cloud that shades you in the center field bleachers is grace. The ability Babe Ruth had to hit home runs came to him by grace. He worked to develop his ability, but he did nothing to deserve it. It was a gift.

I have a Father in heaven who is a great giver. *He* is where I find grace. At the time I need strength, he puts it in my heart or provides it through someone close to me. I don't earn it. I don't deserve it. I don't bring it about. It's a gift. And it's offered to you, too.

Dave Dravecky

WHAT OTHERS HAVE SAID

A state of mind that sees God in everything is evidence of growth in grace and a thankful heart. —Charles Grandison Finney

FATHER, DADDY

Read: Galatians 3:26—4:7

Because you are sons, God sent the Spirit of his Son into our hearts, the Spirit who calls out, "Abba, Father."—Galatians 4:6

When my children were small, I remember the excitement of their first steps. I met each wobbly lurch forward with enthusiastic hurrahs and hugs. They went from heavily padded bottoms to reinforced knees—shock absorbers for their anticipated tumbles and tears. I *expected* them to fall, to cry. I knew they were learning, and I delighted in each stage of their progress. That's what parents do. It's effortless to love our children, to nurture them, to delight in their growth.

We quickly forget that God is a Father who—like our earthly parents—loves us passionately. He delights in our growth. He knows we're learning. He expects bruised knees and bruised hearts along the way. He doesn't want guilt over our occasional tumbles to paralyze us in fear of his response. He wants us to brush off the dust, figure out what tripped us up, grab his strong hand, and keep walking.

True victory over guilt comes when we see ourselves as God views us—as children who are learning to walk the uneven emotional and spiritual road of life, children whose *"Abba,* Father" (or "Daddy") spared no expense to walk beside them.

Dave Dravecky

POINTS TO PONDER

✳ What does it mean to you that, "God sent the Spirit of his Son into our hearts"?

✳ Can you relate to a God who sees himself as your "Daddy"? Why or why not?

✳ How does it feel to know that God loves you far more passionately than you do your children?

IN STEP WITH THE SPIRIT

Read: Galatians 5:16–26

Since we live by the Spirit, let us keep in step with the Spirit. —Galatians 5:25

When you're hurting, life is lived in steps. Very small steps. The sufficiency of Christ is more than enough to meet the needs of a lifetime, but life can only be lived one day, one moment, at a time. The meaning here is not about "keeping pace," as if the Spirit were racing ahead and we'd better keep up with him; it has to do with measuring one's moments in a slow and circumspect way. God's strength is available one day at a time. And frankly, when you're suffering, you are only able to take one day—or one hour—at a time.

There are things in my life, Lord, that are slowing me down. Help me to see these "problems" as opportunities to keep in closer step with the Spirit.

Joni Eareckson Tada

TAKE ACTION!

Write the name of each the fruit of the Spirit on a 3x5 inch index card. Carry them with you and each day over the next few days. Choose one and meditate on it. If you wish, look up Scripture verses on each topic in a concordance or topical Bible and jot them down on the appropriate card.

HELP ALONG THE ROAD

Read: Galatians 6:1–5

Carry each other's burdens, and in this way you will fulfill the law of Christ.
—Galatians 6:2

*B*y its very nature, suffering and adversity brings uncertainty, confusion, and isolation. It is difficult to talk about these things, and so many who suffer feel they need to bear their burden alone. After all, if they don't understand what is happening, how can anyone else understand?

Yet those times are the very times we need others most—and especially fellow members of the body of Christ. Through our own experiences and the suffering we have witnessed in the lives of others, we have learned how profoundly we need one another as believers. At the very beginning of the human race, God said, "It is not good for the man to be alone." Thousands of years have passed, but our deep, abiding need for one another hasn't changed. We still need friends, spouses, and family members to help us bear life's burdens.

Dave and Jan Dravecky

POINTS TO PONDER

The New International Bible commentary distinguishes between what it means to carry one's own load in verse 5 and to bear one another's burdens in verse 2. The expression in verse 2 means to carry the burdens that are "more than one person should carry." The word in verse 5 means to "carry one's own pack"—one's own unique "work" and responsibilities toward God and others. How do you understand this difference?

WISDOM FROM THE SPIRIT

Read: Ephesians 1:15–23

I keep asking that the God of our Lord Jesus Christ, the glorious Father, may give you the Spirit of wisdom and revelation, so that you may know him better.
—Ephesians 1:17

The Holy Spirit confines his power largely to the hearts of men and women, boys and girls who have placed their faith in the resurrected Christ. He uses that power to help them "grasp how wide and long and high and deep is the love of Christ" (Ephesians 3:18)—a work of great power indeed! This power is so great that it helps us to "know this love that surpasses knowledge." Through his power and illumination, we may transcend our poor ability to comprehend and reach out into divine waters far deeper than any we have yet explored.

As children of God, we have been given the Holy Spirit to dwell within us. As we permit the Spirit to exercise his power in and through us, we will begin to see with God's eyes and will gain much wisdom and discernment. When we live like this, it is unbelievable the wisdom and discernment we can receive in order to handle difficult situations!

Dave and Jan Dravecky

PATH TO PRAYER

Use Paul's words in Ephesians 1:15–23 to pray for your family members, friends, and others.

DYNAMITE POWER

Read: Ephesians 1:15–23

I pray also that the eyes of your heart may be enlightened in order that you may know the hope to which he has called you, the riches of his glorious inheritance in the saints, and his incomparably great power for us who believe.
—Ephesians 1:18–19

G od has incomparably great power in store for those who believe, the same power he exerted when he raised Christ from the dead. In other words, the sky is the limit when it comes to the display of God's mighty strength in your life.

The usual word for God's power is the *dunamis,* from which we get our words "dynamite" and "dynamo." A dynamo is just as strong as dynamite, and maybe more so. But the power of a dynamo isn't as obvious. Its power is quiet, controlled, and steady, unlike the explosive "bang" you get from sticks of dynamite. This is the kind of inward power that is displayed by God in the lives of saintly Christians who may never experience a rising up out of their suffering, believers who may never know an outward miracle.

It takes God's power to be a faithful spouse, a conscientious parent, or a responsible office worker. If you're struggling, remember that his power for you is incomparably great. If the Father could raise his Son from the dead, he can raise you above your circumstances.

Joni Eareckson Tada

TAKE ACTION!

Write out the words of Paul's prayer in Ephesians 1:15–23 in the form of a letter, with your own name in the salutation, e.g. Dear_____. Post it in a prominent place and read it everyday for a week.

STRENGTHENED WITHIN

Read: Ephesians 3:14–21

I pray that out of his glorious riches he may strengthen you with power through his Spirit in your inner being, so that Christ may dwell in your hearts through faith.
—Ephesians 3:16–17

*I*t's the Spirit's job to strengthen us with power in our inner being. It's true we don't see him, but my experience with wind tells me that you can see the results of power. And according to Ephesians 3:14, we should be able to see those results in our "inner being."

When the Spirit is blowing in power through our lives, we start noticing that the things that used to petrify us don't frighten us as badly anymore. We recognize a peace in our hearts that we never felt before. We find a greater willingness to reach out beyond ourselves, a deeper hunger to know Christ, a more acute desire to help and comfort others. In other words, no matter what is happening with our "outer being," we see that our "inner being" is being renewed day by day.

Dave and Jan Dravecky

WHAT OTHERS HAVE SAID

The gift of the Holy Spirit closes the gap between the life of God and ours. When we allow the love of God to move in us, we can no longer distinguish ours and his; he becomes us, he lives in us. It is the first fruits of the Spirit, the beginning of our being made divine. —Austin Farrer

EVERY OPPORTUNITY

Read: Ephesians 5:8–20

Be very careful, then, how you live—not as unwise but as wise, making the most of every opportunity, because the days are evil. —Ephesians 5:15–16

We make the mistake of thinking God is always preparing us for future ministry. We rush through the present moment to quickly reach the next one. As a result, we don't pay sufficient attention to the immediate. Oswald Chambers has said, "Grace is for right now."

That's what Ephesians 5:16–17 is talking about. Some translations say, "Walk circumspectly" and "Redeem the time." The NIV says, "Make the most of every opportunity." God is very interested in the situation we find ourselves in *this instant.* It is incidental that he may use our circumstances to prepare us for the future. We need to be praying for guidance for today as well as for tomorrow.

Joni Eareckson Tada

PATH TO PRAYER

God, I hold this day you have given to me in my hands. Please help me pay attention to the grace, power, and opportunity you have made available to me in this day. Not for the future, but for right now. Amen.

OPPOSITION

Read: Ephesians 6:10–18

Finally, be strong in the Lord and in his mighty power. Put on the full armor of God so that you can take your stand against the devil's schemes. —Ephesians 6:10–11

Spiritual warfare against the world, the flesh and the devil is one long, continuous struggle. The enemy has a strategy, and he's out to kill, maim and wound. But God's strategy is to advance his kingdom and reclaim enemy territory.

As in any battle, the troops can get demoralized. That's when you and I need to remember that when we signed up in the army of Christ, it was like having radical heart surgery. In Christ we have died to the power of the enemy over us, and we've been given victorious new weapons of warfare in prayer and worship. God's battle plan can't fail.

If you are experiencing battle fatigue, please remember that your fight won't go on forever. The spiritual warfare will soon be over. Revelation 21:7 promises that we shall inherit all of heaven and earth, God will be our God and we will live as his children if we overcome. So don't shrink from the front lines if you feel the heat of the enemy artillery. Stand strong in the Lord, the captain of your salvation, and you will overcome.

Joni Eareckson Tada

PATH TO PRAYER

Read through the list of "spiritual armor" again. Ask God to help you lift each piece of armor and help you as you imagine yourself putting on piece after piece, meditating on the meaning of each one.

November 20

EXPECT SUFFERING

Read: Philippians 1:12–30

It has been granted to you on behalf of Christ . . . to suffer for him.
—Philippians 1:29

God hates suffering. Jesus spent much of his short life relieving it. Scores of passages tell us to feed the hungry, clothe the poor, visit inmates, and speak up for the helpless.

But it simply doesn't follow that God's only relationship to suffering is to relieve it. He specifically says that all who follow him can expect hardship. Life is *supposed* to be difficult, says the apostle Paul. But he doesn't stop on that morbid note. He adds: Be strengthened. Be encouraged in your faith. And don't let trials unsettle you.

Yet it's amazing how many people believe that life should be easy. They bemoan the enormity of their problems, feeling as though their difficulties are a unique kind of affliction that should not be.

Life is a series of problems to be solved. It is a painful process, but it is this whole process that gives our life meaning. Benjamin Franklin said, "Those things that hurt, instruct."

Do you think you should be exempt from suffering? Then listen to Hebrews 5:8: "Although he [Jesus] was a son, he learned obedience from what he suffered." If he suffered, we can expect it, too.

Joni Eareckson Tada

PATH TO PRAYER

Lord, you have not redeemed me to make my life happy, healthy or free of trouble. You've redeemed me to become more like Christ, and this is why I'm destined for trials. Give me the wisdom, strength, and grace to go through them giving honor to your name.

Caring for Each Other

Read: Philippians 2:1–11

Each of you should look not only to your own interests, but also to the interests of others. — Philippians 2:4

To be a real winner on the field of life, a believer must look out not only for his or her own interests, but also for the interests of others. To be a good team player, you cannot afford to think only of yourself. You have to use your talents to cooperate with your teammates for the common good. Sometimes that means letting somebody else get the glory. If that's what it takes for the team to win, that's what you do. And you do it gladly.

In every line of work there are times when the pressure is on. There are times when somebody on the team drops the ball or misses a play. In those situations, the way we treat each other is what makes the difference between winning and losing; it certainly makes or breaks team morale. I think God cares about our performance *toward each other* in those kinds of situations just as much as (if not more than) he cares about whether we make the play or close the deal. *Affirming the worth of your co-worker is as valuable as the work you accomplish.*

Dave Dravecky

For Further Reflection

Read also Romans 12:10; 14:19; and 15:1–2 as well as 1 Corinthians 13 for more on how to look to the interests of others.

WITHOUT COMPLAINING

Read: Philippians 2:12–18

Do everything without complaining or arguing, so that you may become blameless and pure, children of God without fault in a crooked and depraved generation, in which you shine like stars in the universe. —Philippians 2:14

Your commitment to praise God—in spite of your suffering and adversity—counts for a great deal. Beyond those people with whom you rub shoulders every day, there are many others who watch. God uses your praise as a witness to angels and demons about his wisdom and power. When you bite your tongue and shun the luxury of complaining, you are gaining victory against the devil. You are showing the heavenly hosts, powers, and principalities—the demons of darkness and the angels of light—that your God is worthy of great praise—no matter what your circumstances.

Joni Eareckson Tada

WHAT OTHERS HAVE SAID

As selfishness and complaint pervert and cloud the mind, so love with its joy clears and sharpens the vision. —Helen Keller

Press on Toward the Goal

Read: Philippians 3:12–16

Forgetting what is behind and straining toward what is ahead, I press on toward the goal to win the prize for which God has called me heavenward in Christ Jesus.
—Philippians 3:13–14

I never would have stuck with my grueling rehab regimen unless I had a definite goal in mind. I was fixed on returning to the major leagues. Every weight that I lifted, every muscle that I stretched, every hour that I spent in the gym was focused on the day when I'd once more put on my uniform, trot out to the mound, and throw my first pitch toward home plate.

In the same way, we'll never stick with our spiritual rehab regimen unless we keep our goal in full view. Peter reminds us of that goal when he writes, "the God of all grace, who called you into eternal glory . . ." (1 Peter 5:10). We must be fixed on that eternal glory. Every trial that we face, every burden that we shoulder, every agony that we suffer must be borne with our everlasting destiny in mind.

Dave Dravecky

Take Action!

What are your spiritual goals? To pray more? To study the Scriptures more often? To be more compassionate or less judgemental toward others? Sit down and write five spiritual goals, asking God to bless them and help you achieve them, knowing that they will help you attain your eternal goal.

CONTENTMENT

Read: Philippians 4:10–13

I have learned the secret of being content in any and every situation.
—*Philippians 4:12*

Contentment is a sedate spirit that is able to keep quiet as it bears up under suffering. Contentment is all about leaning on Jesus.

Of course, we don't automatically know the secret of being content. If you are to know contentment—that quietness of heart, supernaturally given, that gladly submits to God in all circumstances—you must undergo the learning process. That takes time and great effort. To learn means to make choices, to practice over and over.

When Christ gives us strength to tackle a painful situation, gaining contentment doesn't mean losing sorrow or saying good-bye to discomfort. You can be sorrowful yet always rejoicing (2 Corinthians 6:10). You can have nothing yet possess everything.

So don't let anyone tell you that contentment comes easily. It has to be learned. And it requires strength from beyond this world. But once you gain it, you'll never trade that settled contentedness for anything.

Joni Eareckson Tada

WHAT OTHERS HAVE SAID

Contentment is a pearl of great price, and whoever procures it at the expense of ten thousand desires makes a wise and happy purchase.
—John Balguy

IN CHRIST'S IMAGE

Read: Colossians 1:13–29

God has chosen to make known among the Gentiles the glorious riches of this mystery, which is Christ in you, the hope of glory. —Colossians 1:27

Suffering has inspired and forged more sculptures than one can count. And not just the bronze kind that rest on pedestals in village squares. Suffering fashions us into a "holy and blameless" image of Christ (Ephesians 1:4), much like a figure sculpted out of marble. An artist in Florence, Italy, once asked the great Renaissance sculptor Michelangelo what he saw when he approached a huge block of marble. "I see a beautiful form trapped inside," he replied, "and it is simply my responsibility to take my mallet and chisel and chip away until the figure is free."

The beautiful form, the visible expression of "Christ in you, the hope of glory," is inside Christians like a possibility, a potential. The idea is there, and God uses affliction like a hammer and chisel, chipping and cutting to reveal his image in you.

Jesus isn't around in the flesh, but you and I are. When we suffer and handle it with grace, we're like walking billboards advertising the positive way God works in the life of someone who suffers. It's for the benefit of believers. But it's more than a matter of example or even inspiration. It's *you*.

Joni Eareckson Tada

POINTS TO PONDER

* What might the "image of Christ in you" look like if you were a sculpture that was already finished? What characteristics would Jesus "chisel" out of you?

* How might you model those characteristics now?

* How can you cooperate with God as he sculpts your life?

THE UNSEEN THINGS OF GOD

Read: Colossians 3:1–17

Since, then, you have been raised with Christ, set your hearts on things above, where Christ is seated at the right hand of God. —Colossians 3:1

I used to lock my eyes on my catcher's glove when I was pitching in the major leagues. Batters were merely distractions, especially if they were good hitters. My goal was to so focus on my catcher's glove that I wouldn't even see the batter.

It is this kind of stare we are instructed to level at the unseen things of God. Countless distractions will clamor for our attention, trying feverishly to seduce our eyes to drift in their direction, but God urges us to fix our gaze on his eternal truths. Only in that way will we be enabled to look past the vicious cuts life takes at us, and wind up with a big "W" on our final scorecard.

Dave Dravecky

WHAT OTHERS HAVE SAID

The only way to get our values right is to see, not the beginning, but the end of the way, to see things, not in the light of time, but in the light of eternity. —William Barclay

DEVOTED TO PRAYER

Read: Colossians 4:2–6

Devote yourselves to prayer, being watchful and thankful. —Colossians 4:2

I don't for a minute pretend to understand everything about prayer. How it works is a mystery that I will never fully understand. But through it we are changed. We discover God. We become connected with him. Whether it is through the unmistakably powerful way he addresses the needs we bring to him, the quiet but certain way he comforts us in our pain, or the divine gift of encouragement that comes from the people God brings into our lives, our prayers connect us with our heavenly Father. For that reason alone, we should always pray.

Dave Dravecky

FOR FURTHER REFLECTION

Set aside some time for a Bible study on prayer, using a topical Bible or concordance. Be sure to include 1 Thessalonians 5:16–18; James 5:13–16; 1 Peter 4:7; and Jude 1:20.

FOREVER

Read: 1 Thessalonians 4:13–18

The Lord himself will come down from heaven . . . with the trumpet call of God, and the dead in Christ will rise first. After that, we who are still alive and are left will be caught up together with them in the clouds to meet the Lord in the air. And so we will be with the Lord forever. —1 Thessalonians 4:16–17

*E*very once in a while, when our heart grows weary of waiting, the Lord revives us with snatches of joy—previews of the joy that will one day overtake us. And it will happen in the twinkling of an eye! (1 Corinthians 15:52).

Before we know it, we shall find ourselves in the embrace of our Savior at the Wedding Supper of the Lamb. Heaven will have arrived. At first, the shock of joy may burn with the brilliant newness of being glorified, but in the next instant we will be at peace and feel at home, as though it were always this way, that we were born for such a place. At that moment, earth will seem like a half-forgotten dream, pleasant enough, but only a dream.

Joni Eareckson Tada

PATH TO PRAYER

Praise be to you, O God, for this glimpse of the glory that will be. I look forward to that day when you will call all your people to yourself, and when I will meet the loved ones who have gone before me. But I look forward most to being at home with you and in peace. Amen

COUNTED WORTHY

Read: 2 Thessalonians 1:3–12

All this is evidence that God's judgment is right, and as a result you will be counted worthy of the kingdom of God, for which you are suffering. —2 Thessalonians 1:5

Very often when we are forced to endure suffering for a long period of time, we take our prolonged pain as evidence that God has forgotten us. That he doesn't love us. That we have been cast adrift in the middle of a hurricane. Yet Paul considers this same evidence and comes to an entirely different conclusion.

The "evidence" Paul has in mind here is not just the suffering; anybody can have that. What Paul finds extraordinary about these young Christians is the way they persevered through their suffering, how they patiently endured it. In Paul's mind, it was this patient endurance that proved the authenticity of the Thessalonians' faith—and which conclusively demonstrated they were "counted worthy of the kingdom of God." How's that for making lemons into lemonade?

Dave and Jan Dravecky

WHAT OTHERS HAVE SAID

The kingdom of God is a kingdom of paradox, where through the ugly defeat of a cross, a holy God is utterly glorified. Victory comes through defeat; healing through brokenness; finding self through losing self.
—Charles W. Colson

UNMEASURED LOVE

Read: 2 Thessalonians 2:13–17

May our Lord Jesus Christ himself and God our Father, who loved us and by his grace gave us eternal encouragement and good hope, encourage your hearts and strengthen you in every good deed and word. —*2 Thessalonians 2:16–17*

*I*f love could be measured, it would be measured by how much it gives. Of course, true love doesn't even care to measure itself. It just joyfully gives without taking any notice of how much has been sacrificed.

That's how God loves. And the measure of the love of God is in what— or I should say, whom—he gave. He gave his only Son. He gave everything, nothing held back, every last ounce, all in all. He squandered his love extravagantly and unashamedly on vile sinners.

That's why God should be so easy to trust. With you he never uses words of despair or defeat, hopelessness, or frustration. His encouraging love never mentions fear or failure. When God encourages your heart, he speaks words of hope and victory, rest and peace, joy and triumph. In today's verse we discover God's eternal encouragement. It's the measure of his love. If your heart needs to be strengthened today, let him speak to you his loving words of hope and comfort.

Joni Eareckson Tada

TAKE ACTION!

Because God encourages you, thank him by encouraging someone else. Write a note or send a card to someone who is sick, or to a struggling college student, a young mother, or your pastor. Include today's verse in your note.

December

BLESSED GOD

I charge you to keep this command without spot or blame until the appearing of our Lord Jesus Christ, which God will bring about in his own time—God, the blessed and only Ruler, the King of kings and Lord of lords. —1 Timothy 6:13–15

*I*n this verse and in 1 Timothy 1:11, Paul calls God "blessed." To be blessed is to be happy. Scholars use the word *blissful* for blessed. Exultant and joyous, radiant and rapturous. God is not a threatened, pacing deity starved for attention. He is not easily angered, touchy, or out of sorts on bad days. He is not biting his nails or blowing his stack when the world goes awry. Rather he is the exultant and rapturously happy God.

That is why the Good News sounds so great. If *we're* in trouble, God had better not be! If we're miserable, it would not do us good to go to Someone who's miserable. People in deep distress need to reach out and find a strong, secure, and happy anchor. God is just that: a joyful foundation, a blissful rock, a happy fortress. Nothing we can do will disturb the blessedness of God. We will always find him full of compassion and tender mercies.

Joni Eareckson Tada

PATH TO PRAYER

Blessed are you, O God, the King of kings and Lord of lords. I praise you that you are the blessed God, joyous, radiant, rapturous. I praise you as my joyful foundation, my blissful rock, and my happy fortress. I praise you because you are always compassionate and merciful to me. Amen.

GOOD INVESTMENTS

Read: 1 Timothy 6:17–19

Command those who are rich in this present world not to be arrogant nor to put their hope in wealth, which is so uncertain, but to put their hope in God, who richly provides us with everything for our enjoyment. —1 Timothy 6:17

What does it mean to invest in the eternal? How do you make a deposit to the Bank of Heaven? What does a deposit slip look like, and where can you fill one out? The apostle Paul helps us a great deal with this in verses 18–19.

This is phenomenal investment advice! If you're interested in making sizable deposits to the Bank of Heaven, don't waste your time reading money and investment magazines. You can get absorbed in those if you're fond of becoming intimately acquainted with moths, rust, and thieves, but if you're looking for a dynamite *eternal* investment, read Paul's four-pronged investment strategy: 1) Do good; 2) Be rich in good deeds; 3) Be generous; 4) Be willing to share.

Dave and Jan Dravecky

TAKE ACTION!

Write down the four items on Paul's "investment strategy" on a small post-it or other piece of paper. Tape it on your checkbook to remind you of this strategy whenever you write a check.

OUR FATHER

Read: Hebrews 1:1–4, 10–13

The Son is the radiance of God's glory and the exact representation of his being.
—Hebrews 1:3

How do we know God even thinks about us? We know he does, because we know his Son. The Son is "the radiance of God's glory and the exact representation of his being." And what did God look like when he walked in our sandals? People enjoyed the kid who worked with his dad at the carpenter's shop in Nazareth (Luke 4:22 says, "All spoke well of him"). After God "grew up," he earned the undying affection of blind beggars, spine-twisted women, and people who ran out of wine at weddings. It's the everyday people who took to him: fishermen, spinsters, widows, guys out on parole, bakers, and bag ladies.

Does the Father care? Or is he so invisible, omnipresent, and omniscient that he cannot or will not consider you in your pain? Listen to the words of Jesus: "I tell you the truth, the Son can do nothing by himself; he can do only what he sees his Father doing, because whatever the Father does the Son also does" (John 5:19). The Father, for all his grandeur and loftiness, loves the beggars and the bag ladies *just as much as does the Son*!

Joni Eareckson Tada

PATH TO PRAYER

Meditate on the wonder of Jesus, God incarnate, who loves you as you are, where you are, right now, this minute. Bask in that love and respond to Jesus in prayer.

Free From Fear

Read: Hebrews 2:5–18

[Jesus] too shared in their humanity so that by his death he might destroy him who holds the power of death . . . and free those who all their lives were held in slavery by their fear of death. —Hebrews 2:14–15

As human beings, we are prone to fear, no matter how much we believe in God or heaven. And the fear of death can hold tremendous power over us, as this verse makes clear.

God understands the fear common to all humanity. He isn't the author of death; he is the one who came to vanquish death, and one day he will destroy it. But when it comes to facing death, I am like a child, just flesh and blood. Jesus understands because he took on our human condition to deal with this fear of death.

I realize I will have to face off with fear for the rest of my life, but I don't have to live in slavery to it! I believe in a mighty God, the resurrected Christ, who proved his power over the grave. I have to admit I'm still afraid on occasion. Now I am learning to admit my fears honestly to God, who understands my human condition.

Jan Dravecky

PATH TO PRAYER

Jesus, thank you for making it possible for me to live without fear— especially the fear of death. I am all too human, Lord, and I sometimes take my eyes off you and begin to sink in a quagmire of fear and anxiety. I admit my fears to you now, and I ask that you will take away my fear and give me a spirit of power and love and self-discipline instead (2 Timothy 1:7).

HE KNOWS HOW IT FEELS

Read: Hebrews 4:14–5:3

We do not have a high priest who is unable to sympathize with our weaknesses, but we have one who has been tempted in every way, just as we are. —Hebrews 4:15

Jesus empathizes with us. For Jesus to be resurrected, he first had to die. To die, he first had to become human (without ever surrendering his deity). So the resurrected Jesus once walked in our shoes and felt the pain of this earthly life. Even though he's now in heaven, he has a "divinely" good memory that recalls his days upon earth. He knows what we go through.

Are we broken? He is broken with us. Do neighbors no longer come by to help? Jesus couldn't get his three best friends to spend an hour in prayer with him. Do we feel like the world has passed us by? He too was ignored. Are we sinking into sorrow? He sunk low as "a man of sorrows, and familiar with suffering" (Isaiah 53:3). Does he descend into our hell? Yes, for I may cry, "The darkness is all around me," but "even the darkness is not dark to [you]" (Psalm 139:12).

You are not alone in your hardships. You have not been blindsided and ambushed by suffering only to trudge on in senseless disappointment. God is with you. He is deeply involved in your circumstances. You have a Savior who can completely empathize with your weaknesses. In other words, you have relationship—and this, like nothing else, is what gives your circumstances powerful meaning.

Joni Eareckson Tada

POINTS TO PONDER

* What does it mean to you to have Jesus as your "high priest"?

* Can you identify what temptations you are facing right now?

* How does it make you feel knowing that Jesus empathizes with your weaknesses? Do you believe that this is true?

A Clean Conscience

Read: Hebrews 9:9–28

How much more, then, will the blood of Christ, who through the eternal Spirit offered himself unblemished to God, cleanse our consciences from acts that lead to death, so that we may serve the living God!—Hebrews 9:14

Sometimes our pain is caused not by others, not by illness, not by serious accident and not even by the grinding march of time. Sometimes we cause our own pain by the gnawing memory of a hurt or offense we ourselves committed against another. So when our pain arises from deep within, is there any hope for relief?

Hebrews 9:14 gives us the answer. We do not have to live with a guilty conscience. We do not have to bear the pain of our own "acts that lead to death." Jesus bids us place these crushing burdens at his feet. In exchange he promises to cleanse our conscience so that we may serve the living God—surely the best trade in the universe.

The greatest healing of all occurs when we own up to our sin, confess it, and turn to Jesus in faith. Then his blood washes it all away and transforms us into new creatures, spiritually whole and healed. That is the greatest healing of all, and it prepares us to cope with affliction when it comes barging into our lives. Thanks be to God—through Jesus Christ our Lord!

Dave and Jan Dravecky

Path to Prayer

Make a prayer of confession. Take an inventory of your failings and sins, things you have done that you shouldn't have and things you should have done but did not. Turn your sins over to Jesus in faith and ask for his cleansing grace. Pray that you will be healed and transformed into a new creature.

BETTER

Read: Hebrews 11

Instead, they were longing for a better country—a heavenly one. —Hebrews 11:16

Some people worry that they'll be bored in heaven. But how could they be—unless they think boredom is "better" than anything earth has to offer. *Better* is the key word throughout the book of Hebrews. Chapter 11 lists an honor roll of great people of faith from the Old Testament who often left their native countries to serve God because "they were longing for a *better* country—a heavenly one." And while all of them were commended for their faith, none of them received what had been promised. Why not? "God had planned something *better* for us so that only together with us would they be made perfect." And where would that happen? In heaven!

Think of the best day you've ever had. Remember the joy? The excitement? The thrill? The sheer happiness that welled up in your heart and burst into uncontrollable laughter and ear-to-ear smiles? Well, that was good—but heaven is better. So if that's boredom, bring it on!

Dave and Jan Dravecky

WHAT OTHERS HAVE SAID

Jerusalem, the golden, descending from above, / the city of God's presence, the vision of God's love— / I know not, oh, I know not what joys await us there, / what radiancy of glory, what bliss beyond compare!
—Bernard of Cluny, 12th century

ENLIGHTENED EYES

Read: Hebrew 12:1–13

Let us fix our eyes on Jesus, the author and perfecter of our faith, who for the joy set before him endured the cross, scorning its shame, and sat down at the right hand of the throne of God. —Hebrews 12:2

We're told to "fix our eyes on Jesus," but how do we do that when we can't see him? Answer: through faith. It's a different kind of seeing than our physical eyes are equipped for. As Paul prayed, "I pray also that the eyes of your heart may be enlightened in order that you may know the hope to which he has called you" (Ephesians 1:18–19).

That's how we fix our eyes on Jesus. We do not go looking for visions or mystical appearances or the like. We obey the command by filling our minds with his Word, by studying the gospel accounts of his earthly life, by staying in constant touch with him through prayer, and by maintaining fellowship with his people. We remember what he suffered on our behalf to free us from our sins, and we look to his example as someone who through faith obeyed his Father's commands, even though it cost him his life.

Dave Dravecky

PATH TO PRAYER

Jesus, open my eyes so that I can see your face always before me. Open my mind to hear your Word and let it live in me. Open my heart so that I hear your voice in prayer and in the guidance you give me through your Holy Spirit. Amen.

FOREVER NEW

Read: Hebrews 13:1–8

Jesus Christ is the same yesterday and today and forever. —Hebrews 13:8

One evening my friend Francie brought out an old, tattered Bible. "This is my Grandma Grace's," she smiled.

The binding was torn, and Francie carefully turned each delicate page, so we could read Grandma Grace's faded scribbles in the margin. We got an up-close look at this woman's love for the Lord Jesus. Her words were nearly a century old, but the love of which she wrote was anything but obsolete.

I felt as though this woman shared the rhythm of my heart. We were kindred spirits. We could have been best friends. Her notes weren't reminiscent of dusty days gone by, for each word was a powerful and poignant reminder that Jesus is the same yesterday, today, and forever.

There's nothing old or worn out about the love of God. His love has not yellowed with age. It is neither fragile nor ragged at the edges. God's love is as current now as it was a century ago . . . and as fresh today as it will be tomorrow.

Joni Eareckson Tada

FOR FURTHER REFLECTION

See also John 1:1; Colossians 1:15–17; and Revelation 11:15 for more about the timeless reign of Jesus Christ.

THE GOD OF PEACE

Read: Hebrews 13

May the God of peace, who through the blood of the eternal covenant brought back from the dead our Lord Jesus, that great Shepherd of the sheep, equip you with everything good for doing his will, and may he work in us what is pleasing to him, through Jesus Christ, to whom be glory for ever and ever.
—Hebrews 13:20–21

What a crazy world we live in. Oh, how we need God to breathe peace on our planet. Actually, he has, according to these verses. No matter how wild the world gets, we can experience this glorious peace because hostility no longer exists between the Father and us. The war between God and human beings is over. God is no longer against us, but with us!

Still, it's a crazy world. We need the peace of God that rules in our hearts (Colossians 3:15). God is with us, right in the middle of our world. And anywhere, at any time, we may turn to him, hear his voice, and know his peace.

It's my prayer that you turn your thoughts toward his calm and quiet. Hold the world at bay. Live in many moments of rest. May the peace of God go before you, leading you into each day. For whenever we look up into the face of our Father, whenever we quiet our spirit to hear his voice, we have found divine peace this crazy world can never take away.

Joni Eareckson Tada

TAKE ACTION!

Make two bookmarks inscribed with John 14:27. Give one to a friend and keep another in your Bible until it becomes imbedded in your heart: "Peace I leave with you; my peace I give you. I do not give to you as the world gives. Do not let your hearts be troubled and do not be afraid."

SEIZE THE TRIAL

Read: James 1:2–18

Blessed is the man who perseveres under trial, because when he has stood the test, he will receive the crown of life that God has promised to those who love him.
—James 1:12

Trials and temptations may sound like one and the same, but they are not. A trial is a test God places before us to prove our faith and produce perseverance. Trials are something we can face with joy.

There's nothing joyful about temptation! Unlike trials, God does not even place temptations in our path. Temptations occur when we are enticed and dragged away by our own evil desire.

So how are trials and temptations related? When we fail a God-given trial, when we resist the grace he gives to persevere and obey, we miss the God-given opportunity to have our faith refined. At that point, a failed trial can turn into a temptation when we are enticed to go our own way, seek our own desires, or even grumble or complain.

God never intends for trials to turn into temptations; trials are his good and perfect gifts intended to refine our faith, develop perseverance, and make us mature and complete (James 1:2–4).

Joni Eareckson Tada

TAKE ACTION!

Take out your pencils or markers and draw your crown of life. What will decorate your crown? What kind of jewels will be in it? How colorful will it be? Let yourself wonder and meditate as you draw.

No Mists in Heaven

Read: James 4:13–17

What is your life? You are a mist that appears for a little while and then vanishes.
—James 4:14

L ife is uncertain. It really is true that no one has a guarantee of tomorrow. Everyone on the face of the earth has a prognosis of terminal—it's just a question of when. As others have pointed out, the statistics on death are impressive: 1 for 1. If you're born, you will die. We all know that, we all see that, but somehow it never sinks in until that uncertainty attaches itself to us personally. Sooner or later the truth comes knocking at our doorstep, and it won't go away without taking us with it.

When I was diagnosed with cancer, suddenly I was in a place where I had no idea whether I would come back to play baseball, whether I would ever pitch again, or even whether I would live to do anything at all. As I stared into the uncertainty, I realized how short life is.

Uncertainty about whether we will live or die is a wrenching ordeal. Yet this isn't all bad. Often it's just this that causes us to look for answers and to turn to God. In the uncertainty of life we tend to trust God more. And if the uncertainty of life here below leads us to the certainty of life above, we will have found the biggest prize of all. For I've read the Book and I know one thing for sure: there are no mists in heaven.

Dave Dravecky

Points to Ponder

* In what respect are we like a "mist that vanishes?
* Have you ever thought about the day of your death?
* How does thinking about your death turn your thoughts toward God?

HEALING PRAYER

Read: James 5:13–16

And the prayer offered in faith will make the sick person well; the Lord will raise him up. — James 5:15

*L*ack of complete physical healing is not proof that our prayers have gone unanswered or that we didn't have enough faith in prayer. The healing may be an extension of life beyond the normal course of the disease. It may be that the fever is suddenly and inexplicably gone. The healing may be emotional or spiritual. It may be instantaneous or take place over a period of time.

Whatever comes, we are simply called to obey God's prompting to pray for healing. We don't tell God how or when. We trust that he is working, perhaps in ways we don't see or understand. We may not know how our prayers for healing were answered until we stand before the Great Physician. This is walking by faith, not by sight, which we know is pleasing to God and is able to move mountains.

Dave and Jan Dravecky

PATH TO PRAYER

Make a list of all the people you know who are sick in body, mind, or soul. If you don't know anyone, look through the local newspaper and find the names of people who are sick or injured. Put the list in your Bible and pray faithfully for those people everyday for ten days or until you know that your prayers are answered in some way.

THE LONG WAY HOME

Read: 1 Peter 1:3–9

In his great mercy he has given us new birth into a living hope through the resurrection of Jesus Christ from the dead, and into an inheritance that can never perish, spoil or fade—kept in heaven for you. —1 Peter 1:3–4

Sometimes we're tempted to think that life's hardships have some-how managed to wipe eternity off the map. We imagine that our suffering demonstrates there is no such place as heaven. When thoughts like that begin to bedevil us, we need a dose of minor league thinking. Every minor leaguer knows that no matter how uncomfortable and long the trip to the next ball field might be, the trip won't last forever and the diamond will be waiting for him at the end.

The Bible promises us that no matter how difficult our journey may be-come, *the length of our journey never alters the reality of our desti-nation.* That's what Peter meant when he declared that all those who have been given "new birth into a living hope through the resurrection of Jesus Christ from the dead" are also guaranteed "an inheritance that can never perish, spoil or fade." And why is that inheritance secure? Because it is "kept in heaven for you."

Dave Dravecky

PATH TO PRAYER

Abba, Father—Daddy—my prayer for all of us is, that as we travel on this journey of life, we would be able to say with confidence that our deaths mean coming home to you. Help us to see that heaven is a place where, for all eternity, we can heap praises upon our infinitely precious God. And may that cause us to yearn for glory. For heaven. For paradise. FOR HOME! Amen!

A Reason for Your Hope

Read: 1 Peter 3:8–22

But in your hearts set apart Christ as Lord. Always be prepared to give an answer to everyone who asks you to give the reason for the hope that you have. But do this with gentleness and respect. —1 Peter 3:15

"*R*eligion is a private matter," some people say, by which they apparently mean, "Don't mention it in public." But Jesus did, and so should we.

I never want to push my beliefs on anybody. There's a time to talk about Jesus Christ, and a time that's inappropriate. In my ball playing days, when a reporter asked me what pitch I threw to a certain batter, I didn't bring God into it. He asked the question expecting a factual answer, and I gave it to him.

I never thought it was quite fair, though, for a reporter to insist that I censor the true story of my comeback. Certainly God didn't lift any weights for me, but he did give me the courage and the perspective to deal with adversity—and even with heartbreak. Faith makes a visible, demonstrable difference in my life. It permeates my thinking and my behavior. If I stop talking about it, I'd have to stop talking about practically everything important to me.

Dave Dravecky

Take Action!

If you have never written out a testimony of what you believe, consider doing so. Write in your own words how you came to believe in Jesus and what he means to you now. Keep your testimony in a safe place and review it occasionally, so that you can share your story naturally when God presents you with an opportunity.

PLIABLE

Read: 1 Peter 4:12–19

Dear friends, do not be surprised at the painful trial you are suffering, as though something strange were happening to you. —1 Peter 4:12

When you first became a Christian, did you realize what you were getting into? Did you read the fine print in the contract? God plainly spelled it out: "It has been granted to you on behalf of Christ not only to believe in him, but also to suffer for him" (Philippians 1:29). God made it clear that following him would mean real hardship. Life is supposed to be difficult!

When I first came to Christ, I sort of knew it meant suffering, but I had no idea it would involve paralysis! I was surprised at the painful trial at first, thinking something strange had happened to me. But now I praise God for this wheelchair. It has taken me down Calvary's path. It's the path to deep-down joy and peace.

Joni Eareckson Tada

PATH TO PRAYER

Lord Jesus, help me to remember that following you mans taking up my cross. Keep me pliable rather than resistant when fiery trials greet me.

NO GUILT

Read: 2 Peter 1:19—2:3

But there were also false prophets among the people, just as there will be false teachers among you. — 2 Peter 2:1

I remember one young man who confronted me during my battle against cancer. He told me I had cancer because of sin in my life and that if I confessed that sin, God would restore my health. What a load of guilt that was! By that time, I had struggled enough with the "whys" of my cancer to recognize the false guilt inherent in the young man's solution.

I was fortunate to have the grace to politely, but clearly, reject that guilt. I responded to him by saying, "I appreciate what you're saying. I do have sin in my life, but I can't say this has happened because of it. I do know that cancer has caused me to draw closer to God, and that God can use this as a way of encouraging others. Who am I—or you—to say what God should or should not be doing in my life? God is in control of that. We are not."

Dave Dravecky

POINTS TO PONDER

* How do you decide who is giving you false counsel?
* Where do you find trustworthy counsel and advice?
* By what standards should we judge the counsel of others?
* How can you develop the discernment to accept or reject counsel?

UNCONDITIONAL LOVE

Read: 2 Peter 3:1–9

The Lord is not slow in keeping his promise, as some understand slowness. He is patient with you, not wanting anyone to perish, but everyone to come to repentance.
—2 Peter 3:9

*C*ould this mean that God continues to love us despite our sins, just as we continue to love our kids despite theirs? Absolutely! God does not rejoice when I fall, nor does he rub his hands and say, "Aha! I told you so!" I find great comfort in that.

This thought has been a real eye-opener for me because I tend to get down on myself whenever I fail miserably. I do not want to go to God at those times because I don't feel worthy. Yet that's when I need him more than at any other time. God hates our sin and regrets the consequences that come to us because of our sin, but he doesn't love us any less. His love remains constant.

Dave Dravecky

FOR FURTHER REFLECTION

Read Romans 9:22–25; 1 Corinthians 13:4; and 1 Timothy 1:16 to discover more about the patience of our loving Lord.

WHEN HIS GLORY IS REVEALED

Read: 2 Peter 3:8–14

But in keeping with his promise we are looking forward to a new heaven and a new earth, the home of righteousness. —2 Peter 3:13

I've never succeeded in painting a picture of heaven—it defies the blank canvas of the artist. The best I can offer are scenes of breathtaking mountains or clouds that halfway reflect something of heaven's majesty. I'm never quite able to achieve the effect. And neither is earth! Actual mountains and clouds are exalting, but even the most beautiful displays of earth's glory are only rough sketches of heaven. Earth's best is only a dim reflection, a preliminary rendering, of the glory that will one day be revealed.

We rarely let that fact sink in. That is, until we are stopped short by one of those brilliant nights when the air is clear like crystal and the black sky is studded with a million stars. It takes such a moment to make us pause, watch our breath make little clouds in the night air, and think, "What is your life? You are a mist that appears for a little while and then vanishes" (James 4:14).

Heaven is the home that endures.

Joni Eareckson Tada

TAKE ACTION!

Go outside and walk until you find a sight that gives you a glimpse of the wonder of creation. Or find a picture in a magazine or book that makes you yearn for the new heavens and new earth. Reflect in your journal on how that picture gives you hope of your life beyond this one.

THE GIFT OF SELF

Read: 1 John 3:16–24

This is how we know what love is: Jesus Christ laid down his life for us.
—1 John 3:16

*R*eal love is an action—a selfless, sacrificial giving. The greatest act of love anyone can perform is to give himself or herself for others.

Sometimes it's easier to say, "I'd die for you," than it is to say, "I'll live for you. Let me put your desires first. Let me think of your interests before my own." I think we would all agree that living sacrificially is a real death to self. It's a killing of your selfishness, your own desires. To die for others, to live for others, is a gift of love that can only come from God. Why only from him? Because it takes superhuman strength to live—I mean really *live*—for others.

Joni Eareckson Tada

PATH TO PRAYER

Jesus, as long as I live, I will never understand the depth of your love for me—that you laid down your life. My mind can hardly comprehend the wonder of it. And it is only with your love and grace that I, in turn, can live for others in the same spirit of sacrifice. Help me die to self so that I can live selflessly for your kingdom. Amen.

STRONG LOVE

Read: 1 John 4:7–12

Dear friends, let us love one another, for love comes from God. Everyone who loves has been born of God and knows God. —1 John 4:7

During my long rehabilitation, it was friends—acquaintances, casual, loose, or even intimate—who made all the difference in the world. If I were to pinpoint the one common denominator these friends shared, it would be love. Love strong enough to overcome the stale, stuffy smell in my hospital room. Love strong enough to break through the fear of "having nothing to talk about." Love that refused to be squeamish when they had to empty my leg bag. And love that saw potential in me, even though I was reduced to doing not much more than writing with a pen between my teeth.

Joni Eareckson Tada

WHAT OTHERS HAVE SAID

Redemptive love, that which the New Testament calls *agape*, is marked by a passionate and tender concern for the needs—physical as well as spiritual—of other people. This love, which is the gift of Jesus Christ and is the manifestation of his Spirit, invades human selfishness with a power that wins self-centered men and women, as persons and in groups, to find a new center for their lives in the love and life of God. No other faith but Christianity has either magnified or practiced this love, and the church has practiced it all too little. —John A. Makay

SACRIFICIAL FRIENDSHIP

Read: 1 John 4:7–19

This is love: not that we loved God, but that he loved us and sent his Son as an atoning sacrifice for our sins. Dear friends, since God so loved us, we also ought to love one another. —1 John 4:10–11

*B*efore I went through my season of suffering, I had friends, but I didn't understand how important those relationships really were. Sure, I enjoyed my friends. It was nice to have them. But it didn't seem to me that I needed those relationships. Boy, did that change!

I learned that you can't get through pain and suffering on your own. You eventually come to the end of yourself, and you need another person there to stand beside you and lift you up. To have a friend who is willing to make the personal sacrifice to be with you so that you are not alone is a powerful thing. When I was struggling, it was really important to know that my close friends were willing to sacrifice for me. Their sacrifice was a demonstration of God's love for me.

Dave Dravecky

WHAT OTHERS HAVE SAID

God's love is always supernatural, always a miracle, always the last thing we deserve. —Robert Horn

A NEW NAME

Read: Revelation 2:12–17

"To him who overcomes, I will give . . . a white stone with a new name written on it, known only to him who receives it."—Revelation 2:17

Only in heaven will we find out who we truly are. Our true identity will unfold in the new name God will give us. And the name is a secret between God and you. In heaven, you will not only find what was irretrievably lost, but when you receive it, you will be a thousand times more yourself than the sum total of all those nuances, gestures, and inside subtleties that defined the earthbound "you." On earth you may think you are fully blossomed, but heaven will reveal that you had barely budded.

What's more, you will be like none other in heaven. The fact that no one else has your name shows how utterly unique you are to God. You touch his heart in a way no one else can. You please him like none other. It is a royal seal of his individual love on you.

Joni Eareckson Tada

PATH TO PRAYER

Lord Jesus, I picture it: a white stone with my name carved on it, a new name that you have given me. How can I thank you, dear friend, for your goodness and love to me. Amen.

IN GOD'S BOOK

Read: Revelation 3:1–6

"I will never blot out his name from the book of life, but will acknowledge his name before my Father and his angels."—Revelation 3:5

*U*nlike some address books, God's isn't collecting dust. It's in use. And once your name is recorded, once you are listed under C—for "child of God"—you'll never have to worry about the Lord ripping out your page in disgust over some sin or blotting out your name out of sheer disgust. That's the message of Revelation 3:5.

And even beyond that, we can be thankful that the Book of Life isn't jam-packed with names that Jesus can't remember. Names on honor rolls, the Hollywood Walk of Fame, stained-glass windows, and brass plaques are all too quickly forgotten. Not so with the Book of Life. If your name is entered in God's book—and it is if you claim Jesus as your Savior and live like it—take a moment right now to praise the Lord for this wonderful fact. Praise him also that he has written your name in permanent ink—the blood of his Son. And thank him that there are no erasers in heaven.

Joni Eareckson Tada

PATH TO PRAYER

I praise you, Lord, for you are my Savior and my God. I thank you that you have written my name in your book of life, in the blood of your Son Jesus. May I always live in awareness of this promise in a way that shows just how much I love you.

December 25

COURAGE TO CRY

Read: Revelation 7:9–17

"For the Lamb at the center of the throne will be their shepherd; he will lead them to springs of living water. And God will wipe away every tear from their eyes."
—Revelation 7:17

Years ago when I was in the hospital, I noticed something peculiar. Even though there was so much pain in the lives of my roommates, no one cried. Sometimes I would lie awake in the middle of the night, wanting so much to cry, but afraid to. I was afraid I would wake up my roommates and maybe, just maybe, they would make fun of me the next day. So I kept my tears to myself.

Later, I learned about David, the warrior-king who cried. The pages of the Psalms are salted with this man's tears. I learned about big, burly Peter who wept bitterly when he recognized his sin. I read about Jesus who offered prayers and petitions "with loud cries and tears."

Learning about these people in Scripture gave me courage to cry. No longer were tears a mark of weakness or shame. And I have the confidence that one day God will wipe away all my tears. How ironic that in heaven, where I will be able to once again wipe my own tears, I won't have to.

Joni Eareckson Tada

WHAT OTHERS HAVE SAID

Facing the darkness, admitting the pain, allowing the pain to be pain, is never easy. That is why courage—big-heartedness—is the most essential virtue on the spiritual journey. —Matthew Fox

GOD'S DELAYS

Read: Revelation 10

"There will be no more delay! But in the days when the seventh angel is about to sound his trumpet, the mystery of God will be accomplished, just as he announced to his servants the prophets."— Revelation 10:6–7

*D*elays can drive us crazy. They cost us time, they cost us money, and often they cost us our composure. That's doubly true when we're suffering and it appears that the relief we expected has somehow been delayed.

It's comforting to know that God both understands and anticipates our anxiety over what seem to be his maddening delays in coming to our rescue. He is never late, as we imagine, nor is he otherwise occupied. God's timing is a mystery to us. Our suffering is often a mystery. But the day is coming—right on heaven's timetable—when all will be accomplished, just as our Lord promised us through the prophets. The mystery *will* be unfolded—in due time.

Dave and Jan Dravecky

FOR FURTHER REFLECTION

Read John 19:30; Hebrews 10:37; and 2 Peter 3:8 for more on God's perfect timing.

REWARD

Read: Revelation 11:15–18

"The time has come . . . for rewarding your servants the prophets and your saints and those who reverence your name, both small and great."
—Revelation 11:18

*M*aybe some adults pooh-pooh the idea of rewards, but I don't. The child in me jumps up and down to think God might actually reward me with something. I remember when I took piano lessons as a kid and would squirm with delight on my bench whenever Mrs. Merson pasted gold crowns on my sheet music for a job well done. I wasn't so much overjoyed with my performance as I was in pleasing Mrs. Merson. My focus wasn't on what I did; it was on her approval.

In the same way, nothing is so obvious in a heavenly–minded child of God as his or her undisguised pleasure in receiving a reward—a reward that reflects the approval of the Father. Get ready for God to show you not only his pleasure, but his approval!

Joni Eareckson Tada

WHAT OTHERS HAVE SAID

Today, let us rise and go to our work. Tomorrow, we shall rise and go to our reward. —Richard Buckminster Fuller

HARD SOIL

Read: Revelation 13:1–10

This calls for patient endurance and faithfulness on the part of the saints.
—Revelation 13:10

*E*ndurance is a lot like patience. All of us want it, but none of us look forward to what we have to go through to get it. We somehow know that endurance, like patience, grows only in hard soil—like that pictured in Revelation 13.

How often we feel a deep kinship to the hard-pressed saints described in this bleak chapter! We feel as if we've been taken captive by hostile forces; we stare death in the face all day long. The pressure mounts and rises until we consider giving up and caving in. But for weary believers like us, God has a special word: "This calls for patient endurance and faithfulness on the part of the saints."

Hard soil is where such patient endurance grows best. And the crop it (eventually) produces—faithfulness—is well worth the wait. In God's eyes, that's a harvest worth every ounce of sweat.

Dave and Jan Dravecky

TAKE ACTION!

Memorize Romans 15:5–6 to remind you where your patience and endurance come from and why:

"May the God who gives endurance and encouragement give you a spirit of unity among yourselves as you follow Christ Jesus, so that with one heart and mouth you may glorify the God and Father of our Lord Jesus Christ."

END OF STORY

Read: Revelation 20:4–10

And the devil . . . was thrown into the lake of burning sulfur, where the beast and the false prophet had been thrown. They will be tormented day and night for ever and ever. —Revelation 20:10

*I*f Hollywood were writing the script for the end of time, you might expect one final, face-to-face conflagration between God and the devil, packed with fireballs and earthquakes and supernovas, with the outcome in doubt until some odd twist sprang out of nowhere.

What you wouldn't expect is this: "And the devil . . . was thrown into the lake of burning sulfur, where the beast and the false prophet had been thrown. They will be tormented day and night for ever and ever." And that's it. End of story.

When we're in pain, it helps to remember that God is fully in charge. There is no doubt to how this story ends, no suspense as to who might win. When it comes time to wrap up world history, God does the wrapping. And Satan can't so much as singe the bow.

Dave and Jan Dravecky

PATH TO PRAYER

Praise God that he is fully in charge of all of history, including your place in it. Praise him that you are not in suspense about the outcome and that the devil is already defeated. Ask him to help you persevere until the day you meet him in heaven.

EVERY TEAR

Read: Revelation 21:1–5

"[God] will wipe every tear from their eyes. There will be no more death or mourning or crying or pain, for the old order of things has passed away."
—*Revelation 21:4*

*I*t's not merely that heaven will be wonderful *in spite* of our anguish; it will be wonderful *because* of it. Suffering serves us. A faithful response to affliction accrues a *weight* of glory. A bounteous reward. God has every intention of rewarding your endurance. Why else would he meticulously chronicle every one of your tears? "Record my lament; list my tears on your scroll—are they not on your record?" (Psalm 56:8).

Every tear you've cried will be redeemed. God will give you indescribable glory for your grief. Not with a general wave of the hand, but in a considered and specific way. Each tear has been listed; each will be recompensed. We know how valuable our tears are in his sight—when Mary anointed Jesus with the valuable perfume, it was her tears with which she washed his feet that moved him most powerfully (Luke 7:44). The worth of our weeping is underscored again in today's verse, "he will wipe every tear from their eyes." It won't be the duty of angels or others. It'll be God's.

Joni Eareckson Tada

PATH TO PRAYER

Meditate on today's verse until its meaning reaches deep into your soul. Respond to God in prayer.

"I AM COMING SOON"

Read: Revelation 22:7–20

"Behold, I am coming soon! My reward is with me, and I will give to everyone according to what he has done."—Revelation 22:12

Never forget that God has a reward with your name on it, and all you have to do to receive it is to remain faithful and hang in there. Don't give up. It may seem like a long road ahead, but from the Bible's viewpoint, "in just a very little while, 'He who is coming will come and will not delay' " (Hebrews 10:37). And what will he do when he comes? I'll let him tell you himself: "My reward is with me, and I will give to everyone according to what he has done."

So do well. Hang in there. Don't lose hope. And I'll see you at the rewards ceremony.

Dave Dravecky

WHAT OTHERS HAVE SAID

We are not a post-war generation; but a pre-peace generation. Jesus is coming. —Corrie ten Boom